GANDHIANS' RISE TO POWER

National Movement, Power Politics & Independence (1920—47 AD)

GANDHIANS' RISE TO POWER

National Movement, Power Politics & Independence (1920—47 AD)

Prasant Kumar Pradhan

Commonwealth

Gandhians' Rise to Power

ISBN : 81-7169-520-5

Edition : 2019

Published by :
COMMONWEALTH PUBLISHERS (P) LTD.
4831/24, Govind Lane,
Ansari Road, Darya Ganj,
New Delhi - 110002
Ph. : 23272541, 23242541
e-mail : commonwealthpublishers2016@gmail.com

Distributed by :
ARJUN PUBLISHING HOUSE
4831/24, Govind Lane,
Ansari Road, Darya Ganj,
New Delhi - 110002
Ph. : 23272541, 23242541
e-mail : arjunbooks2001@gmail.com

Laser Typesetting by :
Dimple Computers
Delhi

Printed at :
Balaji Offset
Delhi

Dedicated

to my History-teacher

Sj Binod Chandra Routray, B.A. B.Ed.
Prachi Academy, Adaspur, Cuttack, ORISSA

who made HISTORY a passion for me

Preface

M.K. Gandhi successfully launched the *Satyagraha* or non-violent civil-resistance against the racial policies of the government in South Africa and arrived in India in January, 1915AD. The advent of Gandhi provided a monolithic leadership, unity and ideals of the decolonialistic nationalist movement of the Congress. India witnesses the emergence of a mammoth mass-based agitation against the colonialists under his leadership from, 1920 AD to 1947 AD. Not only in political field but also in social sphere his movements highlighted the causes of the exploited people and turned their attention to their rights and duties to which they were not aware of. Championing the causes as well as capabilities of the ignored masses in a big way and providing the unarmed common Indians the scope to participate in movement Gandhi captured their imagination completely and proved himself as the most popular mass-based leader of Indian History.

Gandhi launched Non-Co-Operation Movement in 1920 AD which quickly engulfed the entire sub-continent. By that time, a movement for the amalgamation of different Oriya-speaking tracts for the safety of Oriya language and culture was going on in Orissa. A few educated elites with the help of some native princes and zamindars had formed a conference called *'Utkal Sammilani'* in 1903AD for the purpose. They had no faith in the National Congress because of its indifferent attitude to the cause of the Oriyas. But the emergence of Gandhi as a unique full-time social worker, his ideals, devoted activities and above all, his instant concern for the poor of Orissa created hope in many of the young social workers of Orissa. Among them Gopabandhu Das was the most prominent who had already proved himself in many fields of general life of the province. He foresaw that the Oriyas could achieve both regional and national goals only by joining the national movement under Gandhi's leadership. Subsequently Orissa joined Gandhian movement and occupied one of the most prominent places in the political map of the country so far as the history of the national movement was concerned.

From 1920 AD to 1947 AD, many common Oriyas joined the Gandhian movement of the Congress and worked for the national movement. They became known as 'Gandhians' or 'Gandhiwalas' in the countryside. They acknowledged Gandhi as their leader. Many of them followed or tried to follow many of the Gandhian ideas in their personal lives. Some also could not adopt or practice, even believed in few ideals of Gandhi, but helped his movements devotedly for the betterment of the poor people. There were both staunch and general Gandhians within the Congress. Working in the countryside all these workers or 'standing army' of Gandhi widened the popularity of Indian National Congress to achieve independence. Both in political and social spheres most of them proved their abilities as the real leaders of the localities and perfectly highlighted the class interests of the poor people to which most of then belonged.

Indentifying a group of Gandhian freedom fighters of India who were middle ranked leaders of the early phase of the Gandhians movement, J.M. Brown ("Gandhi's Men, 1917-22 AD, the Role of the Major Leaders in the Congress Middle Rank Politicians"; In *Studies from Africa and Asia* (ed), W.H. Morris-Jonnes University of London, Atnole, 1976) opines that the Gandhians' commitment to the central figure was the distinguishing mark of these groupings and their wide range of joint activity was the another characteristic. The Gandhians provided for their members solidarity and strength in spheres of public life other than the overtly political. He also opines that these Gandhians were easy to isolate and they knew the localities pretty well and could interpret in their language to the people. They had the time and expertise to record people's sentiment.

Likewise the Gandhians in Orissa, irrespective of their cadre, positions in the organisation group identities and own interests, tried to appear in the same ways to distinguish themselves as an exclusive group. As propagators of different Gandhian ideas, these people succeeded in mobilising the common people to make different sister organisations and movements of the Congress banner successful, and as social workers could infuse awareness in the exploited classes. Most of them personally suffered and ruined their carreers and families. They bore atrocities of the police and exploitations of the landlords. They also faced the hostility of the orthodox sections of the society because of their tirade against superstitions and social inequalities. But due to the devoted lives of many of them common people supported these groups at different stages of the movement.

Most of the Gandhians could not follow Gandhism in the strict sense of the term. Different groups adopted and practised different ideas according to their temperament, convictions and group identities. So far as strategies were concerned almost all of the activities adopted Gandhian styles of '*Satyagraha*' to mobilise the common people. There were different types of freedom-fighters in Orissa and most of them belonged to the Congress organisation. They all wore *khadar* and many of them stayed in Congress *Ashrams* or offices. There were both committed and non-committed Gandhians. Some were deeply committed where some also less committed in their devotion to the cause of the people. Some believed Gandhi entirely after much scrutinies. Some also followed him blindly. There were social workers as well as politicians. Many became constructive workers. The workers of princely states also became *Satyagrahis* and adopted Gandhian techniques and strategies to be identified as Gandhians among the people. The socialists used Gandhian platforms in the province. The power brokers also entered the Congress organisation in large number without any respect for many programmes of Gandhi. They also succeeded in projecting themselves as Gandhians. So this work includes the activities of those workers of the national movement in Orissa who were called as Gandhians by the common people irrespective of their commitment, group loyalties and areas of activities.

This work has two aims, in the first place, it is an attempt to give exclusiveness to the groups of Gandhians of Orissa who were working at the lower-rung of the Congress organisation in the provincial Congress without giving special emphasis on any leader or oligarchy. Secondly, it is intended to find out the space of Gandhism in lower level Congress organisation and its variations of use at different stages of the national movement. It will analyse both positive and negative fallouts of the national upsurge which was going on under Gandhis leadership from 1920 to 1947 AD so far as the areas of Oriya-speaking people were concerned.

Writing history on national movement in regional character has become both exciting and far more difficult than before. The efforts of the scholars during the last fifty years in writing the activities of the leader as well as about different currents of the freedom-struggle from different angles could not exhaust the scope anyway. Rather they had made the period more interesting and critical to visualise. The study of the regional character of the movement particularly under M.K. Gandhi, could reveal more interesting findings other than the normal course of the agitation. Different peculiarities of the region could be projected in relation to the study of the era of the national movement.

The lapse of fifty years since 1947AD has lessened the scope of personal biases, patriotism and emotional attachments to infiltrate into or influence the work to the present scholars. The study of the history of freedom struggle can be taken as a purely scholarly work and not an attempt only to pay tribute to the leaders to glorify nationalist or regional aspirations. The works of the official historians of the Congress party or its workers who became historians of the freedom struggle are no more vogue. Their process of glorification of leaders or events of the struggle can not be taken as an entirely impartial attempt. The present scholars have, thus, the scope and environment to avoid such personal beliefs, pre-conceived notions on the leaders and events of the national movement to create an 'objective history' as far as possible.

In the beginning, the history of the national movement of Orissa was mostly written by the participants like Harekrushna Mahtab and Surendranath Pattnaik, who served the state as politicians after independence. Once upon a time these works were being taken as the main sources of freedom movement in Orissa. Then gradually teacher-scholars of three universities of Orissa took this arduous task to provide an impartial and objective history. The pioneers were M.N. Das, B.C. Ray, P. Mukherjee, etc. These scholars created mostly informative history elaborating the courses of the national movement using different sources empirically. These works lacked much needed analysis and interpretations. This trend continued for decades together. The scholars like K.M. Patra, P.K. Mishra, S.C. Patra, J.K. Samal, J. Pattnaik, Nivedita Mohanty Purusottam Kar, etc.. who wrote history of modern Orissa, though highlighted the national movement from different angles, could not provide a complete history of the time and failed to inter-relate different aspects of the then Oriya society which was fighting its battles in different spheres against both indegenous and foreign enemies.

For these scholars national movement in Orissa was somehow a spontaneous event without any sign of animosity among different classes of Oriya society. Most of them had tried to glorify, the then educated middle class for providing a selfless natural leadership to the ignorant masses. These authors visualised political independence and unification of Orissa as the most coveted success of the upsurge without giving importance to its fallouts and by-products. They have tried to highlight the role of common populace but projected them as the ignorant supporters of the leaders and in the process of glorification avoided to discuss the growth of political cycophancy in the Congress organisation even before Indian independence.

Later some scholars like P.K. Mishra (Utkal University) S. Pradhan, N. R. Pattnaik, S. Pati, etc. have tried to glorify the participation of different social forces like tribals and people of princely states in the freedom struggle which were mostly anti-feudal since their inception. Regarding Oriya depressed castes no work has been done on their role during colonial period. Their dormancy during these periods does not exhausts the scope to give them their due place in history. The work of above authors are mostly based an archival sources and their exclusive nature blocked the way to interrelate activities and aspirations of the social forces of coastal area with that of western part of the province and the internal social anomalies of different *garhjats* and their own respective frictional by-products. But these works helped other scholars to visualise the national movement in Orissa in entirely. It also helped to provide history to the so-called 'historyless people' in a larger extent.

Nodoubt it was M.K. Gandhi and this ideas dominated the scene in Orissa form 1920 to 1947 AD. Rest of the leaders, except Gopabandhu Das, were far away from his position and popularity. It is somehow easy to study Gandhi as a personally but to study him as a political agitator in relation with his followers as well as masses was definitely not easy. Study of Gandhians exclusively is also a stupendous task to take up. Though this is an attempt to give a 'collective interpretation of history' in some respect, without giving importance to leaders, it is also not an exclusively isolated study of those thousands of Gandhians without their relationships with the masses as well as the higher leaders. It has its own limitations. The study of the activities of the middle men between Gandhi and the common people can not provide the necessary satisfaction to those who love truely 'collective-history' . This is also not a conscious effort to support elite theory to undo the possibility of an egalitarian study. But this is an attempt to provide a 'history from below' with its typical peculiarities involving larger number of people.

Now-a-day no discipline of Social Sciences is a water-tight compartment, so very often, attempts have been make to give inter-disciplinary approach to the work when required. The picture of the society of Orissa in which the Gandhians worked is also given due weightage to provide backdrops to the activities of the Congress workers.

Besides the works of historians on the freedom struggle in Orissa mostly contemporary vernacular newspapers and journals have been used to suffice the work. The earliest Oriya weeklies were of immense help to find out the currents of the late 19th century and early decades of the 20th century Orissa. *'Utkal Dipika'* of Gouri Sankar Ray, *'Asha'* of Shashi Bhusan Rath, *'Sambalpur Hiteishini'*, *'Seva'*, *'Sambad Bahika'*, etc. which were being published from Cuttack, Berhampur, Sambalpur, Balasore, etc., respectively were such journals. The editors were very reputed and honest personalities of the then Oriya-speaking areas whose editorials and reports were of high quality. They were straight-forward and unbiased in their profession—the fact which was acknowledged by their adversaries. The reports of '*The Samaj*', 'The *Prajatantra*', the mouthpieces of the Congress movement from 1920-47 AD were mostly used as sources of the activities of the Congress workers during the freedom struggle under Gandhi. But the anti-Congress views were taken from the journals like ' The *Lokamat*', '*The Satyasamachar*', '*The Asha*', etc., which were published by leading social figures like Nilakantha Das, Sashibhushan Rath, etc., who turned anti-Congress because of the growth of acute groupism and power-politics. Even the '*Samaj*' also often highlighted such developments. Their allegations against the Congress leaders were taken up to be used when their authenticity were proved from other sources.

The non-availability of the records of the provincial Congress organisation or district Congress organisations in a continuous manner created a big problem. Even the reports of the Government institutions on village level Congress workers and organisations are not available in a systematic manner and those available are often biased in nature. So to make the work more trustworthy some living Gandhians of Orissa have been interviewed. Their opinions on the national movement in Orissa provide immense help to complete the work with satisfaction. Structured-questionnaires are being sent to many Gandhians of different districts of Orissa and their views expressed in these questionnaires also help largely to make the works more authentic and empirical. In spite of certain limitations of this method of data collection, as far as reliable data are used after comparative investigations.

'Social History' being the most neglected part of historical research in Orissa, it is very difficult for a scholar to write the history of regional freedom-struggle without realising the contours and variations of the then society historically. But the contemporary literature of Orissa helped immensely to understand the society of the late 19th and the early 20th century Orissa. Prativa Jain believes, "While journalistic or official reports can be more reliable where objective events and statistics are concerned, creative literary writing can be far more revealing where the subtler background of major social conditions and movements are concerned'. She also further opines, "creative writing is valuable to the historians not merely because it is a specialised kind of mirror to special reality but because it is itself a special kind of reality which needs to be understood historically" . (Gandhian ideas: Social Movements and Creativity, Jaipur, 1985, foreward).

Picture of the 19th century Orissa could well be found from the modern Oriya literature of this time—particularly its prose part which contained the description of the society in larger ways. The writers of the 20th Century till 1960 AD also produced literature taking national struggle as the background, where growth of nationalism exploitation of the poor, impact of education, frustration and decline of traditional aristocracy, growth of modern political workers, existing superstitions, etc., could well be ascertained. The Autobiographies of the leading men of Orissa of the period were used as the sources of information directly. But from novels, short-stories and dramas, even from poems, the social realities were directly taken as facts to be used being corroborated by other sources.

Souvenirs on the Gandhians published by the enthusiastic local people after the movement till date provided the needed understanding of the sentiment of the then society to make the work as objective as possible in nature. Opinions of local people—particularly old, regarding their local Gandhians and the interviews with the retired government servants and teachers who had witnessed the activities of the Gandhians also helped me to be more conscious and critical to complete this work.

This work is divided into six chapters including 'Introduction' and 'Conclusion'. In the 'Introduction', which covers the years 1803 AD to 1920 AD , an attempt has been made to provide a background to Gandhian movement of 1920 AD to 1947 AD in Orissa. Political, social and economic condition of the common Oriyas after the conquest of Orissa by British in 1803 AD upto the rise of Gandhi to national level in 1920 AD covered this chapter Gandhi's doctrines and techniques provided the common people the scope to join this movement because of the suitability and feasibility of these ideas. How far and why the Oriyas of the 19th century were poor, backward, hopeless, weak, inert, fatalists so non-violent, has been discussed here. How the activities of some leaders who championed the cause of language and unification of Oriya-speaking population could not succeed to awaken the poor illiterate people of rural areas to come to the mainstream is another highlight of this chapter.

In the 'First Chapter', which includes the years from 1920 AD to 1930 AD the causes of the growth of Gandhians in the years are found out. The activities of the Gandhians during the Non-Co-operation Movement, their campaigning, role in constructive works, their composition and degree of commitment to Gandhian ideas have been described.

The 'Second Chapter' attempts to find the nature of the mass-based Gandhian movement in Orissa form 1930AD to 1936AD. How Gandhians made the Congress a real mass-based organisation and Gandhi the real man leader is being discussed. Some Gandhians turned socialists or *vice-versa* and championed the cause of peasants and fought against the zamindars including those among the Congress supports. This has also been discussed. Life styles of the Gandhians in villages, jails and in different *Ashrams* and their degree of conviction in Gandhian ideas and their composition are the subject matter in this chapter. The role of Oriya Gandhians in outlying tracts for the unification of Orissa upto 1936 AD is also included here.

The activities of Gandhians from 1937 AD to 1939 AD found place in the 'Third Chapter'. This chapter contains those currents that affected the course of the national movement on Orissa in a big way. The Gandhians of Orissa worked hard for the success of Congress candidates in its first electoral battle in 1937AD. But some unwanted elements, the power broken or hypocrite Gandhians, entered the Congress organisation and gradually side-tracked the true and committed Gandhians. Their rise to stability within the provincial Congress have been discussed in this chapter. Role of Gandhian workers in *Garhjat* movements—who followed, in many respect, Gandhian techniques and ideas, also drew the attention.

The 'Fourth Chapter' discusses the activities of the Gandians from 1940 AD to 1947 AD and also highlights the condition of the Congress organisation before, during and after the "Quit India Movement" of 1942 AD. The Gandhians had succeeded in mobilising the people and those, who were not arrested, led the people for violent activities disregarding the concept of non-violence of Gandhi because of sheer excitement. But when the movement subsided the power, brokers again became active and subsequently monopolised the Congress provincial organisation. The socialist-gandhians became quiet. The constructive workers isolated themselves gradually and silently from the Congress at the dawn of independence to provide ample open field to the 'politicians' to groom-most of whom were non-committed to the people and were opportunists. These have been the centre of attraction in this chapter.

In the 'Conclusion' a brief analysis of the role of Gandhians in Orissa at grass root-level and growth of power-politicians from 1920-47 AD has been given.

This is the book form of my Ph.D. Thesis which I have developed to this shape. I have translated the Oriya lines or stanzas of the informations into English to express their meanings as perfectly as possible. I make myself responsible for any type of lapse.

I am very thankful to my revered supervisor Dr. Prasanna Kumar Mishra. Reader. P.G. Department of History, Utkal University, Vani Vihar, Orissa for his guidance and necessary advice to complete this work. If this work bears any sort of clarity, it is due to his priceless guidance. I am thankful to Srimati Manorama Mohapatra, Honourable Secretary of Orissa *Sahitya Samaj* Library, Cuttack who allowed me to use the old vernacular newspapers and books kept in the library. I am indebted to Sri Bhartruhari Mahtab, Editor of Daily *Prajatantra*, Cuttack for his kind permission to collect valuable materials from his library. My since respect to Srijukta Dasarathi Pattnaik, *Jadumai Sahitya Sansad*, Udaypur, Nuagan, Puri, whose library provided me priceless data for the work. I am also very much thankful to the staff members of National Archives, New Delhi, State Archives, Bhubaneswar, Nehru Memorial Museum and Library, *Teen Murti Bhavan*, Delhi, Gandhi Memorial Museum and Library, Rajghat, Delhi, Delhi

University Library System, Delhi, Ratan Tata Library, Delhi, *Sahitya* Academy Library, Delhi, Sapru House Library, Delhi for their kind co-operation in collecting the source materials.

My honest and sincere respect and gratitude to those Gandhians of Orissa who provided reliable informations through structured questionnaires sent to them. I am also greatly indebted to those Gandhians whom I interviewed personally—who in spite of their old age and illness, helped me to get valuable informations and directions for the work. No less grateful I am to some old companions of the village level Gandhians and retired government servants who offered me their views verbally on the Gandhians of their localities. Though many of those Gandhians and the old people are no more alive, yet their help enabled me to complete this ardous task.

I express my sincere respectful regards to my late father, mother and thank to my brothers and sisters for their continuous encouragement. I am also thankful to my scholar friends for their valuable suggestions and encouragements—particularly Subrat Rout, Bishnu Charan Satpathy and also Radhakanta Barik, who during the eight years of my stay at Delhi, continued a discussing on the history of Orissa from different angles with me and suggested gaps and possible hypotheses of the work. I am also thankful to my friends of Bihar who also informed me about different social problems of their province in connection with the national movement. My sincere affections are for Bimal (Mohapatra), Jyoti (Pradhan), Mamata, Kuni, Hem who shared with me some tender but critical moments of my life. I am very much grateful to my wife Mrs. Chirashree Indrasingh, who, in spite of her busy literary life, supported me continuously to be a serious student of history. I am, at last, thankful to the publisher of this book: "The Commonwealth Publisher, Delhi" who published this book within a short time and a great care.

Prasant Kumar Pradhan

Contents

List of Maps

(These Maps have been drawn by the author himself)

Abbreviations

AICC	All India Congress Committee
BBSR	Bhubaneswar
B.O.D.G.	Bihar-Orissa District Gazetteers
CWMG	Collected Works of Mahatma Gandhi
DCC	District Congress Committee
D.G.O.	District Gazetteers of Orissa
IHC	India History Congress
IHRC	Indian Historical Records Commission
JOH	Journal of Orissan History
N.A.	National Archives
NMML	Nehru Memorial & Museum and Library
O.D.G.	Orissa District Gazetteers
OHC	Orissa History Congress
OHRJ	Orissa Historical Research Journal
OSA	Orissa State Archives
PCC	Pradesh or Provincial Congress Committee
Proc.	Proceedings
S.D.O.	Sub-Divisional Officer

1

Political, Social and Economic Condition of Orissa Before the Advent of Gandhian Movement (1803—1920 AD)

I

POLITICAL, SOCIAL AND ECONOMIC CONDITION OF ORISSA (1830 AD—1864 AD)

Political Condition

The last great *Gajapati* of Orissa Mukunda Dev was killed in 1568AD in a battle against the Afghans of Bengal and the grand empire of medieval Orissa lost its independence.[1] The Afghans ruled it for few years, but very soon the Moghuls captured the region from them in 1592 AD.[2] Todarmall, the revenue minister of Akbar, divided the province into two distinct regions. He kept fertile coastal area of Cuttack, Puri and Balasore under the direct administration of the Moghuls which became known as *Moghulbandi* and the rest hilly and forest regions known as *Garhjats* were left to few princes to rule.[3] The *Marathas* got Orissa in 1751 AD from Alivardi

---

1. R.D. Banarjee, History of Orissa, Vol. 1, Calcutta, 1930, pp. 340-48; K.C. Panigrahi, History of Orissa, Cuttack, 1981, p.p. 235-45.
2. K. C. Panigrahi, *op.cit.*, p. 242.
3. A. Stirling, An Account (Geo, Sta. and Hist.) of Orissa proper or Cuttack, London, 1846, p. 32.

Khan of Bengal and thoroughly plundered the region.[4] But finally in 1803AD the British captured the region from them.[5]

The British failed to understand the difference between Bengal and Orissa. Being influenced by their Bengali *Amlas*, they gradually excluded Oriyas systematically from the courts, police revenue and salt departments. It was resented by the people.[6] The Magistrate of Cuttack wrote in 1821AD, "Scarcely a single real Oriya received a salary of more than Rs.10/- per mensem",[7] and the officer also opined, "I scarcely know a single Oriya to fit for being a common scribe".[8] The British introduced different types of land settlements in Orissa and exacted revenues disregarding the capacity of the people. The land and the estates of the defaulters were auctioned.[9] These ultimately caused a rebellion of the *Paiks* of Khurdha region in 1817AD under Baxi Jagabandhu, the titular commander-in-chief of the then *Gajapati*. The revolt was suppressed. It failed to become an all Orissa issue and no assistance came from any of the reputed princely states of the *Garhjats*.[10] British superiority was completely accepted by the then traditional, divided and aimless indigenous political forces of Orissa.

Meanwhile in the *Garhjats*, the princes concluded treaties with the British and were left to rule freely. 'Their loyalty to the British *Raj* was considered more important than the welfare of the people they governed.[11] They ruled

4. R. D. Banerjee, *op.cit.*, Vol.-II, p. 99; B.S. Das, Studies in the Economic History of Orissa : From Ancient Times to 1833, Calcutta, 1978, p. 82.
5. R. D. Banerjee, *op.cit.*, p. 263.
6. P. Mukherjee, "Employment of the People of Orissa in Govt. Services in the 19th Century", *OHRJ*, Vol.-VIII, No-2, July, 1959, pp. 110-16.
7. A.G. Toynobee, A Sketch of the History of Orissa (1800-1828), *OHRJ*, Vol.-IX, April-July, 1960, p. 70.
8. *Ibid.*
9. *Ibid.*, pp. 12-13.
10. R.D. Banerjee, *op.cit.*, pp. 286-87.
11. S.S. Pradhan, Agrarian and Political Movement : States of Orissa, 1931-49, Delhi, 1986, p. 1.

the people by a strong hand and oppressed them to the maximum. After the revolt of the 1817AD the coastal Orissa remained silent for a long period.[12] During the revolt of 1857AD not surprisingly, the areas of Orissa, except one or two, remained quiet. The *Garhjat* princes proved to be sincere in their loyalty to the British *Raj*. *Raja* of Mayurbhanj helped[13] the government against the mutineers. The people of *Moghulbandi*, where the influence of *Gajapati* was very strong*, were totally quiet since the royal household of *Gajapati* was no more hostile or could be mutinous.

By 1850AD, Orissa was not unitedly ruled as one administrative unit. Oriya-speaking areas of Ganjam, Koraput, Gunthur, Vishakhapatna were still left under the administration of Madras Presidency and in 1862AD Sambalpur was also made over to the newly constituted Central Province.[14] Many *Garhjats* like Gangpur, Bonai, Bamanda, Kalahandi, Redhakhol, Sonepur, etc. were under the administration of neighbouring provinces.[15] Only Orissa Division of Cuttack, Puri and Balasore alongwith nineteen *Garhjats* were ruled by a Divisional Commissioner under Bengal, Bihar and Orissa Government from Calcutta. This type of division did not allow the natives to be united and raise their head when the *Marathas* in Bombay Presidency and Central India, Sikhs under Ranjit Singh and Bengalis under newly emerging modern elites could muster strength to carve out areas of their own influence in modern India. Political inactivity of the natives for centuries made them very backward as compared to other neighbouring regions.

---

12. P.K. Mishra, Political Unrest in Orissa, In the 19th Century, Calcutta 1983, p. 44.
13. N. Senapati, D.C. Kuanr, (ed) O.D.G. - Mayurbhanj, Cuttack, 1977, p. 74.

* Coastal Orissa always remained the heart-land of Orissa Empires.

14. S.C. Patra, Formation of the Province of Orissa, Calcutta, 1979, pp. 40-42.
15. *Ibid.*, p. 54; S.S. Pradhan, *op.cit.*, p. 17.

Social Condition

During the medieval period, the Oriyas became successful to carve out a grand empire and the cosmopolitan Cult of Jagannath or *'Jagannath Dharma'*[16] provided the needed ideological support to all classes of people to contribute for the State—which was of *Jagannath*—as the common Oriyas still believe. Religious and emotional attachment to the Lord and to his chief servants—the Ganga Emperors and the *Gajapatis* provided the spirit of cohesion to the society in spite of the presence of social segregation, casteism and superstitions throughout the age. The poverty-stricken sections of medieval Oriyas were provided with some sort of satisfaction where the kings and the *Brahmins* in the name of religion provided them a grand Empire to be content. The success of kings with the help of the *Brahmins* and the construction of gigantic temples amazed the masses and, thus, the kings became successful in arresting their loyalty for centuries.

Feudalism grew throughout the medieval period in Orissa and when Moghuls ruled, it was at its highest extent.[17] The by-product of this system made common people being exploited by the landlords. In the later centuries, overseas trade declined and artisans lost their patrons due to the lack of interests in the administrators who were mostly engaged in frequent warfare and most of them were outsiders also. It gave extra pressure on agriculture. *Bhakti* movement of medieval period continued its strong influence on the society even in these years. The people became very poor and helpess and gradually alienated themselves completely from the mainstream. Fatalism and superstitions engriped them and desperation destroyed their interest in lives. So, there

16. A. Eschman, H. Kulke, G.C. Tripathy, The Cult of Jagannath and the Regional Tradition of Orissa, New Delhi, 1978, p. 80, 93, 94 & 95; K.C. Mishra, The Cult of Jagannath, Calcutta, 1971, pp. 86-96, (It is regarded cosmopolitan as it reflects the tenets and customs of many Indian Cults, religions and also races).
17. Proc. OHC; 1977, p.106; A. Stirling, *op.cit.*, pp. 246-48.

helpess people got solace in different religious sects to avoid mental agony and frustration. As cultivation was the only source of employment almost all of them engaged in it. The closed agrarian atmosphere made the natives unprogressive in outlook and lethargic in temperament.

Confinement in villages for long periods without any geographical mobility[18] made the Oriyas intensely traditional, orthodox and mentally static. So, caste system became rigid and the operational values of the society, which were very much productive before, became worthless under the rule of the outsiders. Most of the outsiders were also of different religions. The glory-starved higher castes tightened their noose over the society to safeguard their identity, status and livelihood. Continuous loot by the Moghuls, *Marathas* and by the British with the help of Indian officials of neighbouring provinces and also by native feudals never gave the people of Orissa the scope to think seriously about their conditions. Because of acute poverty the people became blind rationally. The spiritual leaders of the traditional Hindu Society of Orissa, the *Brahmins*, became dumbfounded finding unexpectedly as well as suddenly new political powers having different outlooks and objectives[19] who need not patronise them. A complete collapse of the vitality of the society took place in the province of Orissa.[20]

During the years of British occupation of Orissa, same condition has been prevalent also in the region. Caste system was quite acute. *Brahmins* remained highest in the Caste hierarchy followed by the *Karanas* and *Khandayats*.[21] The

18. K.M. Patra, "Growth of National Consciousness & Freedom Struggle in Orissa", *Orissa Review*, Vol.-XLII, No.-1, August, 1986, p. 7.
19. N.K. Das, Atmajivani (O), Cuttack, 1973, pp. 7-11.
20. S.L. Maddox, Final Report on the Survey and Settlement of the Province of Orissa, 1890-1900AD, Vol.-1, Cuttack, 1900, pp. 149-50; J. Singh, Prachina *Utkal* (O), BBSR, 1964, p. 246.
21. *Ibid.*, p. 124, 495 (These feelings are clearly described by the early British Officials in Orissa in their works).

Brahmins were of different sub-castes and as in other parts in India dominated the social scene in the province. Though their pivotal position, which they were enjoying under the patronage of Hindu Kings, no longer existed, their titular social position was not disturbed in spite of their non-functional existence. They lost vision and direction in the new political atmosphere. But, they still remained supreme in an orthodox society where helplessness and superstitions controlled social behavior and norms. The fatalist masses without any sense of rationality and new hope failed to regenerate vigour in this region and were left to be suffered from degradation and degeneration in the eyes of their neighbours.

The *Brahmans* failed to take theses masses into confidence to rebuild a national character. They themselves became orthodox which followed suit by the rest. The traditional priests took asylum in different *Sasanas* and became parasitic.[22] Their traditional knowledge without any modern revision and orthodoxy due to fear to loose social identity definitely could not help them to come out of their medieval jinx. The *Brahmans* of Orissa, no doubt of the 19th century, failed to adjust themselves with the new age when their brethren in Bengal, Madras and Maharastra became the proud active members of modern Indian renaissance as well as of the modern elites of India.

The *Karanas* were conspicuous during the medieval period for their activities as scribes and royal officers. Though few in number, these *Karanas* were also of different kinds having social inequalities in themselves. It is difficult to find out the origin of these castes. It may not be untrue if their origin can be traced from the *Khandayats*. Even it is

---

22. Interview—Late Mayadhar Mohapatra, Adaspur, Cuttack; Late Lokanath Mohanty, Ghodansh, Jagatsinghpur, Late Prahalad Pradhan, Adaspur, Cuttack and many other Old Men expressed the Social Condition of their child-hood in 1900AD; W.W. Hunter, Statistical Account of Bengal, Vol.-XIX, Delhi, 1877, p. 40.

still said today that if a peasant grows becomes a *Karana*.[23] These people were famous for their adoptive nature and quick adjustive characters which they perhaps acquired during medieval period. British style of administration helped these castes to improve their social status quickly surpassing the *Brahmans* and *Khandayats*. These castes actually worked as the real harbinger of modernisation in Orissa. During the early years of British administration these castes became prosperous and active. They got the lower-level governmental jobs easily for their traditional profession as scribes as compared to the people of other castes in Orissa. Their number also grew when many *Khandayats* became *Karanas*. 'Karanisation' was the main way of social mobility of the *Khandayats*—who were declining rapidly, for social mobility to get higher status and recognition in the society.[24] Thus the *Karanas* symbolised social progress of Orissa in the 19th century.[25]

The traditional militias of Orissa, the *Khandayats* lost their patrons with the demise of old Hindu empires in coastal region. They were mostly peasants or *Chasas*,[26] and were large in number because of the military nature of Oriya empires in its history since time immemorial. These 'quast-military'[27] castes constituted a prominent part in the history

23. P.M. Pradhan, Mukti Pathe Sainika (O), Cuttack, 1979, p. 12; B.M. Pattnaik, Amari Gan Kahani (O), BBSR, 1989, p. 12; P. Mukherjee, (ed), *Utkal* University History of Orissa, Vol.-VI, Cuttack,1964, p. 460; S. Mohanty, Maralara Mrutyu O Anyanya Galpa (O), Cuttack, 1962, p. 165; G.B. Das, Bhima Bhuyan (O), Cuttack, 1988, p. 37.
24. These developments can be ascertained from the Reports of S.L. Maddox, *op.cit.*; W.W. Hunter, *op.cit.*, and the Autobiographies of all the leading men of Orissa and the contemporary literature.
25. P.M. Acharya, Odisara Itihas (O), Cuttack, 1977, p.18.
26. S.L. Maddox, *op.cit.*, p.p. 149-50; W.W. Hunter, op.cit., p. 40; K. Champati Ray, Paikakheda (O), Sadashiv Rath Sharma (ed), Puri, 1953, pp. 7-10; P.K. Pradhan, "The Peasant - Militias of Orissa, The *Khandayats* : Their Sociol-Historical Identity", *JOH*, Vol.-XIII-IV, November, 1995, pp. 167-75.
27. Hutton, Castes in India, Bombay, 1986, p. 26.

of this region because of their peculiar professions—as soldiers and as farmers. Though they regarded themselves as *Kshyatriyas,* because of their profession as farmers during peace time, also called as *'Sudras'* by the Brahmin-dominated society as the *Marathas, Jats, Patidars* and *Vellalas* in other provinces of India.

The castes constituted more than 40% of the coastal population having their regional variations and own social inequalities within themselves.[28] They were also present in princely states—where because of the continuation of semi-independent feudal princes, they could retain their traditional identities more prominently than those in coastal region. The coastal areas were ruled by the Moghuls and the British directly abolishing the traditional royal households and feudal chiefs.

These *Khandayats* were of different *Jatis* or sub-castes like *Chasas, Garhuas, Sudhs, Mahanayaks, Orhs, Kalingis, Baluas, Banayats,* etc.[29] Almost all were commonly known as cultivators except a few feudal landlords. Their financial condition was suddently disturbed when they were disbanded in large numbers. Gradual pauperisation reduced them into marginal farmers and even agricultural workers.[30] The inactivity and orthodoxy of these dominating but large number of unprogressive people made the society more static and superstitious in nature.

Though socially considered forward these castes became paupers like the untouchables. Becoming cultivators solely they lost their chivalry and great historical identity. Only the nobles or *Samantas* among them could continue their social status establishing their marital relationship with newly emerging *Karanas*. The *Khadayats* had no respect for

28. K.C. Panigrahi, *op.cit.*, p. 462; S.L. Maddox, *op.cit.*, pp. 145-49; R.D. Banerjee, *op.cit.*, p.18.
29. B.M. Padhi, Puratana Kalingara Samajika Itibruti (O), Cuttack, 1992, pp. 10-30; R.D. Banerjee, *op.cit.*; S.L. Maddox, *op.cit.*, p. 149.
30. S.L. Maddox, *op.cit.*, p. 261; J.B. Singh, *op.cit.*, p. 267.

the British and the later also did not recruit them in the armies declaring the Oriyas 'non-martial'! The hatred for government jobs or business also aggravated the condition of these peasant-militias of Orissa. The process of demilitarisation made these great people very backward, orthodox and dispirited for the first time of their history. They had been of backbone of Oriya Nationalism and identity since time immemorial. Forcible peasantisation of these castes and lack of modern trends gave the final blow to the downfall of the Oriya race. Their downfall was permanent and very quick in nature which was unparalleled in the history. Their traditional leaders, the nobles, could not identify themselves with the rest and isolated themselves into the realm of false ego, pride, frustration and newly acquired status of *'Rajputs'*. The social bond between the nobles and the peasant-soldiers never revived and the nobles failed to identify themselves with the agonies of the rest to be ignored by the mass completely.

Besides the *Brahmins, Karanas, Khandayats* and also *Gaudas* (milk-man-caste), there were artisans and trading communities. They were *Badhei* (carpenter), *Kamara* (black smith), *Bania* (gold smith), *Kumbhara* (potter), *Thatari* (brass smith), *Daraji* (tailor), *Tanti* (weaver), etc. and trading castes like *Putuli Bania* (merchant of medicinal herbs), *Teli* (oilman), *Thoria* (grain merchant), etc. These castes constituted the backward castes socially.[31] Though were prosperous during early years of colonial rule they were ruined. It is very difficult to trace the existence of traditional merchant classes of Orissa *i.e.* the *Sadhavas*. Perhaps people of different castes including the *Brahmins, Khandayats, Teli* or *Thorias* having surnames as *'Sahu'* were the offspring of those dare-devil sea-voyagers of old *Kalinga*.

Among the lowest castes, there were both touchables like *Keuta* (fisherman), *Bhandari* (barber), *Tanti* (weaver), etc. and untouchables or *achhuts* like *Bauri, Kandara, Dama, Pana,*

31. A. Stirling, *op.cit.*, p. 32.

Dhoba, etc.[32] These people were homogeneous in their presence throughout the province and were living within the close proximity of higher castes.[33] But their condition was worse than the tribals—who were living a life of isolation but had not suffer the stigma of social ostracism and ignominious agony of the practice of untouchability.

The untouchables were numerous in number having different social status. In India the lower castes have a tendency to adopt lifestyles of the dominating upper castes to develop their status in the eyes of other nearer castes. The process has been christened as 'Sanskritisation' by M.N. Srinivas.[34] But the traditional Hindu society has also legal and ritual sanctions to prevent lower castes to do so.[35] So, very often, while imitating the upper castes, the lower castes followed only superstitious, unscientific, dogmatic, expensive customs and caste surnames that helped for the dominance of casteism and social inequalities without destroying these. While except a few *Karanas*, the traditional dominating castes like *Brahmans* and *Khandayatas* were very orthodox and backward in outlook in villages, the untouchables and lower castes who took these dominating castes as social models, thus, helped for the growth of superstitious customs and unscientific traditions in the society becoming more backward in outlook.

Inequality within the lower castes created a great hindrance for the growth of a common front among these stratas. The higher Oriya castes were divided into thirtysix *Patakas* or *Jatis* on the basis of their services which also

32. W.W. Hunter, *op.cit.*, Vol.-XVIII, pp. 72-76; P.K. Pradhan, "Socio-Political Identity of the Depressed Castes of Orissa during the Colonial Phase; Study of the Untouchables, 1803-1947", Proc., *OHC*, Vol.-XX, 1995, pp. 122-27.
33. B. Sahoo, Weaker Section, Poverty & Development, BBSR, 1985, p. 5.
34. M.N. Srinivas, Social Change in Modern India, Bombay, 1982.
35. A. Beteille, "Castes : Old & New", *Essay in Social Structure and Social Stratification*, Bombay, 1969, p. 90.

included few untouchables. These untouchables regarded themselves higher than the rest.[36] The acted as the agents of segregation imposed by the touchable higher castes in the untouchables. There was no common social platform for the depressed castes.

While glorifying the era of medieval *Odra* kingdoms, scholars forget to highlight the role of tribals and untouchables who were living in a very highly religious but unequal environment. They were recruited in army in large number.[37] The untouchables, particularly, were definitely being used as manual labourers while temples were built in different places in Orissa. They were poor, illiterate and could not have a proper respectable place in this highly feudal and Brahmanic society. But surprisingly these people continued their existence amazingly for centuries in spite of many inhuman atrocities inflicted on them. Their non-violent attitude was the product of their environment, age-old beliefs in fate and status-quo and feeling of guiltiness to think anything negative against the existing social systems. Strong religious beliefs had made them so docilc that they did not revolt against the system, rather laboured hard for generations to build the financial backbone of the Oriya society where they themselves were not considered as a part of the mainstream.

In the temples, the entry of untouchable castes were strictly prohibited.[38] They were not allowed to take active part in religious functions of the villages. Caste organisations existed to protect the interest of various castes.[39] The poorer *Karanas, Khandayats* and artisans totally depended on their small patches of land and due to their unavoidable dependence on agrarian labourers, mixed

36. B.M. Padhi, *op.cit.*
37. K.C. Panigrahi, *op.cit.*; P.K. Pradhan, "The Peasant....", *op.cit.*
38. W.W. Hunter, *op.cit.*, Vol.-XIX, p. 62.
39. G.B. Mishra, Ardha Satabdira Itihas O Tahinre Mo Sthhana (O), Cuttack, 1958, p. 110; K.B. Das, Jivani O Jivana (O), Cuttack, 1981, pp. 245-46.

frequently with the untouchables while maintaining their social status. This somehow lessened the intensity of isolation and untouchability in the non-*Brahmin* castes in the society. Economically there was very little difference between a tiller or so-called marginal farmer or an agricultural labourer. So there was no middle class in this totally agrarian environment. Frequent famines and floods as well as exploitation by the tax-collectors and money-lenders made the land meaningless for the peasants. There were broadly only two classes in the society—the land-owners, and poor peasants and agricultural labourers.

The Report of Famine Commission, in 1866AD, says that Oriyas of the time had much caste prejudice. They seemed to be certainly less quick and pushing than the Bengalis and the higher classes had almost no education. The labouring and lower castes of cultivators were somewhat stupid. The Oriyas were very much conservative and could hardly be made to hurry themselves.[40]

In the *Garhjats*, the officials of the princes exploited and harassed the common people to the maximum taking the help of the neglecting attitude of the princes. The princes were practising polygamy.[41] They kept large number of concubines and many women servants. The women of princely houses were practising *sati*. It is also found that women of different castes were performing this gruesome custom.[42] These petty kings unleased reign of terror with the help of their landed militia—who here 'combined with the most profound barbarism, and the blindest devotion to the will of their chiefs, a ferocity and unquietness of disposition which had ever rendered them an important and formidable class of the province. They were from the peasant classes'.[43]

40. Quofed in S.L. Maddox, *op.cit.*, p. 124.
41. P. Mukherjee (ed), *op.cit.*, p. 462.
42. *Ibid.*, N.B. Samantray, Odiya Sahityara Itihas (1803-1920), BBSR, 1964, p. 26.
43. A. Stirling, *op.cit.*, p. 38.

Impact of Bengal Renaissance was felt a little here due to the total isolation of Orissa from rest of India and also for the absence of strong educated elites. Western education was still out of the imagination of the general public. The traditional elites—Princes, Zamindars, Revenue officials and *Brahmans* in villages and a few government officials who were very much medieval in their outlook, never felt concerned for the poor. Introduction of British-type courts and legal procedures helped these elites to exploit the people to their heart's content.[44] Absence of commercial middle-class and non-formation of strong educated group left the ground open to the land-owners to rule supreme socially for a long period. Political division, lack of interest in education, British apathy towards the region, poverty and lack of communication facilities did not create atmosphere for the growth of any leadership like those of Rammohan Roy, Dayananda Saraswati, Iswarchandra Vidyasagar, Ramaswami Naicker or M.G. Ranade of other provinces.

Financial immobility of the rural society only helped for a continuity towards destruction gradually. People got satisfied with a severely low-standard of living. They became apathetic towards administration and physical labour. They had lost their faith in themselves completely and not aware of their capability and rights as human beings of a civilized world. Missionaries established schools in different places but the then society rejected them completely, because of their engagement to spread Christianity.[45] The *Brahmans* opposed the system[46] and even a teacher was declared outcaste as he taught in the *firingi* school.[47] A medical student was threatened with ex-

44. F.M. Senapati, Fakir Mohan Granthabali (O), Vol.-II, Cuttack, p. 76. (In his novel 'Chha Mana Atha Guntha' also he has vividly described exploitation of a peasant by a land-lord and money-lender).

45. K.M. Patra, Orissa State Legislature and Freedom Struggle, 1912-47, Delhi, 1979, p .4.

46. P. Mukherjee, *op.cit.*, p. 460.

47. W.W. Hunter, History of Orissa, Vol.-II, London, 1872, p. 146.

communication for dissecting corpses.[48]

In spite of opposition from the society British should have tried to spread education in Orissa which they did not. By 1848-49AD the British had established only 9 schools in Orissa.[49] But, anyhow, growing demand of English-Educated persons in the government services and the social status gradually acknowledged by the society, induced many parents to send their children to schools.

The condition of the society turned worst when the Great Famine of Orissa (1865-66AD) visited the land. Poor peasants and the dependents on them were ruined completely. People roamed to get food. It was calculated that only in Cuttack, Puri and Balasore, 8,14,469 persons were killed and 1,15,028 were migrated to other provinces. The missionaries took the orphans and looked after them as they had become outcastes taking food from government food centres.[50] The social system was considerably disturbed during this period.

Economic Condition

Towards the end of the *Gajapati* rule, the economic system of Orissa had lost its mobility and reached a standstill position. Typical village self-sufficiency grew to the maximum within the limited production and limited want which destroyed the circulation and accumulation of capital for prosperity. During the Moghuls peoples' suffering grew because of the growth of rent-free estates. The *Marathas* with their demand of tributes from the princes also collected revenues from the common people. After conquering Orissa the British[51] made arrangements to rule the region permanently. They exacted the dues regularly

48. *Utkal* Putra, 17th June, 1874.
49. W.W. Hunter, *op.cit.*, p.147.
50. *Utkal* Dipika, 14th July, 1868; S. Pattnaik, "Orissa in 1866", *OHRJ*, Vol.-IX, October-January, 1961, p. 71; "Orissa in 1868", *OHRJ*, Vol.-X, No.4, 1962, pp. 45-48.
51. B.S. Das, *op.cit.*, pp. 139-47.

and enhanced it in due intervals.

The British knowingly encouraged the growth of land-owning classes to create their supporters among the natives and to collect revenues without taking any extra responsibility to develop indegeneous industries and trading. The condition of animal husbandry was quite precarious to take as a profession. Local artisans had no market. Rice export was in the hands of outsiders. Textile could not withstand the onslaught of British textile mills.[52] The land-owners did not encourage new patterns of cropping. Rice or pulse cultivation could have been encouraged through irrigation which the British started very late. The landlords and princes could not utilise their wealth in industries or trading, thus, the growth of a trading class of indigenous origin could not take place. No Oriya merchantile community could grow as *Marwaris, Chettiars, Lalas* or *Gujratis.*

Estate's became available to be purchased and defaulters were forced to leave their possessions over the land.[53] This helped the zamindars and money-lenders as well as few Calcutta - based wealthy Bengalis to buy estates whenever the estates of the defaulters were auctioned.[54] The new zamindars kept themselves aloof Oriya culture and aped western life, so, could not realise the support of the common people. The British discouraged traditional Oriya Currency system—*Cowrey,* putting more hardship on the people. Indigenous and prosperous salt industry was ruined due to British restrictions.[55]

Gradually small estates were absorbed by big landlords

---

52. S.C. Dey, "British Conquest of Orissa and Early British Administration", *OHRJ*, Vol.-III, No.3, 1954,pp. 159-61; K.C. Jena, Socio-Economic condition of Orissa : 19th Century, Delhi, 1978, pp. 36-40.
53. S.L. Maddox, *op.cit.*, p. 165.
54. *Ibid.*, p.186.
55. S.C. Dey, *op.cit.*

and most of the small farmers became landless tillers[56] which helped for the polarisation of the rural society. The cultivators fell victims to money-lenders' greed. Some sort of slavery grew and it was reported that there were around 7,000 slaves within the jurisdiction of one *thana* of Balasore district.[57] The peasants, though, had land, bullocks and ploughs, without modern methods of cultivation and irrigation facility and capital, could not grow under heavy pressure of a colonial and feudal agrarian economy. Government dug canals in 1862AD but could not complete the works untill the famine.[58]

Even by this time the coastal districts had a few busy ports and flourishing trade of Ship-building. But restrictions imposed by the company over internal trade ruined these trading centres. Balasore was the centre of salt trade of Eastern coast. Ports of Puri were exporting rice to Mauritius, Srilanka and Maldives. But these places soon were deserted due to lack of proper patronage. This led to mass unemployment for thousands of people.[59]

Though ready money and matter were available for the loanees by the village money-lenders,[60] it was meant to bind the peasants in the relation of perpetual dependence within the confines of the villages to continue their perennial exploitation. Money was spurned as worthless and prices of rice were far beyond those known in any recorded famine in the country.[61] *Mahajans* sold rice taking more than 200% as profits.[62] People died in numbers and agriculture of the

---

56. S.L. Maddox, *op.cit.*, p. 132 & 184.
57. N.A. (Judicial), File No.830 (H. Ricketts to the Register, Nizamat Adalat, 24th June, 1936).
58. W.W. Hunter, Statistical........, *op.cit.*, Vol.-XVIII, pp. 39-47.
59. *Ibid.*, p.p.31-32, also Vol.-XIX, p. 21; F.M. Senapati, *op.cit.*, p. 35.
60. S.L. Maddox, *op.cit.*, p. 126, 130, 135 & 495.
61. P. Mukherjee, "The Orissa Famine of 1866", *OHRJ*, Vol.-VI, April, 1957, p. 69.
62. *Ibid.*, p. 79.

coastal area, particularly, was destroyed.[63] Many a people migrated to other provinces to seek livelihood.[64] The condition of the people which had been continuing from the downfall of *Gajapati* empire finally climaxed in the famine which destroyed the total agrarian population. The suffering of the coastal region was beyond description.

Orissa was being used as a colony by the Moghuls and the Marathas till 1803AD when British occupied it. They also continued to drain the resources of the region regularly. 'All these occupants of Orissa quickened the stagnation and degradation of the entire structure of the natives by plundering its riches and revenues, harassing the traditional leaders, discouraging general progress and also blocking the growth of reawakening.'[65] The non-Oriya *Amlas* heightened the process and the Oriyas reeled under the typical 'double colonialism'. The non-Oriya officials of the company behaved as masters of the natives. This colonialism of Orissa was not only 'double' in nature but also completely 'hegemonic' since the occupation of the Moghuls in late 16th-Century till the out-break of the Great Famine of 1864AD under British rule. Due to the absence of a conscious group of natives, the outsiders completely ignored the Oriyas without any fear. No progressive Programmes were introduced for the development of the natives as happened in other regions of India—where the colonialists had to satisfy the vociferous and conscious elites. The Oriyas were divided into many parts to perpetuate the hegemony of the outsiders for centuries.

'The Class of big land-owners including the princes and zamindars of petty kingdoms emerged to the sub-ordinate exploiters in Orissa next to the Britishers'. 'There were middle class tenure holders who assisted their masters in the collection of revenues and received percentages'.[66]

63. L.S.S.O.' Malley (ed), B.O.D.G. Sambalpur, Patna, 1932, p. 143.
64. *Utkal* Dipika, 11th April, 1868.
65. B.S. Das, *op.cit.*, p. 141.
66. N.K. Jit, The Agrarian Life and Economy of Orissa, A Survey, 1833-97, Calcutta, 1984, p. 212.

Below them were subordinate tenure-holders, who were generally rich and rarely suffered in times of bad harvests'.[67] The newly emerging tiny band of native government servants also became tiny land-owners because of the availability of cash money with them. All these landed classes became money-lenders.

When the coastal Orissa had zamindars of British creation, the Western Orissa had the old households of big zamindars called Rajas by their people. By the end of 1850AD few English educated from coastal Orissa joined government services as *Amlas* or managers and served in Western Orissa as the representatives of the British *Raj*. They became infamous as '*Katakias*'[68] for their hypocritic attitude.

The ratio between urban and rural population remained same for decades together as there were no scopes for employment in nearby towns. The Oriyas migrated to West-Bengal, Madras, Assam or Rangoon to seek livelihood. The Oriya towns like Cuttack, Puri, Bhadrak, Balasore, Jaleswar, Sambalpur, Rambha, Berhampur, etc. were like big unpolished clusters of houses[69] —mostly thached without any factory, industrial or business establishment. These towns had official centres, schools, courts besides old monuments. *Punjabis* and *Marwaries* were coming to Orissa as traders. British and native officials were another group of urbanites.

Centuries of exploitation and oppression by the Moghuls, Marathas and especially by the sophisticated British upto the outbreak of the famine in 1865AD, made some permanent effect in the Oriya character. 'To sow year after year without knowing by whom the fruits would be gathered, to be continually harried and plundered-must necessarily discourage thrift and promote improvidence.'[70]

67. *Ibid*.
68. C.R. Das, Odiya Sahityara Sanskrutika Vikasa Dhara (O), BBSR, 1981, p. 210.
69. P.M. Acharya, *op.cit.*, pp. 5-7; K.B. Das, *op.cit.*, p. 258.
70. S.L. Maddox, *op.cit.*, p. 125.

This system was started during the Moghul and Maratha period, and so continued—rather aggravated—during the East India Company's rule in Orissa as well as upto 1866AD, when even the British 'Crown' took the administration of India in 1858AD. Famine completed the darkest chapter of Orissa's history of modern times.

II

POLITICAL, SOCIAL AND ECONOMIC CONDITION OF ORISSA (1866 AD—1920 AD)

Famine also marked the end of an era of total inactivity, isolation, ignorance and helplessness in Orissa. A new chapter of Orissa's history was opened and gradual awareness entered into the people—particularly in the growing educated elites. From 1866 to 1920AD, these years witnessed certain new developments in the political fields of Orissa. Growth of modern education contributed largely for the growth of political awareness among a part of the population. These modern elite class and the professionals inaugurated a political and cultural awakening that helped, in all respects, to shape the mind and awareness in succeeding decades. They really opened the floodgates of new ideas to come into Orissa after a long isolation.

Political Condition

The Orissa famine exposed the serious defects of British administration in Orissa. Realising its responsibility, the government tried to raise the general condition of the people through better communications, irrigation facilities and extension of education. But these attempts were inadequate to develop the condition of the people. After the Munity of 1857AD the government did not try to dissatisfy the princes. The Princes became more autocratic and paid least attention towards the development of the people. They 'did not maintain regular police stations and the police duties were performed by their own militia, the *Paiks*—cultivators, holding on a tenure of military service',[71] and they were very backward in their outlook. Even some kings were illiterates,[72] so were not aware of modern trends of administration. By 1870s the *Garhjat* people were mostly left untouched by modern system of statecrafts.

There were series of out-breaks in many *Garhjats*—Baud (1862AD), Athamallik (1863AD), Mayurbhanj (1866AD), Keonjhar (1868AD and 1891AD), Daspalla (1897AD), Nayagarh (1893AD). The causes of the out-breaks were mostly the oppression of the kings as well as frequent civil wars for succession. But all these events were isolated in nature and evolved within some particular areas. These were quickly suppressed.[73] Till 1905AD, British administration kept nineteen tributary states out of twentysix under Orissa division and rest were in Central Provinces and Madras Presidency. By 1906AD, due to the partition of Bengal, only seven more states joined Orissa division from Central Province. But the entire princely Oriya areas of Madras Presidency were left out.

So, the British, though occupied entire region of Oriya-speaking population, never tried to rule the region under one administration; rather these people were kept under different Presidencies. Madras Presidency ruled over Oriyas of Koraput, Ganjam, Vizagpatanam (Vishakhapatna) and Gunthur districts.[74] Central Province had jurisdiction over tracts of Sambalpur, Bolangir, Kalahandi and Sundargarh districts.[75] The Oriyas of Medinipur, Manbhum and Dhalbhum were governed by Bengal Division. The Oriyas of Singhbhum were left to be administered by Bihar division of the Bengal Presidency. Rest of the Oriyas were under the administration of Orissa division of Bihar, Bengal and Orissa Government. This ramification caused lots of hardship for

71. W.W. Hunter, *op.cit.*, p. 264; F.M. Senapati, *op.cit.*, pp. 164-65.
72. F.M. Senapati, *op.cit.*, pp. 135-36; *Utkal* Putra, 1st July, 1873.
73. S.S. Pradhan, *op.cit.*, p. 83.
74. R.C.S. Bell (ed), D.G.O. Koraput, Cuttack, 1945, p. 1.
75. S.C. Patra, *op.cit.*, p. 54.

the people and political awareness could not grow due to the lack of political Unity and common identity. Hindi, Bengali and Telgu languages were forced upon the Oriyas students of other provinces.[76] The Oriyas formed a minority under each Government.[77] In Medinipur, the Oriyas, out of their inferiority complex for their racial identity gradually tried to be identified as Bengalis using Bengali caste titles, language and social customs.[78] Same also happened in Madras Presidency.

As already mentioned growth of education in Orissa created a new band of elites in the society. Though, urban based, they ushered a new era of cultural modernisation of Orissa. And the most profound influence was felt in the field of literature, journalism and social work. In these years the Princes and Zamindars contributed handsomely for this development.[79] Though the society was still orthodox in villages, in Cuttack, Puri, Balasore, Sambalpur and Berhampur towns (these were the only urban centres of the region), the people sent their children to the schools to provide them the minimum educational qualification to get a government job—at least to be a clerk or at best to be a Deputy-Magistrate.[80] Rich parents of the rural areas kept their sons (not the daughters) in boarding schools of urban centres after their primary education in the villages.[81] This really helped in breaking up the urban-rural isolation.

Out of these educated young men some emerged as social workers, who championed the cause of the natives. Meanwhile some influential domiciled Bengalis tried to introduce Bengali as the vernacular language of the primary schools of Orissa. It created lots of resentment among the

76. P.K. Mishra, The Political History of Orissa, 1900-36, New Delhi, 1979, p. 20.
77. *Utkal* Dipika, 13th January, 1869.
78. G.B. Mishra, *op.cit.*, p. 137., *Asha*, 25th May, 1914.
79. This can be found from contemporary newspapers.
80. H.K. Mahtab, Prativa (O), Cuttack, 1962, pp. 13-15.
81. F.M. Senapati, *op.cit.*, Vol.-II, p. 203.

conscious Oriyas who reacted strongly against this heinous move. They realised the fact that it was the political vivisection which was responsible for the backwardness of the region and dominance of the neighbours. The educated Oriyas started a language movement which forged a spirit of unity between different Oriya-speaking regions. Meanwhile historical writings of Andrew Stirling, W.W. Hunter and John Beams on Orissa awakened the educated men culturally.[82] The attempt of some writers to malign Orissa's culture and history was also strongly objected by the Oriyas. Unification of Oriya-speaking people became the cry of the educated of the time. Many Oriya periodicals, newspapers*, books were written. Numerous associations were formed.[83] Debating societies grew in different towns. In this process ultimately language crisis became the breeding ground of the 19th Century Oriya nationalism.

Whenever a dormant race rose its head, it was its knowledge on rich cultural heritage that helped to infuse pride and spirit among the people. Oriyas of the late 19th Century were culturally unaware, and for this they had to acknowledge attack on their culture and race. The leaders of the late 19th Century Oriya nationalism took the help of the currents of glorious culture of Orissa to awaken the people.[84] This brought self-respect and pride and confidence in them. Writings of A. Stirling, W.W. Hunter, John Beams and also of Fakirmohan Senapati, Gangadhar Meher, Radhanath Ray, Madhusudhan Rao, Nandakishore Bal, Laxmikant Mohapatra etc. about the role of Oriya historical heroes as well as the flora and fauna and traditions helped the semi-educated and literate persons to be aware of their

82. B.C. Acharya, Oriya Sahityara Sankhipta Parichaya (O), Cuttack, 1975, p. 194.

* *Utkal* Dipika, *Utkal* Star, *Utkal* Sevaka, Cuttack Chronicle, Ganjam News, Swadeshi, P*Raja*bandhu, etc.

83. K.M. Patra, "Growth of Social Consciousness in Orissa in the 19th Century", Proc., *IHRC*, 1970, Vol.-XL, p. 151; N. Samantaray, *op.cit.*, pp. 175-80.

84. B.C. Acharya, *op.cit.*, p. 198.

old glorious past and acquire self-dignity.

Throughout the period various efforts to glorify Orissa were made and it infiltrated downward through the educated people to the semi-educated people and gradually form urban areas to the villagers by the help of books, newspapers, meetings and visits of different leading personalities. To subscribe newspapers in villages became a very prestigious matter and subscribers' names were printed on the front pages of various newspapers. People did gather in their leisure periods to know something new through the columns. Their curiosity helped them to be aware of, gradually, their rights and duties towards the motherland. The growing educated persons in rural and urban areas came out of the schools being educated in the line of modern political and cultural ideas and developments.

A cultural unity between coastal and western Orissa became possible after a long gap due to the language movement.[85] The inspired leaders worked with a new hope to bring all Oriya-speaking people under one political umbrella. Oriya papers gave constant support to the people in their agitation to secure rights and safeguard their language, and simultaneously educated them to challenge an alien culture and even an alien administration in the future. Though the concept of 'India-as-a-Nation' was already realised by these intelligentsia, no doubt, regional question took prominent place in their mind because of its immediate nature.

The urban-based educated elites-consisting of lawyers, poets, writers, novelists, teachers and journalists—supported by few other enlightened social workers and government servants, started the language movement and amalgamation agitation. Mostly they were high caste Hindus. Many domiciled Bengalis took leading part in heightening the case of Oriyas against acute Bengali dominance. These people -

85. *Utkal* Dipika, 16th July, 1902.

making different district headquarters as their centre of activities, were cordially helped by princes and Zamindars. It is a fact that the movement was confined within few urban centres and was not participated by the common people of the villages. But so far as the strategy of this group was concerned, it took pro-British stand as they felt it was the highest authority which could listen to them and realise the authenticity of their appeal, not the neighbours. It heralded a new era of awareness and gradually engripped the total population when it merged with the freedom movement.

In these years a man of great calibre, Madhusudan Das or Madhubabu as he was called popularly, emerged as the leader of Oriya nationalism. He was a great champion of the cause of Oriyas. He was the first Oriya lawyer. His appearance at the Cuttack court heralded a new era in the history of Oriya nationalism. Educated young people saw him as their hero when he fought successfully against the dominance of the neighbours in the court. He became a folk-hero and was regarded as the natural leader of Orissa for his achievements in his different careers. People tried to seek his help and advice and by his intelligence and presence of mind he became a symbol of pride to each Oriya.[86]

He visited different towns of Orissa and localities of Oriya-speaking people in other provinces and created a sensation and political heat throughout the region. He was helped by editors of vernacular papers in popularising the concept of the political unification of Orissa. The contemporary poets and writers glorified Orissa's culture, and this step-through various propagating channels like press, literature, meetings, deputations and appeals, helped the leaders to avail the support or involvement of all the educated Oriyas in this cultural movement.

Madhubabu kept constant touch with different associations and organisations of Oriya-speaking people

---

86. F.M. Senapati, *op.cit.*, p.-II & 206; N.K. Das, *op.cit.*, pp. 65-70.

throughout the region. He, with Gourishankar Ray,* the editor of the *'Utkal Dipika'*, joined *'Utkal Sabha'* in 1885AD and championed the case of Oriyas. As like as the moderates of the Congress party of the nineties here Madhubabu and his associates, keeping faith in British fairplay and justice, demanded concessions for the peasants of Orissa, growth of education, irrigational facilities and to improve the communication facilities like raliways and roadways in Orissa.[87]

Madhubabu kept a close link with the Indian National Congress but he was disappointed to realise that the Congress was too busy on issues concerning the whole country and Orissa as a mere appendix of Bengal found no place in the Congress agenda.[88] Domination of Bengali and Telgu leaders in early years of Congress made him annoyed of the national organisation. In 1903AD at the Madras session under the presidentship of Lal Mohan Ghosh, the Congress rejected the proposal of Oriyas to unite the districts of Ganjam and Vizagpatnam to Orissa Division. A dejected Madhubabu cut off all his relation with the Congress and formed *'Utkal* Union Conference' or *'Utkal Sammilani'* in December 1903AD,[89] to highlight the cause of political unification of Oriyas. The Princes of Orissa, meeting at the Annual Conference of the Ruling chiefs of Orissa, supported Madhubabu to provide a common platform to the scattered and foster close fraternity among the Oriyas.[90]

In 1898AD, Madhubabu was selected to the Imperial Council. Being the first Oriya in this respect he used his office to express the feelings of his fellow people in the council. Oriyas of each area looked him up as their

---

* A Domiciled Bengali and a Champion of the cause of Oriya Language.

87. S.N. Pattnaik, Odisare Swadhinatara Andolana (O), Cuttack, 1972, p. 7.
88. S.N. Das, Deshaprana Madhusudan (O), Cuttack, 1971, p. 25.
89. *Utkal* Dipika, 10th January, 1903; G.B. Mishra, *op.cit.*, p. 68.
90. *Ibid.*

representative in every platform of his activities.[91] The language movement created a spirit of unity among the people after a long period. In Sambalpur, the leaders with the help of a mouthpiece—'*Sambalpur Hiteisini*' (published from Bamanda) and in Ganjam the educated Oriyas with the help of the '*Asha*', championed the cause of the unification.[92] They were supported by the newspapers of Cuttack, Puri and Balasore. Madhubabu visited different places and criticised the government policies[93] of amalgamation. The leaders of these places sought his advice.[94] He created a deep impact on the young people and it is said that whoever went to meet him, Madhubabu would ask whether the man thought five minutes daily about the country.[95]

Meanwhile, two great Oriyas, who were yet to get their due place in the annals of the history of modern Orissa, laboured hard to make the issue strong throughout the region. Anant Mishra, a great propagandist, visited each and every places where the Oriya-speaking people were living and reported about their condition, their historical background and heritage to the leading dailies of Orissa. He visited Singhbhum, Manbhum, Medinpur, Manjusa and almost all sub-divisions of Orissa to foster the unification by mobilising people, arranging meeting, personal contacts and writing on the condition of the localities to the leading dailies which published these regularly. Before the visit of prominent leaders to any place his activities created the congenial soil for the leaders to accumulate popular support. Another man was Sribatsa Panda, the champion of the eradication of social superstitions. A social worker-par-excellence, he fought against the social injustice inflicted on the common people in the name of religion, caste and

91. Sambalpur Hiteishini, 24th March, 1895.
92. B.C. Acharya, *op.cit.*, p. 230.
93. C.R. Mishra, Freedom Movement in Sambalpur, Delhi, 1986, p.160.
94. *Ibid*. p. 174.
95. *Utkal* Sevaka, 22nd March, 1870.

untouchability, and wrote fearlessly against the *Rajas*, zamindars and *Brahmans* who were supporters of this exploitation. He was able to create a sense of awareness in the people-particularly among the educated.[96]

'Utkal Sammilani' held its annual meetings in different parts of the region Kings and prominent laureates presided over the meetings. Emotional songs, written by Gangadhar Meher, Laxmikant Mohapatra and Madhusudan Das paying homage to *'Utkal Laxmi'* were recited on the pandals.[97] The cry of Bengalis of 1905AD against the partition of Bengal, their nationalist literature and their sacrifice also influenced the young students in Orissa.[98] Bengali revolutionaries who made Orissa as their hide-outs, also influenced the Oriya students.[99] As the visit of B.C. Pal in 1907AD influenced the people of Cuttack, so also the tragic death of Khudiram moved the people deeply.

From 1903AD upto 1920AD, the *'Utkal Sammilani'* held sixteen annual sessions concerning the amalgamation of Oriya speaking people. Madhubabu took the leadership, but within these years another young Oriya was emerging as a leader of the masses in the name of Gopabandhu Das, whose career in Orissa as well as in India is a romance of history.[100] He not only gave a new colour to the concept of leadership, but also by his personal activities, teetotal life and true commitment to the people's cause had left an unforgettable memory in the people of Orissa till today. It was he, who gave a new direction to the emerging Oriya nationalism and spread the awareness among the people of villages by 1920AD.[101]

By 1910AD, India had few leaders who had behind them

96. These events were regularly published in contemporary newspapers.
97. B.C. Acharya, *op.cit.*, p. 82.
98. G.B. Mishra, *op.cit.*, p. 82
99. *Ibid.*
100. P.K. Mishra, *op.cit.*, p. 118.
101. S.N. Das, *op.cit.*, pp. 28-29.

mass support. Perhaps it was only Tilak, Lajpat Rai or Bipin Chandra Pal who could be called as leaders of the masses in some respect. Faith in common people's ability in the nation-building had not yet touched the imagination of prominent leaders of Congress. In Orissa, it was Gopabandhu Das who had established himself as sole leader of the people of every walk of life. It will not be untrue, if Gopabandhu is regarded as the only unchallenged leader of the people that Orissa soil had ever witnessed. He had secured the faith, respect and support of all Oriyas of his time.

From his student career in school and in Cuttack College,* he was a devoted social worker. He created his student supporters and formed a volunteer organisation to help the distressed people during famines, droughts, floods and epidemics.[102] Selfless social service and Gopabandhu's name became synonymous in Orissa. Perhaps, before Gandhi, in India, he was one of the few 'full-time-social-worker's devoting his total life for the poverty-stricken and politically backward people. He was so clear and open in his activities that the created very few adversary during his time.

When Madhusudan Das and his associates were fighting from above occasionally mentioning the importance of common people, Gopabandhu and his co-workers, fighting from the below, among the downtrodden, created a sense of awareness and belongingness in them. He became able to touch the very core of the hearts of the poor Oriyas in villages.[103] Staying in urban areas as students, his party worked in villages and created a link between these two areas helping in the 'downward-infiltration' of the political ideas into the masses. Mostly the leaders were *Brahmins* and *Karanas*. The fact that some fellows of higher castes and highly educated were fighting for them in different fields

---

* Now Ravenshaw College.

102. S.N. Das, *op.cit.*, p.14.

103. C.M. Das, Kavi Gopabandhu(O), Cuttack, 1966, p. 2.

leaving aside the life of comfort created an impact in the people. Frequent floods and famines for epidemics gave Gopabandhu the chances to mix with the people-going to their native place, which were unique events for the village people. Because no educated leader had ever come to them. The daring activities of his voluntary organisation in the face of epidemics during the great car festival each year at Puri,[104] no doubt, gave the people an impression that Gopabandhu was a true humanist and champion of their cause. As Puri was regarded the most sacred place in Orissa and Car festival being the national festival, this humanitarian role of Gopabandhu and his associates was highly estimated by the people who assembled there from different corners of Orissa. A close relationship with the people gave him the popularity which was well understood by other leaders of the then Orissa. It enabled him to challenge the moderate views and policies of the early Oriya nationalists to turn the tide against the British authority in 1920AD by way of abandoning the policy of mendicancy.

Gopabandhu gave high importance to the common people and also to the newly educated young men of the villages. He tried to keep close contacts with them. He welcomed the students every year who were coming to Cuttack from different corners to take Entrance Examination[105] and also opened branches of voluntary organisations in different schools. Thus, he created a close link with the students and built representatives of his ideas in villages. The students being influenced by Gopabandhu educated the people in the line of political awareness and self-respect. This helped Gopabandhu to spread the seeds of nationalism and political consciousness on the basis of both regional and national causes. Writing fiery articles[106] and delivering emotional speeches[107] he became the sole

104. *Asha*, 14th July, 1919.
105. *Ibid.*, 24th March, 1919.
106. S.N. Pattnaik, *op.cit.*, p.14.
107. *Asha*, 19th April, 1919.

mouth-piece of the contemporary awakening.

Gopabandhu adopted different activities during his lifetime. He was a champion of the cause of Oriya people and travelled many areas to infuse awareness. A poet extra-ordinary, he heralded the new school the 'Nationalist Poetry' when there was deep influence of mythological trend over the popular literature. He proved the indispensability between 'Mother India' and 'Mother *Utkal*.[108] He realised that Oriya nationalism should soon merge itself into the main current of All India feeling and by this way a wider support and field would be opened for the cause of Orissa, instead of damaging it.

By 1910AD, education had reached the villages and the lower-middle class boys of the agrarian society were joining the schools. Education in schools became a prestigious thing as it led to government services. A new trend grew in the agrarian society to leave the ancestral profession and to join schools to get a white collar job as very few Oriyas were taken for the military forces. But the value of true education had not been understood by the parents which should infuse fellow-feeling and concern towards mother land. Schools were regarded as Government Servant-producing-centres. Gopabandhu gave these boys the new direction and tried to give a new outlook of patriotism.

To open the minds of the people, Gopabandhu, in 1909AD, established a national school of his own imagination at Satyabadi of Puri district and collected some of the finest wise men of Orissa of the time as the teachers of the school. Pandit Nilakantha Das, Acharya Harihar Das, Pandit Krupasindhu Mishra, Pandit Godavarish Mishra along-with Pandit Gopabandhu formed the famous '*Pancha Sakha*' or 'Five Associates' group, who contributed in many respects, for the cultural and political growth of Orissa. Large number of students mostly from villages[109] joined the

108. As found from Bandira Atma Katha(O), Abakash(O), Karakabita (O), Gopabandhu Granthabali, Cuttack, 1948.

109. *Asha*, 16th February, 1914.

school and helped Gopabandhu fearlessly to serve the destitutes in the face of natural calamities and epidemics.[110] Their activities were felt by the people. They travelled Balasore and Ganjam, Singhbum and Medinpur and worked as volunteers at the conferences of *'Utkal Sammilani'*.[111] Many princes helped the school financially.[112] This institution helped Gopabandhu in creating a band of his followers who became leading personalities of Orissa in different fields in the succeeding decades. Puri became strong-hold of his leadership and Cuttack town became the area of educated young supporters. He became so popular in Orissa among the people that the government became panicked[113] and accused Gopabandhu for misleading the students in the name of social service.

Gopabandhu was aware of the political developments in India. His political sagacity could foresee the United India's fight against foreign rule. He came in contact with Lajpat Ray and G. K. Gokhale. To stir people utmost, he felt the need of a mouthpiece by which he could generate the appropriate enthusiasm and political temperature. He founded the *'Samaj'*, a weekly newspaper in 1919AD. This marked a new era of 'extremism' in Orissa. It was branded as an 'extremist' paper by the government. The *'Samaj'* was read by the people and its subscribers grew in number as it represented a very fiery tone.[114]

The princes of Orissa played a crucial role during the period. They became active in language movement and helped the poets and writers in publishing their works.[115] They formed the financial backbone of the agitation.[116] By

110. C.M. Das, Aitihasika Krupasindhu(O), Cuttack, 1962, p. 104.
111. *Asha*, 5th January, 1914 & 14th July, 1919.
112. *Ibid*.
113. S.N. Das, *op.cit.*, p. 271.
114. P.K. Mishra, *op.cit.*, p. 110.
115. *Asha*, 19th January, 1914; K.C. Pattnaik, Kumbhara Chaka(O), Cuttack, 1975, p.105.
116. *Asha*, 2nd February, 1914.

doing so, they perhaps tried to control the political temperature of the time, lest it would ruin their privileges and status. They also helped Gopabandhu in establishing and improving the Satyabadi school.[117] But they were eager to see that the Oriya nationalist movement should be confined within regional factors and only on the basis of cultural causes. It should not turn its direction to other fields of life which might jeopardise their privileges. To keep the movement under their control and in a moderate line they joined the sessions of *'Utkal Sammilani'*.[118] They praised the British government for its benevolence and even helped the British during the First World War by giving donations to the War Fund. Attending the Balasore sessions of *'Utkal Sammilani'* the princes praised the people of Balasore for their help in finding out of terrorist group of Baghajatin* and thanked those who helped in this work of 'loyalty'.[119] They had also condemned the terrorists of Bengal and their bomb attack on Lord Hardinge, the Viceroy of India.[120] The *Rajas*, when fighting for the cause of Orissa, were very oppressive in their own petty states. Gradually they alienated themselves from the agitation which assumed wider proportion in later years.

By 1918AD, Madhubabu realised feasibility of Gopabandhu's ideas and even praised him openly. He felt the need of a man like Gopabandhu in the present situation to lead Orissa as Gokhale, who, visualised Gandhi as the future leader of India. In contemporary newspapers like *'Asha' 'Utkal Dipika'*, and *'Utkal Putra'*, etc. few information were published about Congress and the activities of these leaders. The general intelligentsia thinking the body as an anti-Oriya organisation never paid heed to it. They also ignored the collective strength of the common masses.

117. *Ibid.*, 5th January, 1914.
118. *Utkal* Sevak, 4th January, 1917.
* Jatindra Nath Mukherjee.
119. *Utkal* Sevak, 4th January, 1917.
120. *Ibid.*, 5th January, 1914.

Attending the session of *Sammilani* in 1918AD Gopabandhu openly criticised the leaders for this policy. Speaking on behalf of the people, he declared, "The people of Orissa of all walks of life—uneducated village peasants, common lower caste people want unification".[121] Here also Madhubabu realised the fact that in serving the motherland the *'Bauris'* and *'Kandaras'** have the same right as of the *Brahmans* and *Karanas*.[122] Even the great writer of Orissa of the time, Fakirmohan Senapati, who was not a supporter of people's cause during his *Dewan*ships in various *Garhjats* before, openly sought the help of the people to strengthen their own cause.[123]

In the year 1919AD, Gopabandhu became the president of the *'Utkal Sammilani'*. He, in his speech, talked about the Irish revolutionaries and asked people to fight not only for the unification but also fight against injustice, inequality and for friendship and peace.[124] This proved that he was trying to give a new direction and outlook as quickly as possible to the *Sammilani*. In the year 1920AD, he attended the Nagpur Session of All India Congress Committee and was greatly influenced by Gandhi's policy of non-violence and non-co-operation. When returned he went to the Chakradharpur session of *'Utkal Sammilani'* and placed a resolution to merge the *Sammilani* into the National Congress. He asked the Oriyas to fight for the national emancipation along with the provincial cause in joining the non-cooperation movement under the leadership of Gandhi. This move was overwhelmingly accepted by the *Sammilani*, and Orissa, after a long gap, joined the national mainstream to get its due place in the annals of Indian freedom movement.

---

121. *Asha*, 4th March, 1919.

* So-called untouchables of Orissa.

122. *Asha*, 4th March, 1919.

123. *Ibid*.

124. *Ibid*., 28th April, 1919.

Society and Economy

The famine of 1866AD totally ruined the people. People died in numbers and thousands of children became orphans. The Viceroy took personal interest to mobilize the raising of funds and organising helps. The government took full responsibility to import rice. The Relief Committee did considerable work by collecting and distributing public donations. Grains were made available at the lower rate to the labourers who worked under the Public Works Department.[125] But these were just the healing of the wounds. The condition of general public was as it was before the famine.

The agrarian society was yet untouched by the outside developments in considerable ways. More of less, the villages were still under the influence of late-medieval inertness. It can be proved out of the fact that schools were established in different villages, but very few pupils were available due to the indifference and poverty of the masses.[126] In an under-developed agrarian society, the children were also agricultural labourers; so they felt education worthless for them. In villages, the traditional '*Pathasals*' were the only place of education which were 'useful to the village folk.[127] As parents were not interested to send their children to schools so there was no chance of woman education. The untouchables were far away from the sphere of school life. It was only in the urban areas, people sent their children to the English schools and wealthy people in villages liked their boys to go to schools in the urban centres for higher studies.[128] But either in villages or urban areas, even by 1881—92AD, most of the boys were from upper castes *Brahmins* and *Karanas* with few boys from domiciled Bengalis. Very few *Khandayat* boys

125. Sahu, Mishra & Sahu, History of Orissa, Cuttack, 1980, p. 416.
126. G.P. Mishra, *op.cit.*, p.p. 24-40; F.M. Senapati, *op.cit.*, Vol.-I, p. 60.
127. F.M. Senapati, *op.cit.*, p. 5.
128. *Ibid.*, *op.cit.*, Vol-II, p. 203.

were in the schools.[129]

The caste councils existed which were ruling supreme[130] over respective caste people as before. They formulated caste rules and implemented these rules strictly over their members. Orthodox *Brahmins* in villages or in *'Sasanas'* were very strict in observing their caste symbols like wearing threads and not keeping moustaches.[131] Orthodoxy and superstitions and firm grip over the masses.[132] But it was also a fact that some caste councils being liberal in their outlook helped promising boys of their own castes in higher studies—a marked' consciousness in the growing importance of education.[133]

A new religious sect became very popular in many regions of Orissa. The followers were called as *Kumbhipatias* who rejected the materialistic world and believed in the void. The *Kumbhipatias* were the followers of Mahima Gossain who became very popular in western parts of Orissa. Mostly lower-caste people joined the group. The liberal atmosphere of the sect produced eminent propagators of the religion live Bhima Bhoi. A *khond* by birth this blind saint proved himself a remarkable propagandist and philanthropist of the time. Living in the darkness of jungles and without any tinge with the modern world, he popularised *'Mahima Dharma'* and wrote numerous couplets in which the furstration and agony of the toiling masses and the anger to destroy the social inequalities is found. This sect also became popular in coastal Orissa soon. The followers were against caste system, untouchability and dominance of idolatry and rituals in Hindu life. Surprisingly this great soul, Bhima Bhoi had no contact with the leading elites of the then urban Orissa.

129. *Utkal* Dipika, 15th January, 1881 & 28th November, 1882 (Results of First Arts Examination & Lower & Upper Primary Schools reveal such fact).
130. G.B. Mishra, *op.cit.*, p. 110.
131. *Ibid.*, p. 27.
132. G.B. Mishra, *op.cit.*, p. 110.
133. Asha, 9th November, 1914.

Weavers of Sambalpur also became *Kabirpanthis* in number.[134] Meanwhile the *Mahantas* of different religious centres-*mathas*, were leading very luxurious and illegal life due to the accumulation of wealth and blind donation of the people in the name of religious rites. Innocent people were cheated by them.[135] The popularity of religious sects, their sudden growth and vulgar life and the unchallenged dominance of most of the *Mahantas* in the society proves the fact that the people of the region were still hopelss and dispirited. Their materialistic vigour was completely destroyed by the current of fatalist *Bhakti*, which was, no doubt, the product of mass helplessness originated from regular exploitation and frustration. The educated elites also did not champion the spirit of economic developments. *'Arth'*, an important part of *'Purusartha'* of Hindu life was not taken up seriously.

The peasants were still industrious, but without any extra interest. A Stirling described," The cultivating population were labourious, though they worked with little spirit or intelligence. They were certainly the most mild, quiet, inoffensive, and easily managed people in the company's provinces".[136] The cultivators and the agrarian labourers were still ignorant of being exploited by the dominating class and on the other hand the growing educated elites had no faith in the potentiality of these myriad. They had no confidence in the capability and right of the people on the basis of equality. Generally, many people were not getting a square meal a day and these included people from all castes.[137] Writing about the people, E.B. Harris, Commissioner of Orissa, in 1900AD, said; "The

134. L.S.S.O.' Malley (ed), O.D.G. - Sambalpur, Patna, 1932, pp. 63-67.

135. F.M. Senapati, *op.cit.*, Vol.-II, p. 201 & pp. 555-60 (In his short story 'Dhulia Baba' & poems like 'Abakash Basara' and '*Utkal* Bhramana' (O) such things are being beautifully projected).

136. As quoted in Maddox, *op.cit.*, p. 124.

137. F.M. Senapati, *op.cit.*, Vol.-II, pp. 409-10.

people are very simple in their habits, their wants are few, and they are content if these are satisfied in a moderate degree. Habitually law—biding, they do not commit serious crimes by instance, and even in times of distress serious offences against poverty are fewer than in many other place".[138]

In *Garhjats* the peasants' condition was more precarious. 'A peasant was liable to ejection in spite of long possession and enjoyment for generation'.[139] The *Rajas* were not in favour of modern system of administration or education. Very few *Rajas* has established school in their areas. In 1874AD there were only 68 schools in 24 *Garhjats*.[140] In 1872AD, Commissioner of Orissa, T.E. Ravenshaw wrote, "Orissa being an outlying and backward province its tributary states hardly yet brought within the pale of civilisation."[141] The *Rajas* were hostile to each other and were busy to spend lavishly and in vulgar ways to enhance their status and position.[142]

In these years also, around 75% of the rural population were more or less permanently indebted to the *Mahajans*, proprietory tenure holders or Zamindars.[143] The petty cultivator paid away as rent and interest a whold of his crop except what was left to him for subsistence and had always to borrow again before the next harvest was ripe. Landless labourers were employed in Zamindar's fields or by landed-people mostly of *Brahmins* and *Karana* or *Khandayat* Zamindar castes as servants and *kothias*.[144] The Oriya cultivator was contented with very little that he generally got. Moddox in his Report thus remarked, "A full meal of

138. Quoted in Maddox, *op.cit.*, p. 495. (B. Harris, Commissoner, Orissa Division).
139. S.S. Pradhan, *op.cit.*, p. 82.
140. *Utkal* Putra, 18th November, 1874.
141. Quoted in W.W. Hunter, A Statistical.., Vol.-XVIII, *op.cit.*, p. 60.
142. *Utkal* Sevak, 28th July, 1918.
143. B.S. Das, *op.cit.*, pp. 210-13.
144. S.L. Maddox, *op.cit.*, pp. 136-37.

rice once a day, taken with a little salt, some pulse or vegetables, and perhaps fish, suffices him.... the poorest classes ate to supplement their rice boiled *Kulthi* or *Mandia* cakes. Low castes, at some times respectable people, do eat roots in times of scarcity".[145] The peasant women were habituated with spinning to meet their clothing.[146] The poorer people were living in havels.[147] Rice was the main crop[148] and its failure always gave trouble to the peasants. Irrigation canals were dug, but the absence of branch canals and distributaries caused accidental floods, thus, damaging the ripe crops of the farmers.[149] Government imposed water-tax from the very beginning of the water supply so people were very irregular in paying this in spite of the tax lowered by the government in later years.[150]

Still only a few Oriyas were in government services and being from the upper castes and urban-based Hindus, they were not committant towards the people and kept themselves isolated from the masses to maintain their 'dignity—on the basis of government service'. They were aping Western system of life being influenced by the Bengalis, thus, were alienated from the poor class.[151] Oriyas were appointed as *Amlas, Tahasildars,* Salt *Dewans*. By 1870AD only three Oriya Deputy-Magistrates were in service.[152] Actually the British Officials did not support natives to get government jobs. A District Magistrate told," I find no necessity of making the sons of cultivators *Babus*".[153]

The great famine of 1865-66AD was not the only natural calamity that the people of Orissa faced. Frequent droughts,

145. *Ibid.*, p.126.
146. F.M. Senapati, *op.cit.*, Vol.-I, p. 17.
147. W.W. Hunter, *op.cit.*, p. 99.
148. S.L. Maddox, *op.cit.*, p. 47.
149. W.W. Hunter, *op.cit.*, p. 47.
150. *Ibid.*, p. 45.
151. F.M. Senapati, *op.cit.*, p. 28 & 211.
152. P. Mukherjee, "Employment....", *op.cit.*, pp. 112-16.
153. *Asha*, 30th March, 1914.

floods and cyclones killed the spirit of peasants. Very often droughts were followed by that of floods in the following rainy seasons.[154] In 1877-78AD there was a famine in Ganjam. Failure of rain in 1888AD and 1891AD was followed by heavy flood in 1892AD. The year 1885AD saw Cuttack district being affected by cyclone. The famine of 1900AD was attended by Cholera, Small pox and Influenza. In some districts during 1906-08AD deaths exceeded birth rates.[155]

Frequent plunder by the revenue collectors and money-lenders forced the peasants to be not hardworking in his own village.[156] So they migrated to other provinces to get their livelihood. Large number of herdsmen and cultivators went to Calcutta for employment.[157] In order to settle past debt and meet current cast expenditure.[158] It was found that the *Khandayat* caste—the traditional land-holder emigrants followed by *Gopalas*.[159] These Oriyas in Calcutta were aware of the Bengali carelessness towards their culture.[160] But, no doubt, there was discontent among these caste-Oriyas. Their staying in Calcutta—the political capital of India of the 19th and early 20th century, made them aware of certain new ideas. They also aped Bengali style of living. Their coming to the villages during vacations helped in infusing certain new lifestyles in the village folk in Orissa.

The precarious condition of trade and internal commerce was as before. The *Marwaris* and *Gujratis* coming from Calcutta and from their respective provinces monopolised commerce in Orissa.[161] Governmental

154. S.L. Maddox, *op.cit.*, pp. 138-39.
155. Census of India, 1951, Vol.-XI, p.1, Cuttack, 1953, pp. 34-37.
156. S.L. Maddox, *op.cit.*, p. 125; W.W. Hunter, *op.cit.*, p. 71.
157. W.W. Hunter, *op.cit.*
158. S.L. Maddox, *op.cit.*, p. 134.
159. Census of India, 1901, Vol-VI, p.1, pp. 41-59; Census of India, 1921, Vol-V, p. 2, Table-XXII, Part-IV & V.
160. G.B. Mishra, *op.cit.*, pp. 136-37.
161. F.M. Senapati, *op.cit.*, Vol-II, pp. 202-3.

measures of irrigation and co-operative banking system could nolt help the peasants to improve. In Sambalpur, by 1918AD, people failed to maintain their family through agriculture and started rickshaw-pulling and cart-riding. All were in debt and still spent unnecessarily in ceremonies and death anniversaries under the influence of superstitions.[162] Birth of unhealthy children caused the growth of child mortality. The indigenous textile industry was in a precarious condition.[163] In Koraput (under Madras Government) influenza took heavy tools of men in 1913AD and 1919AD.[164]

The society was still superstitious. Dowry system had made inroad into the region due to Bengali influence.[165] The people were quiet and submissive, very ignorant of their rights and privileges, and passive under oppression. Except in urban areas and administrative centres of *Garhjats* education had no impact. Only primary education was more in practice; so drop-outs were large in number. There was still only a single college—'Cuttack College', throughout Orissa, and here students were decreasing[166] gradually as it was very costly to stay in hostels and read in college.

As it is known people were very poor, particularly, the *Garhjat* people, who were exploited by the kings and their associates. They were not at all conscious of the political developments outside the areas. The land-holding rural people were paying the bulk of the demands of the *Rajas*. The taxes and policies imposed on them were vindictive in nature and they were unable to meet.[167] They influenced the tribals and the poor agricultural labourers to take part in the revolts against the kings. The war of 1919AD caused deep troble to the poor. Everything of daily use became

162. *Utkal* Sevaka, 28th February, 1918.
163. *Asha*, 3rd April, 1918.
164. R.C.S. Bell (ed.) O.D.G. *op.cit.*
165. *Asha*, 20th April, 1919 and 7th July, 1919.
166. *Ibid.*, 18th August, 1919.
167. F.M. Senapati, *op.cit.*, Vol-I, p. 83, 85 & 136.

scarce. '*Utkal Sevak*' reported, "There is no war, revolution, no disturbances, no natural calamities in India, but there is want everywhere".[168]

By the end of the 19th Century, while the agrarian Orissa was not yet able to come out from its severe blow of the famine of 1864-65AD, the society was in a peculiar state. Only the rural rich and the educated had contact with urban areas. As found from the Contemporary literature these were mostly *Karanas* followed by some feudal *Khandayats*, few princes and Brahmins. Most of them were land - owners. The marginal farmers were mostly from intermediary castes like *Khandayats* of different kinds, *Gopalas* and artisans. But the lower castes and untouchables had no such land. The village people had very limited contact with the urban people and were afraid of their presence because of later's hypocrite tendencies and hatred for their poor fellow Oriyas.[169]

In the urban areas the new group of educated people became prominent. They were social workers and nationalists. They were publishers, editors, social volunteers, professionals, teachers etc. Most of them came from rural Orissa. They gradually became a challenge for the hegemony of officials of the British administration. In rural areas also a new band of educated people made their presence felt. Their education had made them aware of the limitations of the power of the government servants. Their concern for the fellow Oriyas and the political condition of the region made them soon a compact group of activities or full-time social workers.

The government servants as already indicated, though educated, were adamant and complexed. They had no sound financial root as the princes or the non-Oriya businessmen. These lowly-paid servants grew some sort of

---

168. *Utkal* Sevak, 7th March 1919.
169. F.M. Senapati, *op.cit.*, (His entire literature reflect such conditions of the then Oriya Society).

jealously for the rest. Most of them became supporters of British Raj and also indulged in maladministration and bribery. They failed to take the masses into confidence and they had no respect for social equality and sense of fraternity.[170]

The members of many royal households also in these years failed to take the people towards any goal. These contractors of British hegemony, who once were used to be the leaders of countless peasant-militias of medieval or late-medieval Orissa, lived a life of isolation. Some took education in cities of India but most of them remained illiterates and irrational. They could not change themselves according to the time and lost the faith and confidence of their own people. The educated princes, except a few could not ready to believe in the concept of justice or equality acquired through western education. These people alongwith their relatives lived in their tiny capitals and became excessively lavish and adamant without care. They felt it degrading to give the people leadership which they could have. Rather they accepted British superiority completely and helped for its continuity.

Except Madhusudan Das, no leader of Orissa of late 19th or early 20th century did work to infuse the spirit of enterpreneuring for material prosperity of the masses. The educated people in Orissa thus, "developed a split personality living predominantly in a tradition bound agrarian society.... They posed as westernised but in emotional plain remained attached to traditional values"[171] They failed to encourage people for an industrially advanced Orissa. Taking the importance of cultural and unification causes as immediate issues these people became more philosophical than social and financial. Their intense attachment to Jagannath cult and its philosophy, did not allow them to think for an economic renaissance. Most of

170. *Ibid.*, (His novel, 'Mamu' also is the best specimen to find such problems in the 19th century Orissa).

171. N.K.—Jit, *op.cit.*, p. 291.

them behaved as old Indian *rishis* giving importance to the concept of `simple living and high thinking'.[172]

III

In the year 1920AD, Orissa joined the national mainstream declaring non-co-operation as its way of protest. Gandhi was instantly acknowledged as the leader and the India as the nation. It was Pandit Gopabandhu Das who worked tirelessly and with determination to join Orissa in the national mainstream of political awareness. But these political developments and awareness were then confined within a very few localities. The towns of Cuttack, Puri, Balasore and Sambalpur of Orissa Division and Berhampur in Ganjam area became the centres of the movement. The outlying Oriya-speaking tracts of Singhbhum, Manbhum and Medinipur also felt the worth of the uprising. But the people of *Garhjats* mostly remained untouched[173] from this current. The illiterate poor villagers of both interior and even coastal Orissa remained more or less unattached. They never felt concerned for the language movement and the agitation for amalgamation because of their isolation from the educated elites.

The political and cultural relationship between different Oriya-speaking areas were not yet very sound. Only few educated people of different areas had started the process. Marital relationship between different regions could not exist due to political vivisection. To foster unity through social relationships Gopabandhu Das advocated[174] marriage between the people of different regions of Orissa.

As the people were still illiterate, the society was ruled by superstitions which could be proved from the call of Gopabandhu Das, in which he said; "The cause of the downfall of the Oriyas is the lack of education. The illiterates

172. These could be found from the poems of Gopobandhu Das, Nilakantha Das, Nanda Kishore Bal; See - B. Acharya, *op.cit.*

173. *Asha*, 9th June, 1919.

174. *Ibid.*, 12th January, 1920.

cannot realise them as human beings".[175] Child marriages was in vogue and the orthodox people in the society even drafted a petition against the resolution of legalising inter-caste marriages in the Central Council.[176]

The orthodox society opposed the activities of Gopabandhu Das and his close associate, Nilakantha Das, Who were fighting against casteism and other orthodox traditions. They faced the wrath of the local *Brahmins*. Their school at Satyabadi was set on fire.[177] People representing *Brahman Samajas*, Hindu religious organisations and other higher caste councils criticised them. A social confrontation thus continued between the orthodox people and these progressive social workers.[178]

Due to poverty and ignorance of the people, the police was misusing their power and became oppressive.[179] The absence of industry and commerce and heavy dependence on fluctuating agriculture made the people quite hopeless. They were still unaware of the concept of political independence as there was still a great gap of communication between them and the political activists. Their political backwardness due to poverty made them alienated from the mainstream since centuries, otherwise, they could not have informed[180] the police about the hide-outs of Jatindranath Mukherjee. It proves the inability of the political activists to awaken the people taking them into confidence.

A report in brief had been published on 28th Feb, 1918AD in *Utkal Sevak* which had expressed the condition of the then society in true sense. The report was like thus,

"Thus subjects are pulling rickshaws being unable

---

175. *Asha*, 5th, January, 1990.
176. Ratnakar, 18th March, 1920 & Asha, 12th January, 1920.
177. S.N. Das, *op.cit.*, p. 12.
178. G.B. Mishra, *op.cit.*, p. 175.
179. *Asha*, 10th February 1919.
180. *Ibid*.

> to meet their house-hold expenditure from cultivation. Indebtedness has made them paupers. Natural calamities like flood, drought are frequent. People take very poor quality food. Because of child marriages infant mortality is very high and birth of weak babies are taking in large numbers. There are the presence of the beasts like quacks. People are becoming perjurers. New types of bad customs are being adopted. Many rich people spend money lavishly for the death or marriage anniversaries. In the process to imitate them rest of the poor people has been ruined. The educated rather support these developments".[181]

These facts tell how the society was under the grip of orthodoxy and backwardness even by 1920AD. Losing their sense of belongingness due to repeated exploitation and harassment Oriyas had become superstitious, ignorant and submissive in temperament. Being suppressed under a colonial rule, defeated militarily, so also morally, very often, denied of a natural leader, the Oriyas had to be mostly submissive non-violent in nature. Not only their religious attitude but their lack of confidence in themselves forced them to be non-violent in temperament believing in fate and *status-quo*. This made them inert in face of even acute oppression. A few changes had taken place on the surface only, but the underwater was still motionless. Centuries of inertia of rest had killed the very root of their wisdom. The works of few social workers was not sufficient to bring out the masses from the static state of inertia quickly. The awakening among the masses which was started in these years bore fruit in later decades.

181. *Utkal* Sevak, 28th February, 1918.

2

Growth of the Gandhians : Their Role (1920-30 AD)

The year 1920AD marked turning point in the course of political consciousness in India. Non-Co-Operation movement was launched by Gandhi and the degree of mass-consciousness in the political line grew rapidly. This year also marked the end of an era of inertness at the grass-root-level and beginning of a phase of busy political activities in Orissa. Cultural and Political awakening on the basis of immediate regional wants had somehow agitated the surface of the early 20th century Orissa but the new era could involve the greater number of common people with wider dimensions and outlook. The cause of regional salvation got merged into the national interest and Oriyas supported the movement for the independence of India. A long span of isolation was ended. Orissa aspired to achieve unification only through National Independence.[1] Its participation in the struggle not only strengthened the cause of the unification of Oriya speaking population but also putforth Orissa in the forefront of the political map of India.[2]

By the year 1920AD, Gandhi was not well-known in

1. *Samaj*, 29th January, 1921.
2. S.N. Das (ed), Yugapurusha Gopabandhu Das (O), Cuttack, 1972, pp. 56-57.

Orissa.[3] Gandhi's role in South Africa and his activities in later years in India were published occasionally in different newspapers. His Rawlott *Satyagraha* had no impact in Orissa. Only some educated people became informed of his activities by reading newspapers. Common people in villages, who were living a condition of isolation from the mainstream, were not aware of these developments initiated by Gandhi.

Even when Gandhi attended the special session at Calcutta to persuade the Congress to adopt the method of non-violence to launch the Non-Co-Operation Movement, *'Asha'*, a leading newspaper of Orissa, sarcastically reported, "Gandhi attended the session with his *chellahs*. Non-Co-Operation may be accepted but many people would not believe in the methods of boycotting schools, colleges and courts".[4]

But Gopabandhu's firm belief, determination and tireless labour completely changed the political course of the region. *'Utkal Sammilani'*, the sole representative of Oriya aspiration, which had the sympathy of the total educated elites of Orissa, got merged into the Indian National Congress in 1921AD. Gopabandhu openly acknowledged Gandhi as his leader, so also his entire coworkers. Members of Gopabandhu's volunteer Group[5] and his associates supported him whole-heartedly and became *'Congressias'* or *'Gandhiwallas'*. They formed the first batch of Gandhians in Orissa.

These men were mostly educated and they became prominent leaders of the time. Pandit Gopabandhu Das

3. N.K. Das, Atma Jivani (O), Cuttack, 1963; G.B. Mishra, Odisara Ardha Satabdira Itihasa O Tahinre Mo Sthana (O), Cuttack, 1958; F.M. Senapati, Granthavali (O); Vol-1, Cuttack, 1963; K.C. Pattnaik, Kumbhara Chaka (O), Cuttack, 1975; R.D. Chaudhury, Jivana Pathe (O), Cuttack, 1984; Newspapers-Utkal Dipika, Asha, *Samaj*.
4. Asha, 6th September, 1920.
5. Interview—Udayanath Sarangi; *Samaj*, 29th January, 1921.

and his close friends like Pandit Nilakantha Das, Pandit Godavarish Mishra, Pandit Kripasindhu Mishra, Acharya Harihar Das, with Harekrushna Mahtab, Bhagirathi Mohapatra, Niranjan Pattnaik, Chakradhar Behera, Jagabandhu Singh, etc. who formed the leadership of the early provincial Congress organisation, were men of great repute. The students who had joined them formed the first group of common Gandhians and some of them rose to prominence in later years. These people made Orissa a strong base of Gandhism of decades to come. Thousands of people, instigated by them, came forward to be active members and supporters of the Congress organisation.

Eighty Seven delegates from Orissa attended the Nagpur session. On their return they formed *Utkal* Provincial Congress Committee and launched the Non-Co-Operation Movement in Orissa. By that time an Orissa or *Utkal* province had yet to be formed; so before the actual unification a sort of amalgamation became possible in the minds of these workers of the *Utkal* Provincial Congress— as the AICC acknowledged jurisdiction of the PCC over some tracts of Oriya-speaking people living in different neighbouring provinces.[6] It provided the needed boost to the leaders of Orissa and their co-workers, particularly those of outlying tracts who were great supporters of the cause of unification. They developed faith in the National Congress and its leaders, as—the Congress became attentive to the cry of Oriyas unlike before.

I

CAUSES OF THE GROWTH OF GANDHIANS (1921 AD—1930 AD)

From 1921AD to 1930AD, within this decade, Gandhism spread into the villages of Orissa. Very seen the echoes of Gandhian ideas could be heard in the remote interiors of the region in spite of its severe communication drawbacks. This decade witnessed the making of Orissa as a formidable fort for the Congress organisation. Within

6. *Samaj*, 4th September, 1920.

these years, the attitude and degree of awareness of the Oriyas had undergone a great change. District, *Thana* and Village level Congress organisations were formed. Great emphasis was given to enroll as much people as possible from the villages. Leaders travelled far and wide and vernacular newspapers published regularly and prominently on Gandhi which made him a great personality among the people—particularly among educated and semi-educated villagers. Gandhism became the only revolutionary doctrine in the region and Gandhians also the only group of revolutionaries.

The PCC tried hard to enroll common people to be primary members of the local committees. The minimum age to be a primary member was at least twenty-one years and annual fee was four *Annas* per head. Gandhi asked PCC to collect three lakhs primary members.[7] But in June, 1921AD, there were only 40,000 primary members.[8] Their number increased gradually and by January 1922AD they were 52,000 in total.[9] In the initial period people of urban and semi-urban areas could be persuaded to join the Congress organisation where influence of the movement was strong due to frequent activities of district organisations. But gradually village people joined the Congress when the movement entered the interior.[10]

Out of these nearly half a lakh members, around three thousand* could be considered as full-time activists. They

7. CWMG, Vol-XVII, Delhi, 1966, p. 474.
8. *Samaj*, 9th June, 1921.
9. *Ibid.*, 14th January, 1922.
10. Interview—Udayanath Sarangi, Sarat Chandra Maharana.

* This is an approximate calculation taking the help of the reports published in the *Samaj* from December, 1920 to February, 1922. The Gandhians also, more or less, agreed with the number. There were around one thousand activists in prominent towns. They were the students and teachers of nationalist institutions and governments schools and school and college drop-outs. Around a thousand were constructive workers and Ashramites. Nearly five hundred were from Kanika Zamindari. More than a thousand activists were from sub-divisional, *Taluk* and *Thana* head-quarters of different districts.

devoted their whole time for the Non-Co-Operation movement throughout the tenure. They were mostly young college and school dropouts. Some illiterate and semi-educated but somehow conscious villagers also became full-timers. A handful of school teachers also joined them. Rest of the primary members remained permanently in villages and during very high political temperature many of them came out to join the movement. They were the part-timers. Though not active permanently, they remained constant supporters of the movement and participants in some programmes of the Congress without devoting their entire time. Generally most of them were illiterates or just literates but in some respect were conscious politically. But full-time activists and part-timers, thus, formed the group of common Gandhians of Orissa.

Rest of the primary members were sympathetic to the movement and had great respect for Gandhi, but were not active.[11] Most of them were also not adequately aware of different ideas of Gandhi. Many people among the masses were sympathetic to the movement but were reluctant to become primary members as it would brand them anti-British. Though thousands came to attend the meetings few became primary members not to invite trouble for them.[12] It was also a fact that to contribute four *Annas* annually as a primary member of the Congress was difficult for the aspirant poor people.[13]

There were different factors those contribute for the growth of the number of Gandhians in Orissa during the decade of 1920-30AD.

Feasibility of Different Gandhian Ideas and Techniques

For Gandhian Movement, different ideas and techniques were physically suited to the poor, unarmed and inert

11. Interview—Udayanath Sarangi, Sarat Chandra Maharana.
12. H.K. Mahtab, Sadhanara Pathe (O), Cuttack, 1972, p. 45.
13. Interview—Harekrushna Biswal, Advaitballav Ray.

Oriyas to join. *Hartals*, fastings, marches, picketings, dharanas, etc. in non-violent way appeared feasible for the poor Oriyas. 'These were felt convenient and seemed within the capacity of the poor people'. It is already found that by 1920 AD, the common Oriyas were both emotionally and physically submissive because of their helplessness due to lack of self-confidence. Gandhi was also aware of acute poverty of the Oriyas.[14] Non-violent method of Gandhian movement suited them from all respect to join. Even Gandhi also knew that the common Indians would not be able to join a violent movement instantly in numbers. From the interviews of Gandhians and contemporary literature it is also seen that non-violent marches, *dharanas*, picketings etc. enabled the then Oriyas to join it without much hidrance. They could not have joined a violent movement as spontaneously as they did in Gandhian movement in numbers.[15] In this respect Oriyas of the early 20th Century provided the most suitable fields for Gandhian ideas to flourish—the ideas which Gandhi had developed to be used by poor Indians against colonialists

Women and children also became able to join the agitation. The movement saw the participation of the people of all age-groups. Anybody could be a gentle anarchist. Religious-minded and fatalist Oriyas found in Gandhi a leadership that was very much identical to the concept of incarnation, so joined him as pilgrims.

It is also found from the opinions of the Gandhians that as a strategist Gandhi became more successful and

14. CWMG. *op.cit.*, Vol.-XVIII, p. 549.

15. G. Sharp, Gandhi as a Political Strategist, Boston, 1979; Gandhi. Sharp, "Non-violence, Moral Principles or Political Techniques", Political Thinkers of Modern India—M.K. Gandhi, V. Grover (ed), New Delhi, 1990; M.M. Verma, Gandhi's Techniques of Mass Mobilization, Delhi, 1990; Bipan Chandra, "Long Term Dynamics of the National Movement", Proc. *IHC*, Delhi, 1986, pp. 3-41; Interview—*op.cit.*

appealing than an idealist. Though the Gandhian of the decade had great respect for non-violence and also followed some other ideas of Gandhi so far as their personal lives were concerned, it was their physical, mental and material shortcomings which induced them to adopt non-violence 'more as a way than a creed'. It was the non-violence displayed by physically weak persons. The unarmed, unorganised and weak Oriyas were very much afraid of British oppression. The condition of the masses was very pitiable. Frequent natural calamities and epidemics[16] had made them hopeless and inert. So they were reluctant and were not interested to join the anti-British movement. But Gandhian ideas and techniques gradually attracted their attention and interest because they would not involve in a violent movement which would make the British severely oppressive. Most of the common workers along-with the massess offered 'non-violence of the body' which was suitable to their capabilities. Though they believed in the divinity of 'non-violence of mind' often failed to use it in face of oppression as opined by G. Sharp in Indian context.[17]

The practicability of Gandhian non-violent techniques provided the Ghandhians the scope to join the movement and express their anguish in a systematic manner. This underdeveloped[18] agrarian society was quite unable to adopt any other method. Suitability of Gandhian ideas and practicability of Gandhian techniques to the poor people saw Orissa as a strong base for the Congress movement. Large number of people became Gandhians because most of the Oriyas of the time were backward, poor and non-violent people.

16. *Utkal* Dipika, 28th November, 1925; *Samaj*, 30th October, 1925, 16th January, 1926 and 30th October, 1929.
17. G. Sharp, *op.cit.*, pp.60-83; G. Sharp, Gandhi weilds the Weapon of Moral Power, Nav Jivan Publishing House, Ahmedabad, 1960, p. 6.
18. *Utkal* Dipika, 4th February, 1928.

Socio-Economic Factors

The growth of education and lack of suitable employment also caused the growth of Gandhians in Orissa. By 1920AD the number of educated people increased. Though high caste and wealthy parents could send their children to the urban and semi-urban areas to complete their high school education, the poor could send their children up to local primary schools. In spite of their financial difficulties many poor boys completed their primary education and even could enter high schools. Though many became dropouts, the education in schools provided them the needed awakening to think seriously about their condition as well as of the society in which they were living. The Nationalist Schools established by rank-nationalist which were meant for the poor students, provided opportunity to the poor boys to be awakened in the line of self respect and political awareness.[19]

These school-educated dropouts had no job opportunity to be engaged. Political division had made many of them minorities in different neighbouring provinces. Even in Orissa division, the dominance of Bengalis was strong.[20] So being denied of their rightful place these Oriyas realised their helplessness. Frustration grew in them. They could not depend on agriculture which was very fluctuating. Declaring the Oriyas a non-martial race, in spite of their bravery past, the British did not take them in military services. So unemployment grew. Some of these educated youths became teachers in primary schools,[21] but they were not satisfied and were in

19. Interview—Udayanath Sarangi, Sarat Chandra Maharana, Harekrushna Biswal, Advaitballav Ray and Rajkrushna Bose; P.M. Pradhan, Mukti Pathe Sainika (O), Cuttack, 1979, pp. 3-5; Souvenir, Nilamani Pradhan (O), Baharana, Cuttack, 1984.

20. *Utkal* Dipika, 1st July, 1922.

21. Interview—Udayanath Sarangi, Sarat Maharana and Harekrushna Biswal; Souvenir-Nilamani Pradhan, *op.cit.*, P.M. Pradhan, *op.cit.*

search of a way to express their anguish. Many became supporters of Gandhi which proved the degree of their hostility to and dissatisfaction with the British system. The village educated youths-teachers and the unemployed, saw the miserable and humiliating life of their own folk. They experienced the helplessness, ignorance and miserable life of the agrarian society to which they also belonged.

As late starters of education the youths had crossed their teens or were in late-teens when they discontinued school education. So they were matured enough to think independently. Education had made them self-respected and they were esteemed[22] in the society as English-educated men. They had some sort of dignified life in the poverty-stricken agrarian Orissa. They became aware of the causes of their sufferings and saw their kiths and kins facing humiliation and harassment. These educated youths of all castes were in search of a way to express their frustration and dissatisfaction with the system. They turned dissidents.[23]

By the time, Gandhi's sudden rise to fame and his instant and massive popularity captured the imagination of these educated men, as no leader before Gandhi had enjoyed such reputation as an all-India figure. They joined him as his followers acknowledging him as their leader. Gandhi's great emphasis on the condition of poor people had created hope in them. When Gandhi talked about the ability and rights of the common poor people, it appealed them most because they were from such class. They followed Gandhi because his movement gave the common people scope to work for their own causes which they never thought eligible for.[24]

Absence of terrorist activities in Orissa also made the ground open for the growth of the freedom-fighters only

22. P.M. Pradhan, *op.cit.*, p. 30.
23. Interview—*op.cit.*
24. *Ibid.*—Ghanashyama Pati.

as Gandhians in the region. It is interesting to note that when the neighbouring Bengal saw the growth of terrorism and non-Congress platforms, the Oriyas remained supporters of Gandhi and the Congress by and large. Gandhism remained the dominant revolutionary doctrine of the region. The freedom-fighters of Orissa were aware of the activities of terrorist groups in Bengal and in other provinces. They had great respect for them. But they did not opt for violence. Among the Oriyas hatred for British officials was not as strong as found among the Bengalis.[25] The number of educated people was very few which caused the lack of diversities of political opinions in them. The people around those Gandhians were very backward and inert. The condition and opportunity for the growth of terrorism as found in Calcutta, Bombay, Ahmedabad & other urban centres was absent in Orissa. Lack of international connection[26] also caused the absence of terrorism in Orissa which had played a vital role for the growth of revolutionary groups in Punjab, Bengal, Maharastra and Madras. It was the poverty and isolation of Oriyas which never allowed themselves to go abroad and establish any international connection. They could not go abroad or were encouraged to go to seek employment there. So absence of this facility could not give the needed confidence, asylum, encouragement and financial help to the Oriyas to be armed revolutionaries or to be activists of terrorism.

The educated people also joined the Congress not only for the national independence but also to realise political unification of Orissa. The agitation of the educated Oriyas in the past years was still fresh in their mind. The dominance of neighbouring people and their indifferent attitude to Oriya culture and language was not yet forgotten. The terrorist organisations of Bengal never

25. *Ibid.*—Harekrushna Biswal.

26. S. Sarkar, Modern India : 1885-1947, New Delhi, 1983, pp. 123-34 & 250-52.

sought the help of Oriyas or had expressed sympathy for the causes of Oriya people. The total educated elite Oriyas were aware of the neglecting attitude of non-Oriyas towards the cause of Oriya amalgamation. As armed rebellion of Bengali terrorists was directed against the British Officials without any popular cause for the upliftment of common exploited people, it did not attract the imagination of the then Oriyas, though they had expressed respect for the revolutionaries. Perhaps Gandhi's method of 'appeal to conscience' suited to them more than terrorism because in spite of the hostility of the neighbourers to the cause of Oriya unification, the Gandhians of Orissa could get the support of the British officials for the sympathetic lock.[27] Even some of the Gandhians welcomed Simon Commission disregarding PCC directives which indicated the importance of unification for the Oriya freedom fighters. So they chose Gandhian method to realise so while working for national independence and highlighting the causes of poor classes.

Being confined within the close and dependent atmosphere of villages, surrounded by sea of apathetic and illiterate masses, themselves being very few in number as compared to the population, those educated people, still, wanted to do something for the social and political emancipation of the masses. So they thought it correct to choose Gandhi as their leader. They, remaining busy in social work, could also increase the popularity of Gandhian movement in Orissa. Terrorism could not have attracted such popular response in the then Orissa as the voluntary relief works of the Gandhians could. Complete demilitarisation of the great race for more than three hundred years had made the masses sluggish and docile.

Gandhi's movement need not require an altogether new life-pattern and isolation from the society. The common man could work for Congress without disrupting his normal life. So it suited the agrarian common people

27. Interview—*op.cit.*

to join the movement. A common peasant could turn easily a Gandhian without discontinuing his life pattern. At least, to be part-timers in Gandhian movement, Gandhi's ideas and techniques suited the common Oriyas largely.[28] Hundreds of people—literate and semi-literate or illiterate could become Gandhians as their physical, temperamental and economic life could permit them.

Hindu-joint-family system also helped for the growth of this class of volunteers of the Gandhian movement and also for its sustenance. Under a Hindu-joint-family system, the land was kept jointly and looked after by almost all working and able-bodied members of the family under the supervision of the living eldest male member. It was due to the existence of close family bond and very low standard of living, even a non-working could get shelter and food. This system indirectly helped the interested social workers to be full-time Gandhians. Only the part-timers who were not active permanently throughout the year, lived in villages and got engaged in fields. But the full-time activists were saved by their joint families. The relatives of these so-called *Nikamas* provided them and to their wives and children shelter even at the cost of their own comfort and honour. Close family bond saved these Gandhians from total isolation.[29]

Absence of any caste conflict in Orissa also contributed for the growth of Gandhians in the region. Though the society of the then Orissa was caste-ridden and caste orthodoxy was very severe, no caste movement grew to challenge the dominance of Gandhian activities in the decade. In South India [30] different caste movements

28. K.C. Panigrahi, Kalandi Rachana Chaya (O), P-1, Cuttack, 1971, pp. 238-39 (His novel *'Matira Manisa'* depicts the feelings of a would-be common Gandhian in the character of Baraju).
29. Interview—*op.cit.*, Ghanashyama Pati & Udayanath Sarangi.
30. E.F. Irschick, Politics and Social Conflict in South-India; The Non-Brahmin Movement and Tamil Separatism : 1916-1924, Bombay, 1969, pp. 180-88.

became popular during the period which affected Gandhi's movement there. But though the untouchables constituted a bulk of total Oriya population their complete ignorance out of 'illiteracy' [31] and isolation did not give them scope to be organised.

The backward depressed castes including the untouchables of Orissa could not produce their own leaders to fight for their own cause. The leaders of the depressed castes of other provinces could not come to Orissa to awaken them. The depressed people were agricultural labourers. They had no scope to be recruited in the British army as the *Mahars* of Maharastra or could be influenced by the activities of Poona's social workers of the 19th Century to get a leader of backward caste like Jyotib Phule or R. Naicker of Madras to start an anti-*Brahmin* agitation. Severe anti-*Brahmin* feeling was not accumulated in the depressed castes of Orissa. The British need not have to encourage the depressed castes of Orissa as they did in Madras to incite them against the anti-British and nationalist *Brahmins*.[32] Fortunately or unfortunately the higher casts educated elites of Orissa were not severely anti-British. Because they wanted cultural safety and political unification of Oriyas which could be possible under the patronage of the British. These castes in Orissa by 1920AD were for away from the mainstream alongwith many higher castes because of the acute poverty and lack of self-respect in them in a static and unprogressive society. These people had no sense of belongingness or sense of self-respect.

The Tribals had revolted against the British and the feudal chiefs in *Garhjats*. But they were for away from the influence of the concept of nationalism and Gandhian ideas. They had their own respective mainstreams and were feeling restless because of the infringement by non-tribal exploiters. Systematic formation of an all Orissan

31. *Utkal* Dipika, 26th January, 1927.

32. E.F. Irschick, *op.cit.*

tribal platform was not possible in these years which could have given a tough time to the Gandhian force of the province to spare lot of their energy to bring them to their fold. To organise the tribals was the latter agenda of the Congress workers in Orissa. The absence of any agitation on caste in Orissa during these years helped the Gandhians to spread their activities systematically and gradually in the province without any hindrance of social tension.

The-presence of intermediary castes like *Karanas, Khandayats* and *Gopals* had lessened the pressure of caste hierarchy over the untouchables. Poor people, irrespecive of caste, were suffering from acute poverty and[33] such pitiable material condition never created any jealously on class consciousness among them. So[34] Gandhian movement found an open field to spread when it highlighted the purely agrarian problems.

Gandhi, in this region, got the opportunity to be the first great champion of the untouchables. He targetted this inhuman practice in his works and words. Many high Caste Gandhian leaders and workers of the region became ardent champions of anti-untouchability. The lower-caste people realised that many Gandhians were not hypocrites and were openly working with them without caring their orthodox caste societies. The untouchables who became Gandhians were touched by Gandhi's effort for them, but their enthusiasm grew when they found the local Gandhians of higher castes mixed with them breaking the age-old chain of segregation—a product of their own conscience. This deeply moved the untouchables and no

---

33. F.M. Senapati, *op.cit.*, pp. 5-30; K.B. Das, Jivani O Jivana (O), Cuttack, 1981, pp. 245-46.
34. Interview—Late Mayadhara Mohapatra, Late Jayakrushna Dixit, Late Uchhab Sahoo, Prahalled Pradhan (These people of village Adaspur, Cuttack, who were in their nineties when interviewed told that during their childhood almost all of the population of their village were very poor. This could not help for the growth of class consciousness among different castes).

leader could capture their imagination except Gandhi, even upto 1947AD.[35]

The people were aware of the neglecting social attitude of British authorities towards the Indians. They had also felt the discriminatory role of non-Oriya government servants working among the natives. But the growth of the group of Oriya government servants and their adamant behaviour towards the masses made the people really hurt deeply. As already mentioned in the 'Introduction', these ebony coloured Indians became the open supporters of British Raj countryside. They looked down upon the people—particularly the social workers who were also educated like them. Some sort of jealousy were growing in between these two groups. The social workers opposed the excess behaviour of the government servants and made the people aware of their limits. Through newspapers the activities and highhanded attitude of the *'Sarkariloka'*[36] were published. Their oppressive attitudes were very high in *Garhjats* or princely states.[37] Open demands were made by the conscious social workers to provide local self-government for these people.[38] The presence of government servants and their discriminatory role compelled many young people to be Gandhians. Being enlisted as the members of a great organisation like Indian National Congress, these Oriyas destroyed their isolation from the rest of the area and become confident of getting support from other Gandhians of the locality.

Orissa had no class of skilled[39] workers due to the absence of industrial centres. The mining workers, mostly tribals, were under the control of their contractors. Many

35. Interview—Udayanath Sarangi.
36. *Asha*, 10th February, 1921 & 7th April, 1921.
37. F.M. Senapati, Atmajivani Charita (O), Cuttack, 1971, pp.70-180.
38. *Asha*, 9th June, 1919.
39. *Ibid.*, 7th July, 1919.

were working in jute mills of Calcutta and tea[40] gardens of Assam. But their long absence from Orissa and indifferent attitude could not unite them in a single platform within Orissa. Destruction of indegenous industries had made the scenario completely agrarian. The migrants were mostly from higher intermediary castes.[41] They had gone outside to pay back their past debts. Surprisingly the Calcutta based skilled or un-skilled Oriyas could not bring adequate awareness to Orissa in the line of patriotism and self respect as compared to the volatile atmosphere in Bengal. Later Gopabandhu Das became able to organise them and could use this platform to get their support for the cause of Oriyas. But few of them turned Congress workers and could help for the growth of Gandhians in villages when retired.[42]

These few socio-economic factors largely contributed for the growth of Gandhians in Orissa during the decade. The same factors also remained strong throughout the movement and contributed for the growth of Gandhians in the region. The abscnce of communal tension, due to absence of large number of Muslims in Orissa, never affected people's sentiment permanently and never became a headache to provincial Congress workers as in some other provinces of India. The orthodox Hindi organisations, though opposed Gandhi's move against[43] untouchability, never instigated the people to behave as communal. So Gandhian movement in the province became fortunate in this respect as total Congress force could get thousands of common Gandhians without any obstacle from emotional disturbances.*

---

40. G.B. Mishra, *op.cit.*, p. 136.
41. Census of India, 1921, Vol.-V, Pt.-II, Table-XXII, Part-IV & V.
42. Interview—Ghanashyama Pati.
43. *Ibid.*, Udyanath Sarangi, & Advaitballav Ray.

* Whenever there was the dominance of anarchy on the Earth and honest suffered, the God took birth of kill the wicked to save the honest.

Concept of 'Avtarvad'

The concept of *Avtarvad* was very strong in the minds of the then common Oriyas regarding Gandhi. People believed him as an incarnation of Lord Jagannath who had taken birth to save them from oppression.[44] Contemporary literature and the reflection of the feelings of the common people in the newspapers indicate that Gandhi's emphasis on pure religious life, morality, ideals of *'Varnashrama'*, *Ramarajya*, non-violence and *'Gita'* had made him a Godly man for the poor Oriyas who had deep faith in the theory of incarnation[45] and in Hindu religious texts. Even conscious and educated people were not free such belief.[46]

Though most of the leaders of the provincial Congress saw Gandhi as a competent political leader, but the literate, semi-literate, school dropouts and illiterate common Congress workers found Gandhi as an extraordinary man. They were from a highly religious and orthodox society which was under the strong grip of fatalism and superstitions. To think of Gandhi as an *Avtar* or an extraordinary man influenced many people to be Gandhians. Even a section of them saw Gandhi as a champion of Hindu traditions.[47] Old men and women worshipped Gandhi's photographs and uttered his name as hymns.[48] In many respect these caused the growth of Gandhians for whom Gandhi's personality rose larger than of his life size. Religiousness of Gandhi's works and deeds induced many common men to be his co-workers.[49]

---

44. Interview—*op.cit.*
45. S. Mohanty, Andha Diganta (O), Cuttack, 1964, p. 79; G.N. Mohanty, Mati Matala (O), Cuttack, 1977, p. 174; K.C. Panigrahi, *op.cit.*, (These authors have depicted beautifully the mentality of the agrarian masses elaborately in their novels).
46. G.B. Mishra, *op.cit.*
47. *Asha*, 20th December, 1920; Interview—Ghanashyam Pati.
48. Interview—Biswambar Parida.
49. L.K. Mohapatra, Kanta Sahityamala (O), Cuttack, 1972, pp. 78-93.

Gandhi's Personality

Gandhi's own open personal life and his arresting qualities also influenced people to follow him. The conscious and educated people saw in him an unique person whose life was fully dedicated for the cause of humanity. In this respect Gandhi was extraordinary among his contemporaries.[50] During the decade Gandhi's personality rose to wider dimensions due to his many-sided activities that made him leader of almost all sections of society. He not only championed the political independence but also highlighted social emancipation of the Indians. He observed fasting astonishingly for many days continuously and repeatedly and such type of personal sufferings for the cause of common people were not heard for many years. It enlarged his personality in the eyes of the people. People were more eager to see him than to listen.[51] Magnaminity of Gandhi attracted many people.

Gandhi was not attached to any particular province or place. Most of his activities were not confined to a particular city or town. He was not identified as man from particular province or area. His concern for each Indian made him a non-controversial figure so far as regional feelings was concerned. In an age of regional inequality, social segregation and inhuman exploitation he felt concerned for all the poor the came accross. People believed him. He became a model for the social workers.

Reporting the cause of Gandhi's influence on the society on this basis, the *'Asha'* published an anonymous letter which contained the following,

> "There were many people who were more wise, intelligent, having more oratory capacity, rich and honourable than Gandhi in this country, and are also living now. But why their influence is nothing in front of Gandhi's? There are many causes-

50. Interview—Udayanath Sarangi.
51. *Samaj*, 28th March, 1921.

(i) His suffering in South-Africa with his family.

(ii) Though his forefathers were ministers, *dewans* and he himself is a barrister, he has accepted the life of poverty; he spins with his own hand, lives like a saint and travels in third class compartment.

(iii) He openly crticises the government without any fear of law.

(iv) He recognises the applicability and need for four *Ashrams* of Aryan life.

(v) He hates untouchability and the caste system.

His main point of attraction was his selfless work, so no longer people, only speaking high, can win the hearts of the people. No longer a man of wealth can rule the hearts of the people by spending luxuriously and investing the wealth to accumulate it. No man could win millions' heart by donating lakhs of rupees acquiring it through illegal ways. You have to sacrifice everything, you have to leave the illegal way of earning money, then people would accept you as a leader".[52]

Influence of Gandhi was so strong that the people who has not seen him also became his followers.[53] Even the opponents of Gandhi's movement acknowledged that Gandhi was not an ordinary person. The imagination of the people was totally captured by Gandhi's personality.

Contribution of the Methods of Propaganda

The force of propaganda has been used since time immemorial by the leaders of mankind at different junctures of history to shape the mind of the common people in the line of their own ideas and thinking. Gandhi

52. *Asha*, 20th December; 1922.
53. C.R. Mishra, Freedom Movement in Sambalpur, Delhi, 1986, p. 214; S. Mohanty, *op.cit.*, p. 79.

was a great user of this force to mobilise the people. The provincial[54] leaders of the Congress also carefully chalked out programmes through different channels to instigate people in a big way to strike their imagination. The intense propaganda by the Congress provincial force was the first such instance in the region when the entire force of propaganda of an organisation was used for the common masses. The leaders highlighted the personality of Gandhi while magnifying the cause of the common people. Many provincial leaders published newspapers, prepared and circulated pamphlets, toured the distant parts of Orissa, held meetings and invited top national leaders of the Congress to address the people. Observation of National Days, symbolic fastings, marches, *hartals* for different causes also added dimensions to the movement.

Throughout the decade, the provincial leaders spread inside Orissa and addressed meetings. Leading Gandhians were deputed by the PCC to take charge of various districts. Meetings were held in urban and semi-urban areas in the beginning of the movement.[55] Gradually the leaders entered the nearby rural areas. District and sub-divisional headquarters witnessed frequent meetings held by the local Congress workers where the office of the District Congress Organisations were situated. The village level workers who were by then very few in number, also organised such meetings to develop awareness among the people and to attract them to join the movement. The meetings provided the leaders the scope to have a face-to-face contact with the people. For the illiterate people, who could not read newspapers, these meetings became helpful to make them conscious of their rights and strength. It also helped the progagators to bring the ideas of Gandhi directly to the illiterate people.[56]

54. L.K. Mohapatra, *op.cit.*, pp. 85-86.

55. *Samaj*, 25th January, 1921, 12th February, 1921 & 25th February, 1921.

56. Interview—Udayanath Sarangi.

In the meetings, the leaders criticised the government directly and abused its henchmen in rural areas openly in the presence of the officials whom the people were afraid of. These incidents were novel things for the common people which helped them to eradicate their fear for the officials gradually. Role of Gandhi in South Africa and later in India was described by the leaders to magnify his personality.[57] The oppressive attitude of the police on the organisers of the meetings attracted public sympathy for the Congress. The respect for the local Gandhians grew among them, when they were arrested.[58]

Frequent meetings at different villages in a locality made the local Gandhians well-known to each other. They became a conspicuous group of political and social workers in their areas and such congregations made them confident when the feeling of collectivity grew. The presence of top provincial leaders in the meetings made them assured of. Meetings provided them the scope to assemble at crucial periods of the movement to talk about their own difficulties and about the reaction of the people towards their activities. Emotional support from the fellow Gandhians strengthened the spirit of the Gandhians. It helped them to look forward even at the time of personal miseries and despair. Thus, the meetings not only encouraged the people to be Gandhians but also strengthened workers will to sustain their spirit.[59]

Except holding meetings the leaders also published vernacular newspapers from different places of Orissa. Both national and international affairs got their places in the columns. Role of Gandhis in other areas[60] of India and his messages to the people got published regularly. The educated Gandhians read these newspapers and

57. *Samaj*, 19th March, 1921.
58. S. Mohanty, Patha O. Pruthvi (O), BBSR, 1986, p. 33; Interview—Udayanath Sarangi.
59. Interview—Rajakrushna Bose & Udayanath Sarangi.
60. *Samaj*, 15th January, 1921.

discussed the contents among their colleagues. Gopabandhu Das had started the *'Samaj'* from Cuttack, Harekrushna Mahtab published the *'Prajatantra'* from Balasore and Sashibhushan Rath continued *'Asha'* from Berhampur of Ganjan. These newspapers made the atmosphere surcharged with patriotism. Every corner of Orissa got its place in the pages. It reported the work of Gandhians of different areas and thus encouraged them to do more and more organisational works.

When the works of the local Gandhians were reported in these newspapers, they became encouraged. Many Gandhians acted as the area representatives of the newspapers and saw their reports were published highlighting their problems as well as the people around them. It helped them to gain importance and status in their own localities. To work as the area reporter to representative of the *'Samaj'* or the *'Prajatantra'* was a matter of great pride for the Gandhians.[61]

The newspapers reported the developments of international[62] scene and tried to connect Indian movement with these events. The works of Gandhians of other provinces were highlighted.[63] The newspapers tried to educate the common people about the limitation of the police, [64] and, thus, made the Gandhians gradually daring in their works. It also shaped Gandhi as a phenomenon of the time and describing him a man above average humanity through systematic portrait, attracted common people to be Gandhians.

Besides newspapers, the leaders circulated pamphlets and leaflets containing slogans on various issues. Common Gandhians were used to circulate these in different areas secrety. During the Non-Co-Operation

61. Interview—Biswambar Parida and Shyamakanta Mohapatra.
62. *Samaj*, 15th January, 1927.
63. *Ibid.*, 15th January, 1921.
64. *Ibid.*, 19th March, 1921.

Movement Gopabandhu prepared a leaflet containing the line, "Triumph of Non-Co-Operation is sure".[65] It was widely read. Mahtab used cyclostyled-pamphlets.[66] Small booklets were published containing patriotic couplets. Gandhi's Autobiography was translated into Oriya and its copies were sold in cheaper rates namely `Gandhi *Purana*', `Gandhi *Bhagabata*' etc.

The visit of top national leaders also created strong sensation among the people. Their visit made the cadres of the area Congress organisation more educated, trained and active. Fresh enrolments took place due to these hectic activities and high political temperature. Gandhi's call that 'Swaraj can be achieved within seven months'[67] infused tremendous enthusiasm among the people. People became very much excited to see an independent India quickly.[68]

All these channels of propaganda very quickly carried the ideas to the people. It not only made them informed of their pitiable condition but also about their duties and rights. Even the people of *Garhjats* were not left out. It helped the conscious people there to know Gandhi as a champion of the cause of the common people. The *Samaj* became so popular in *Garhjats* that many kings banned it's reading within their states.

Role of Different Nationalist Institutions, Ashrams and Organisations

When Non-Co-Operation Movement was started, many national institutions like schools and *Ashrams* were opened in different corners of Orissa. Gopabandhu had established a residential model school at Satyabadi of Puri

65. H.K. Mahtab, History of Freedom Movement in Orissa, BBSR, 1957, Vol-III, p. 61 & 64.
66. *Ibid.*, p. 61.
67. Interview—Rajkrushna Bose, Udayanath Sarangi; S. Mohanty, Andha..., *op.cit.*, p. 67; CWMG, Vol-XVIII, *op.cit.*, p. 476.
68. S. Mohanty, *op.cit.*; G.N. Mohanty, Matimatala, *op.cit.*, p. 179.

and he converted it into national school. Godavarish Mishra, a close friend of Gopabandhu, went as the headmaster to Chakradharpur of Singhbhum to start a national school. Nilakantha Das went to Samabalpur for the same purpose. Nationalist schools were opened at Bhadrak, Balasore town, Sore of Balasore district and Jagatsinghpur of Cuttack district.[69] Leading Gandhians also opened *Ashrams* in their own areas of activities. Even some common Gandhians opened *Ashrams* in their own home premises.[70] *'Sawaraj Ashram'* [71] of Cuttack town became the head-quarters of *Utkal* provincial Congress. It prepared hundreds of freedom fighters and had witnessed the daring activities of Gandhians—both young and old, till 1947AD.

Gopabandhu Chaudhury and Bhagirathi Mohapatra opened and nourished an *Ashram* known as *'Alakashram'* near Jagatsinghpur of Cuttack. Around a hundred people lived there to learn the life of dignity and self-sufficiency.[72] Harekrushna Mahtab established *'Swaraj Mandir'* at Balasore.[73] National Schools were opened at Kendrapara,[74] Delanga, [75] Jaleswar, Basta, Bhandaripokhari of Balasore district.[76] Niali, [77] Chandabali and Jajpur of Cuttack district had such *'Ashrams'*.[78] These *Ashrams* and national

69. *Samaj,* 15th April, 1921; *Utkal* Dipika, 13th May, 1922; H.K. Mahtab, *op.cit.,* pp. 60-64; Gandhi. D. Behera, Kanika Biplaba (O), Chandabali, Balasore, 1987; M.D. Mallick, Baplabi Chakradhara (O), Cuttack, 1973, p. 1.
70. G.B. Mishra, *op.cit.,* p. 25-27.
71. H.K. Mahtab, *op.cit.,* p. 57.
72. Interview—Sarat Chanda Maharana; Utkal Dipika, 12th May, 1923; Gandhi. N. Mohanty, Dhuli Matira Santha (O), Cuttack, 1985, pp. 59-72.
73. H.K. Mahtab, *op.cit.,* p. 60.
74. *Samaj,* 19th February, 1921.
75. *Ibid.,* 24th January, 1925.
76.. *Ibid.,* 24th January, 1925.
77. *Ibid.,* 28th May, 1921.
78. *Ibid.,* 12th March, 1921; H.K. Mahtab, Sadhanara..., *op.cit.,* p. 93.

institutions became training centres of young volunteers of Gandhian movement.[79] The interested people who wanted to join Gandhi as his co-workers stayed there to be full-time workers.[80]

The influence of these institutions was very strong in nearby villages. The activities of the Gandhians of these centres also awakened the people who never felt concerned before towards the national cause. People came to pay visit to these places and became aware of the aims and objectives of these institutions. The nearby villages and the *Ashrams* [81] and nationalist schools produced many Gandhians of the decade and also of the coming years.

Congress district organisations also worked their best to prepare many Gandhian common workers. The leaders of the PCC were deputed with the charge of different districts.[82] Efforts were made to enlist primary members from different areas of a district.[83] The DCCs convened their annual sessions regularly to discuss important issues concerning district organisations. Local problems were highlighted. Meetings were held in different places of the district. Very often local influential people were invited to attend the meetings to add importance to the event.[84]

A women organisation was also founded at Puri. Other women organisations were formed in Orissa. Women of different classes met at *'Swaraj Ashram'* of Berhampur (Ganjam) and founded the female group of *'Utkal Sammilani'*. All acted as sister organisations of the

79. *Samaj*, 26th February, 1921, 23rd April, 1921.
80. A. Maharana, "Kusuma Parashe", *Utkal* Prasanga (O), Vol-43. No.1, August, BBSR. 1986, p. 14.
81. Souvenir, Gouranga Charan Das, Cuttack, 1982, p. 14.
82. H.K. Mahatab, History of the............ *op.cit.*, p. 64.
83. *Samaj*, 16th April, 1921.
84. *Utkal* Dipika, 17th April, 1926, 1st May, 1926, 8th May, 1926, 15th May, 1926 and 6th April, 1929; H.K. Mahatab, Sadhanara....., *op.cit.*, p. 42.

provincial Congress organisation.[85]

All these institutions and organisations became asylum for budding Gandhians of both sexes. It saved them from frustration and isolation. Many people could become Gandhians because of the presence of these institutions.

Impact of Gandhi's Visits

Perhaps the most important factor for the growth of Gandhians in Orissa was the visits of Gandhi to Orissa. It was first of its kind of the people of Orissa. A man of such a stature—Gandhi, came to Orissa to hightlight the cause of Oriyas. Never before any leader of India had liked or expressed sympathy for the poverty stricken populace of the region. Gossips and rumours that *Gandhi Maharaj* had come to end the *Kaliyug* filled the atmosphere.

Gandhi came to Orissa four times within this decade. He came in 1921 AD, 1925 AD, 1927 AD and 1928 AD to strengthen the morale of his co-workers.[86] In March 23, 1921 Gandhi came to Orissa for the first time to see the condition of the people affected by severe famine. Its impact was far-reaching in consequence. He toured different districts and was received by thousands of enthusiastic people. At Puri, his meeting was attended by more then 70,000 people, even larger than of the *Rathayatra* of the year. In his later visits he supervised constructive works of the volunteers and propagated his ideas of social upliftment. His appeal accelerated the growth of common members of the Congress in the province. Even some illiterate people joined[87] the Congress without knowing properly what they would to in the movement.

---

85. Souvenir, Pradesh Congress Committee, Orissa, BBSR, 1986, p. 36.
86. Publication Division, Gandhiji in Orissa, Cuttack, 1970, pp. 2-3, 4-5 & 7.
87. Interview—Sarat Chandra Maharana, *Samaj*, 28th March, 1921.

To make his visits successful many volunteers came forward to work for the local Congress organisations. Many school boys left their schools to see Gandhi and then joined his movement. His visits generated tremendous interest among local Gandhians to recruit new workers for their organisation. Gandhi's coming made them brave which ended their isolation from the national mainstream.[88]

Role of Gopabandhu and Other Provincial Leaders

By 1920 AD, Gopabandhu Das had established himself as the unchallenged leader of Orissa and was successful in merging the Oriya movement into Indian mainstream. His organising ability and extraordinary sense of fellow-feeling made him immensely popular in Orissa.* He travelled far and wide and came into contact with the common people. By his tireless work, open life of devotion and remarkable achievements in many fields of life he became an idol. It was he, who acknowledging Gandhi as his leader, pupularised him in Orissa. People believed him what he said about Gandhi.[89] Gandhi also was extremely impressed by Gopabandhu's personality whom he described as 'a selfless leader'.[90]

Gopabandhu knew all his co-workers personally. His vision suited to the most of the newly emerging educated elites who followed him without any doubt or hesitation. His arresting personality attracted many people to leave their lucrative careers to be social workers. Inaugurating the school of nationalist [91] literature in Orissa, he captured

88. Souvenir, Orissa Province Freedom Fighters' Samittee, Cuttack, 1986; S. Mohanty, Patha O.Pruthvi.........., *op.cit.*, p. 24.

* To utilise Gopabandhu's popularity some companies used Gopabandhu's photograph and name as lebels of their products, *Utkal* Dipika, 14th January, 1925.

89. Interview—Udayanath Sarangi.

90. Young India, 13th April, 1921.

91. S.N. Das (O), *op.cit.*, pp. 242-43; Interview—Udayanath Sarangi.

the vision of the educated youths. They followed him and joined the Congress as Gandhians. He was a cementing force for Congress Organisation of Orissa and after his death, no leader could check the growth of factionalism in PCC. Many of his co-workers also left Congress after his death in 1928AD.

Besides Gopabandhu Das, there were many leading Gandhians in Orissa for which many people also joined the Congress movement. Nilakantha Das, Godavarish Mishra, Jagabandhu Singh, Acharya Harihar Das, Gopabandhu Chaudhury, Rama Devi Chaudhury, Sarala Devi etc. were much leaders whose lives became examples for other. Leaving aside the life of comfort these people made their lives purposeful. Mostly they were from high caste Hindus and were Zamindars. They were also highly educated and eminent writers. But when they came down from the high pedestal[92] of the society and mixed with the common people, the later realised their honesty of devotion.[93] These leaders were leading organisers of different district Congress organisations. They had areas of their own influences and own group of followers within the district organisations. Many a women broke the age old *Purdah* system and came out of their home to join the movement. These leading Gandhians had created such stature of themselves among the people by their selfless activities that many people joined them even without any sound knowledge in different Gandhian ideas.[95]

Role of Constructive Programmes

Gandhian constructive programmes were indispensible part of his movement were directed for emancipation of society from its backwardness. Removal of untouchability,

92. Questionnaire—Baishnab Charan Mohanty, Cuttack; Interview—Annapurna Mohaprana.
93. G.N. Mohanty, *op.cit.*, p. 36; Interview—Sarat Chandra Maharana.
94. Interview—Advaitballav Ray.
95. *Ibid.*, Sarat Chandra Maharana.

Prohibition of liquor, *Khadi* and village industries, Village Sanitation, New Basic Education, Adult Education, Upliftment of women, Education on Heigene, Cultivating love for one's own language, Working for Economic Equality, Communal Harmony etc. were the areas of his constructive movement. Gandhi's political struggle for independence along with these constructive activities made the movement stronger, multifaceted and mass-based. Curious people saw these activities of Gandhian volunteers and felt the presence of the movement among them through these programmes. It gave continuation to the course of the struggle during its low political temperature. More people became Gandhians for the emancipation of the society.

Very often immediate local needs were taken into consideration which made the local Gandhians enthusiastic in these works.[96] Relief programmes during natural calamities under the direct supervision of local Congress workers were conducted. Programmes for the upliftment of backward classes of the areas were also looked after by these workers. The concern and the sincerity of these Gandhians for the poor were felt by the people. Many eminent leaders came to Orissa to supervise these works in different localities and praised the volunteers of the Congress in Orissa. Works for the untouchables created a stir in them which prepared a strong base for the Congress among these sections of the people.

All these attracted young people in the villages who were observing these activities with great care. It contributed tremendously not only for the growth of Gandhian workers but also the sympathiser—much more than the active workers. The movement permitted different social groups to join hands with one another without giving up their distinct and even contradictory interests. As constructive programmes were chalked out

96. *Ibid.*, Harekrushna Biswal and Advaitbailav Ray.

for different classes of the society and as it was not meant for the destruction of the contributing traditional customs and values, even orthodox elements[97] of the society supported Gandhi's movement. Because Gandhi was not a big and direct threat to their existence.

As a champion of women's cause, Gandhi created a strong place for himself among the women-folk in Orissa. During this decade, though, very few women active workers joined Congress and Mahtab[98] observed that the Congress had failed miserably to liberate the women in Orissa, still, there were some women workers who enrolled themselves as the primary members of the organisation. This was a new experiment for the Orissan society. At the initial years mostly the wives of top Congress[99] leaders joined the movement. Seeing them the wives of few common village Gandhians also followed them.

Gandhi's Special Attention for Orissa and Cause of Unification

These were too very important factors for the emergence of Gandhians in Orissa. These deeply moved the young people who were thriving for identity. Gandhi was a master technician of highlighting regional causes. Whenever came to Orissa, he talked about the poverty of the region. He highlighted pitiable condition of Oriyas in national platforms.[100] As the editor of 'Young India' and '*Navjivan*', he described the causes of the sufferings of these people. Due to his special effort, relief helps came to Orissa from other provinces.[101] He praised the culture and traditions of the province and felt concerned deeply for the poor. When the Oriyas, saw a man like Gandhi, coming from outside, talked and wrote about them, got

97. *Ibid.*, Harekrushna Biswal and Advaitballav Ray.
98. H.K. Mahtab, *op.cit.*, p. 158.
99. Interview—Advaitballav Ray.
100. Ratnakar, 1st April, 1920.
101. Asha, 13th August, 1920.

encouraged and sympathetic to the movement. Thus, Gandhi's movement captured the attention of the Oriyas before any other leader could do so.

Gandhi wrote, "I was prepared to see skeletons in Orissa, but not to the extent I did. I had seen terrible pictures, but the reality was too terrible."[102] He also wrote, "The new Indian Nation cannot be built upon the ashes of an ancient race."[103] He openly supported the cause of amalgamation and pleaded through his newspapers in favour of the cause. He further observed, "The fine race cannot possibly make the natural advance which is its due. If it is split up into four divisions for no sound reason, and we trust that the Oriya movement will be examined by the people with sympathetic care and attention.[104]

Gandhi vehemently criticised the government for its inadequate relief provided to the people of Orissa during the natural calamities and appealed to both government and non-governmental institutions and agencies to send immediate help to the people of Orissa. The people felt the concern of Gandhi and his special attention for Oriyas. The educated and conscious people were deeply moved by his soft corner for the region in his heart. So many Oriyas felt it as their duty to join Gandhi's movement.

Before 1920AD leading Oriyas were fighting for the safety of Oriya language and for the political unification of Orissa without joining the National Congress due to its step-motherly behaviour.[105] Even some old guards opposed the merger of *'Utkal Sammilani'* with the Indian National Congress. But when Gandhi sympathised with the Oriyas and the Congress recommended the formation of the provinces on linguistic basis, young Oriyas developed faith in the Congress as a national party. Rise

---

102. Young India, 13th April, 1921.
103. CWMG, Vol.XVIII, *op.cit.*, 1965, p. 36.
104. *Ibid.*
105. *Samaj*, 8th January, 1921.

of educated class within the decade and their enthusiasm to see Orissa as a province made them active supporters of the Congress. Whenever any provincial or district Congress sessions were convened the workers laid emphasis on the unification of Oriya speaking population. Common Gandhians of the districts, lying outside Orissa division, became active supporters of the unification. If Gandhi got the support of the educated people of the area, it was his support to the cause of amalgamation induced them to do so in many respects.

These causes largely contributed for the growth of Gandhians and popularity of Gandhi in the region. These factors also were responsible throughout the movement in shaping the attitude of the total Gandhian force in the province. These workers by dint of their tireless work and selfless devotion made the foundation of the Congress and popularity of Gandhi very strong. By 1930AD Orissa represented itself as one of important Gandhian areas of India. In the political map of India it could occupy a very honourable place.

II

ROLE OF GANDHIANS DURING THE NON-CO-OPERATION MOVEMENT

When the Non-Co-Operation Movement was launched in Orissa, the people who became Gandhians were very few, but gradually thousands of people representing different parts of the region, became primary members of the Congress. This made the organisation an all-Orissa stature. In spite of the accidental nature of the movement to the common people, within a year, its impact reached every corner of the province. Gandhi called for the boycott of educational institutions, courts, government services and elections. But the boycott of educational[106] and legal institutions was successful as compared to others. Very few service holders left their profession. Among them

106. *Ibid.*, 22nd January, 1921.

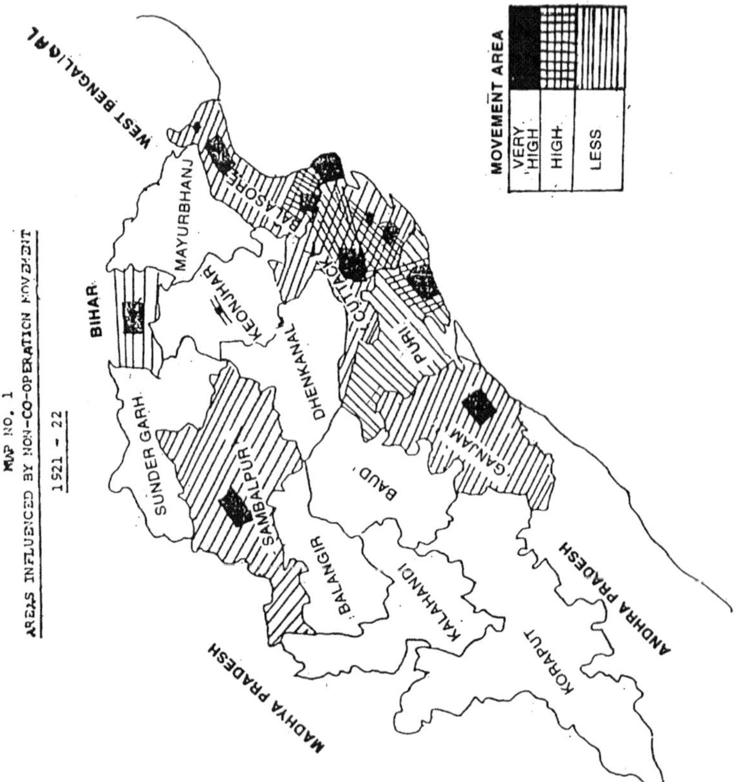
MAP NO. 1
AREAS INFLUENCED BY NON-CO-OPERATION MOVEMENT
1921 - 22
WEST BENGAL
BIHAR
MAYURBHANJ
BALASORE
KEONJHAR
CUTTACK
PURI
DHENKANAL
SUNDER GARH
SAMBALPUR
BAUD
GANJAM
BALANGIR
KALAHANDI
KORAPUT
MADHYA PRADESH
ANDHRA PRADESH
MOVEMENT AREA
VERY HIGH
HIGH
LESS

many were teachers. But to lawyer relinguished his legal practice.[107]

In urban and semi-urban areas, many students boycotted the government schools and many of them joined national schools established by the leading Gandhians of the province. Many teachers also left their job. Thus, the teachers and the students formed a formidable force for Gandhian movement in Orissa. The teachers of national institutions guided the young boys in the line of self-respect and political awakening. But in rural areas, where the schools were few and number of dropouts was very high, boycott of educational institutions was not successful.

Hundreds of villages of different districts formed their *panchayats* to boycott British legal institutions.[108] Everyday '*Samaj* published news in this regard publishing the names of office bearers of hundreds of such *panchayats*. The workers of the Congress influenced their villagers to boycott the courts and settle their disputes in the *Panchayats*. In many cases teachers and student of national[109] schools went to villages to encourage the people to form such traditional village legal organisations. As *panchayat* system was an age-old tradition of Orissa like other Indian provinces, the common villagers of Orissa formed such organisations in number. In actuality every village had this traditional organisation, but during the movement these became reactivated. These, in many respect, helped to spread Gandhism in interior Orissa. The office bearers, though, from dominating upper-castes, came across different ideas of Gandhi taking active role in the affairs of these *Panchayats*. The DCCs advised the *Panchayats* to settle the disputes without punishing any

107. *Ibid.*, 8th October, 1921.

108. *Ibid.*, 12th February, 1921, 28th March, 1921 & 16th April, 1921; H.K. Mahtab, *op.cit.*, p. 49.

109. *Samaj*, 28th March, 1920.

party too heavily to give humiliating punishment to any guilt.[110] This would not offend any person to go to the government courts to avenge his insult.

During the year-long tenure of the movement which continued from December, 1920AD to February, 1922AD, the Gandhians of Orissa became engaged in intense political activities. Frequent *hartals*, picketings and meetings were organised to surcharge the atmosphere with patriotic feelings. They targeted government offices and shops of foreign clothes, liquors and other intoxicants to start picketings. As mostly these were located in urban and semi-urban areas, the Gandhians assembled there. They were divided into different groups under many dictators and sent to different localities to continue the agitation. In Cuttack town, *'Swaraj Ashram'* controlled the activities of the Gandhians.[111] Top leaders stayed here to heighten the agitation in the town.* Young Gandhians from different districts came here to be trained properly by adults. The trainees were taught how to avoid or keep themselves safe from police *lathi*. Many young boys and girls were trained to sing patriotic songs. In the early morning, groups of volunteers would go to different streets of Cuttack town to collect foreign clothes for bonfire. They would recite *Kirtans* dancing round the heap before setting fire. Arranging meeting of the washermen and scavangers they could explain them to leave liquor.[112] The S.D.O. of Cuttack restricted Jadumani Mangaraj, Gobinda Mishra and Rajkrushna Bose to held meetings.[113] But the agitation was going on without caring such restriction. In Jagatsinghpur, Ramakrishna Pattnaik, Nilamani Pradhan, Birendra Barala; Dukhisyama Mishra

110. *Ibid.*, 17th December, 1921.

111. Interview—Harekrushna Biswal, Advaitballav Ray, Udayanath Sarangi.

* Cuttack Town was the capital of the then Orissa Division.

112. *Samaj*, 26th February, 1921.

113. *Ibid.*, 12th March, 1921.

in Banki, Nishamani Das in Patia, Banchhanidhi Mishra in Telengapenth, Manmohan Mohapatra and Kulamani Tripathy in Tangi became non-co-operators.[114]

While picketing in front of liquor shops, the Gandhians were abused by the hired prostitutes. Even the prostitutes threw wine, urine and spit on them.[115] In Jajpur a *'Swaraj Ashram'* was established. Rajkrushna Bose, Jairam Das etc. arranged meetings and displayed photographs of Gandhi to public. School teachers like Jagannath Mishra, Dwarkanath Mohapatra etc. propagated Gandhism in Korei and Kanika. Sub-divisional Congress committee was formed which had more than fifty members.[116] In Salepur Atal Bihari Acharya, Rajendra Chatterjee etc. joined the Congress.[117] In Kujang Narayan Samanta was the leader.[118] In Balasore district, under the leadership of Harekrushna Mahtab the Gandhians worked hard to prepare the district as a strong Gandhian base. Banchhanidhi Mohanty wrote highly patriotic poems which became very popular among the workers and the masses because of their coloquial flavour.[119] The prominent workers were Mukunda Prasad Das and Nanda Kishore Das.[120] In Bhadrak Ghanasyama Sahoo and Munsi Humayun formed a *Khilafat* committee.[121]

In Sambalpur, the leading Gandhians with the help of their common co-workers made the movement a memorable event. Zilla School students took a pioneering role under Nilakantha Das. Many teachers and clerks of different schools joined the movement. National Schools were closed on Friday for Muslim students and not on

114. *Ibid.*, 28th August, 1921.
115. Souvenir, Sangrami Sri Suryamani Nayak (O), Cuttack, 1989.
116. *Samaj*, 28th March, 1921.
117. *Ibid.*, 26th February, 1921.
118. *Ibid.*
119. Souvenir, Kabi Banchhanidhi (O), Cuttack, 1987, p. 15.
120. *Samaj*, 26th February, 1921.
121. *Ibid.*, 12th March, 1921.

Sunday as for Hindu boys.[122] Leaflets were circulated and the people were persuaded to give up intoxicant.[123] The workers arranged meetings of women and Mahendra Nath Verma, Achyutananda Purohit organised the scavangers to leave liquor. *Panchayats* were formed in every street of the town. Rules and regulations of the Panchayats were printed and were circulated among the people.

In Singhbhum the volunteers visited village to village, even went to tribal areas by foot to spread the ideas of the movement. Both in Hindi and Oriya slogans were shouted. The students of *'Jatiya Vidyalaya'* took leading part in the movement under Godavarish Mishra.[124] Ganjam and Puri districts also witnessed the excitement of the common Gandhians in different activities. There were many agitators in Berhampur and Paralakhemundi. Students left college and came to *'Swaraj Ashram'* of Cuttack to get training.[125] Ganjan district was divided into ten divisions by the PCC. They were Gunupur, Parala-khemundi and Tikili; Barua, Sompet; Tarala, Majusha; Sanakhemundi and Badakhemundi; Shergarh; Darada, Chikiti, Ichhapur; Asika, Dharakot, Baragarh; Ghumsur, Jagannathpur, Purusottampur; Chhatrapur, Ganjam, Huma; Khalikote, Athgarh etc. The leaders were Niranjan Pattnaik, Arjuna Panigrahi, Brundaban Nayak etc.[126]

Jagabandhu Singh and Krupasindhu Mishra in Puri made the movement highly successful. In Khurdha region, the workers succeeded in bringing many common people to the meetings. In Puri town, the leader arranged meetings and Ananta Mishra went to Malud of Chilka to propagate Gandhism there.[127] Students of Satyabadi

122. *Ibid.*, 26th February, 1922.

123. *Utkal* Sevak, 21st January, 1921; Seva, 15th April, 1922.

124. G.B. Mishra, *op.cit.*, pp. 110-14.

125. *Samaj*, 26th February, 1921.

126. *Ibid.*, 16th April, 1921.

127. *Ibid.*, 12th March, 1921.

school like Bhagabat Subudhi and Janardan Biswal went to Kanasha and Delanga police stations to form *Panchayats* and propagate Gandhian ideas among the people.[128]

Gopabandhu Das went to Koraput, the Oriya-speaking areas of Madras Presidency where he was assisted by Baikuntha Nath Nayak, Sarat Chandra Maharana, Syamasundar Patnaik, Narasingha Panigrahi and Nanda Kishore Mishra. The workers were active in Salur, Gunupur, Ralingi Rai, Raigarh etc.[129]

As compared to urban areas, in the villages, the activities of the Gandhians were less frequent in spite of the formation of the hundreds of perhaps the illiterate villagers were less active than the educated urbanites. But the villagers near administrative headquarters and *Ashrams* got the warmth of the agitation directly. The movement became successful in these areas as many Gandhians were produced here. Boycott of foreign cloth was successful in these villages. Typical village self-sufficiency and interdependence helped the *panchayats* of these villages to ostracise the man who sold or bought foreign clothes. Even few *panchayats* collected fines from a cloth merchant who sold mill-cloth. The barbers and washermen were directed not to attend the merchant.[130] The cartmen were persuaded not to carry such clothes into the villages.

In towns also, Gandhians persuaded the cartmen not to carry mill-cloths from the railway stations. Gandhians were deputed to supervise the operation.[131] Many Districts committees circulated By-laws for their workers in which rules and regulations of the Congress members were clearly mentioned. No worker was allowed to hold

128. *Ibid.*, 28th March, 1921.

129. *Ibid.*, 16th April, 1921.

130. H.K. Mahtab, *op.cit.*, p. 48; D.K. Panda, Mukti Sangramare Jaleswar (O), Balasore, 1985.

131. S.N. Pattnaik, *op.cit.*, p. 41.

meetings, exhibitions and led processions or to be the leader without the permission of the D.C.C. Neither he could start picketing in front of shops of foreign goods. Only Congress workers could work for *Swaraj*. In villages the caste councils and *panchayats* were to be directed to settle the disputes amicably and no punishment would be ignominious for the culprit. The agitators should offer himself to be arrested by the police peacefully but not for his own private conduct or attitude. He must not create unnecessary scene when arrested.[132]

Opposition to Gandhians

As the movement was a direct attack on the British hegemony over India, and also against its allied forces within India, its beneficiaries also became dreaded enemies of the Congress. From big Zamindars to petty land-lords, from police officials to revenue collectors, all saw the Gandhians the stumbling block in the way of their social dominance. They tried their level best to disrupt Congress influence in their areas. If anybody dared to help the *Congressias* was harassed severely. The villagers were threatened not to give shelter to these *Khadarias*. Even the relatives of the Gandhians were directed not to provide support to them. When village-level meetings were organised, the villagers were severely threatened and even some meetings were disrupted by police declaring these illegal and unlawful.[133]

The *Khadar* dress became a symbol of bad omen to the authorities. Even a government servant using the *Khadar*, though it was his usual dress, was mistaken as a Congressman and had to be wrongly reprimanded by the authorities.[134] In Banki the authorities prohibited the

132. Interview—Rajkrushna Bose.

133. Interview—Udayanath Sarangi, Sarat Chandra Maharana; H.K. Mahtab, History of............., *op.cit.*, p. 61; S. Mohanty, Andhra Diganta (O), *op.cit.*, pp. 75-95.

134. *Samaj*, 20th August, 1921.

people from attending the meetings organised by the Gandhians and even ordered the shop-keepers not to provide rations to the Congress workers who were creating disturbances.[135] Some zamindars of Sambalpur district physically assulted the Gandhians.[136] Even the authorities tried to defame the Gandhians by setting fire many houses of Cuttack and Balasore towns.[137] People become frightened. Some villagers, who wore hand-made clothes would soil it not to be distinguished as a *'khadaria'*, as the common village level Gandhians wore clean white *Khadar* which made them distinguished among many.[138]

During the agitation, the collectors and sub-divisional officers were asked to tour in their respective areas and try their best to restrain the political leaders and dissuade people. The people became so excited and the atmosphere in many areas became so surcharged with patriotic feeling that very often local zamindars or land-lords had to take the help of District Congress Organisations to settle the disputes amicably.[139] Some zamindars also helped the Gandhians. Though people still talked about the brutal oppression of the Chaudhuries of Bhingarpur of Puri district, the Zamindar, very often, helped Nilakantha Das and the district Congress in arranging meetings in his area.[140]

Garhjats and Zamindaries, and Non-Co-operation Movement

In *Garhjats* the *Rajas* became very conscious not to see their subjects being influenced by Gandhi's ideas. They took all types of measures to check the infiltration of outside Gandhians into their areas. Even within these states,

135. *Ibid.*, 20th August, 1921.
136. *Ibid.*, 25th May, 1921.
137. H.K. Mahtab, Sadhanara........... (O), *op.cit.*, pp. 55-59.
138. Interview—Harekrushna Biswal.
139. S.N. Pattnaik, *op.cit.*, p. 16.
140. *Samaj*, 19th February, 1921.

educated boys were kept under strong supervision lest they would opt for Gandhian movement. *Raja* of Keonjhar even ordered his people, not to utter Gandhi's name. The princes and zamindars became frightened seeing the magical influence of Gandhi on the people. The *'Samaj'* reported that the kings were startled just hearing the name of Gandhi.[141]

Gandhi was reluctant to encourage the states people to fight against the oppressive kings and advised the Congress not to instigate them. He wanted that the people of these states should fight themselve. But when Non-Co-Operation' was launched, its impact was felt in nearby *Garhjats* and Zamindaries which were encircled by strong Gandhian bases of the *Moghulbandi*. Kanika*, a Zimindari-comprising of some areas of both Cuttack and Balasore districts, was easily influenced by the Gandhian agitation. The king was cruel and despot and had inflicted heavy punishments on the people—who dared to speak against it. But in spite of such oppression, the people became organised and started agitation very quickly being influenced by Gandhi's ideas and techniques.

The area was affected severely by flood and famine in 1919AD and the king opened relief centres which was totally untimely and inadequate. But Pandit Gopabandhu came to Kanika to supervise the condition and his coming

141. *Ibid.*, 23rd April, 1921 and 28th May, 1921.

* 'Many scholars believe that Kanika agitation was a natural uprising of the people against feudal oppression and Non-Co-Operation Movement was nothing to do with its outbreak. But it is not untrue to say that Gandhian movement in Orissa of the time regulated and organised this movement in a proper way, thus, heightened the confidence and spirit of the agitating people. Both of the movements could not run separately in the same region at a time. Gandhians might not originate Kanika movement, but helped to organise it at its crucial phase. Later most of the workers of the movement followed Gandhian ideas and strategies and accepted the directives of provincial Congress.

created a stir in the people. Some people had already formed an organisation. The king increased various taxes and tolls.[142]

In the meantime a religious mendicant, Babaji Ramdas entered the area to spread the seeds of non-co-operation on behalf of Cuttack District Congress organisation. In the month of November, 1921AD, the leaders of the Cuttack DCC entered the Zamindari of Kanika and established a *'Swaraj Ashram'* at Kantapara, and planted a banyan tree naming it as *'Gandhi Bata'*. Around three to four thousands became the primary members of the Congress. The king tried to supress the movement ruthlessly by taking different measures but failed.[143]

The PCC sent some volunteers to Kanika to supervise the situation and investigate the excesses done by the King.[144] Gopabandhu wrote about the sufferings of the people in the *'Samaj'*. Many students of Rajkanika High School left school to be non-co-operators. When the king took Ramdas Babaji to the court nobody was available to give witness against him. The king closed the school. The organisation formed by the people was directed and controlled by the Cuttack DCC. It started boycotting and ostracising the supporters of the king and his institutions. The District Congress volunteers were not allowed to enter the state, so they went in disguise to avoid royal police. They contacted leading supporters of the Congress agitation in the Zamindari. Some teachers like Ananda Charan Jena, Jairam Rai, Upendra Subudhiraj left their profession and joined the Congress. *Gramasabhas* were formed to organise people to fight against king's *Lathials* collectively. Even rumours flouted that they would be helped by Gandhi's force from Ranchi. People started no-rent agitation supporting the non-co-operation formula.

142. G.D. Behera, *op.cit.*, pp. 48-51.

143. *Ibid.*

144. *Ibid.*

Hundreds of villages united and thousands of people marched to defy the authority.[145]

A strong Gandhian base was thus created in Kanika. Many people proudly called themselves as Gandhi's disciples and opened *Ashrams* in their localities. Gandhians made people aware of the limitations of police activities and questioned openly the legality of police excesses. King's headmen were replaced by *'Mundials'* who were elected by villagers. People spun *Khadar*. They formed *panchayats* to settle village disputes. It became so successful that the kind became frightened as he could lose his stronghold over the masses. The Gandhians used different ways to avoid royal police. They communicated through difficult ways and wore dresses of women to avoid police. The use of long veil *'Odhana'*, very often, saved them to be arrested by the police. Getting the support of the Congress the indigenous workers became organised. The students of Kanika High School established a national school as a symbol of national pride.[146]

In the state of Keonjhar, which was a distant place from *Moghulbandi*, very few joined the Congress. But in spite of the strong warning by the king they launched Non-Co-Operation Movement. They refused to do *bethi, rasad* and other impositions. They defied the royal order by performing *'Sankirtan'* in the roads to attract the people.[147]

By this time people's discontent against the king was very strong in princely state of Talcher. During the Non-Co-Operation Movement the people started an agitation which was brutally supressed by the king. A High School teacher, jadumani Mohanty became a member of the Congress organisation and adopted Gandhian ideas in his

145. *Ibid.*, p. 53.

146. M.D. Mallik, *op.cit.*, pp. 42-60; B. Pati, Peasants, Tribals and The National Movement in Orissa, 1921-36, M.Phil. Dissertation, Department of History, Delhi University, 1980.

147. S.N. Pattnaik, *op.cit.*, p. 43.

personal life. He fought against untouchability and often organised *kirtans* with the help of both *Harijans* and people at a time. But his effort to allow the untouchables to enter the temple was not successful as his mission was opposed by the upper castes.[148] Pabitra Mohan Pradha, an educated young man of Talcher, was perparing himself as a Gandhian. The king's effort to bring him to his camp could not succeed.[149]

As other princely states of Orissa were far away from the influence of the Congress and Gandhi, Non-Co-Opration Movement was not so strong in these areas. But the people of these areas also heard the magical all of Non-Co-Operation Movement. It gave them needed encouragement to be mobilised gradually.

Methods of Propaganda by the Gandhians

To incite the people, the Congress workers were directed by theis leaders to propagate Gandhi's ideas and visions. They used newspapers, journals, and toured areas to awaken the people. Before holding meetings at particular place, the local Congress workers were directed by the DCC to arrange properly to make the meetings successful. The DCC took total responsibility to arrange such meetings for the visiting leaders. These common workers also held meetings for the visiting leaders. These common workers also held meetings in their own areas. As some of the freedom fighters were school teachers they were helped by their old students in arrangements.[150]

The Gandhians hung the photographs of Gandhi and other leaders to attract the attention of the people of the meetings.[151] They often visited weekly market places—where people in villages usually gathered, to influence the

148. A. Mishra, Talcher Andolana(O), Talcher, p. 10.

149. P.M. Pradhan, *op.cit.*, p. 4.

150. *Samaj*, 5th February, 1921; Interview—Udayanath Sarangi.

151. *Samaj*, 26th February, 1921.

people in the line of self-respect. Women Gandhians visited houses in the villages to seek the support of womenfolk.[152] The Gandhians organised mass-*kirtans* and gather at village fairs to address the people in their own language.[153] It was the belief that Gandhi as an *Avtar* induced these *Kirtan* troupes to join the processions and marches. These *Sankirtans* helped the Gandhians to developed religious flavour of Gandhi's movement further. The members of the *Sankirtan* groups shouted *'Bande Mataram'* and *'Mahatma Gandhi Ki Jai'* being persuaded by the Gandhians to make the processions meaningful.[154]

The Gandhians often celebrated important days, anniversaries and National Days. They arranged meetings on these occasions and invited local people to join it. The inhabitants of the *Ashrams* and Congress offices were very regular in this respect. These symbolic observations— which were new to the common people, helped the Gandhians to educate the people in nationalist spirit continuously. Some Gandhians wrote booklets on Gandhi in Oriya and sold and circulated them in cheaper rates.[155] Handmade lithoed pamphlets[156] were also circulated by the workers among the people. Young Gandhians proved competent in this respect. These pamphlets not only attracted the attention of the public quickly, but also became successful in highlighting local issues.

Banchhanidhi Mohanty and Birakishore Das prepared music parties and trained small boys and girls to sing patriotic songs, which they themselves had composed. These songs and music groups were more successful in propagating and popularising Gandhian ideas than any

152. *Ibid.*
153. *Ibid.*, 28th March, 1921 & 7th May, 1921.
154. *Ibid.*, 28th May, 1921.
155. *Ibid.*, 18th June, 1921.
156. C.S. Mohapatra (ed.), Jatiya Kavi Avinandan (O), Cuttack, 1979, p. 10.

other channel.[157] Some of the Gandhians living today recall some lines of popular poems* of [158] Banchhanishi Mohanty. Very often, the Gandhians used tin-made funnels called '*Punga*' or used small tin boxes to make their voice loud.[159]

Very often, meetings were hald near the temples or other religious places like village fair grounds. As the Gandhians had to ignite majority of the population who were generally Hindus, they selected these places to enlarge Gandhi's personality and to popularise his *divinity*' among the people.

Collection of Fund

In Orissa, the provincial Congress always faced financial problems throughout the decade which continued upto the end of the movement. Unlike in Maharastra, Gujrat, Delhi, Punjab and Bengal, Orissa was industrially very backward and so no business group grew here which could have helped the movement financially which had supported *Swadeshi* . Moneyed people were very few and the kings and the Zamindars, who were once supporting the leaders of Orissa during language agitation, did not support the Congress. Rather they became its dreaded enemies. So very often the PCC had to beg for financial support from the National Congress. This question was repeatedly discussed[160] in AICC sessions.

Collection of funds by enrolling people was very limited. There were thousands of active workers whose expenditure were borne by the PCC. So small boys and girls were sent to different lanes of the urban areas and villages of rural area to collect funds by visiting door to

157. Ibid., p. 56.

* One of the lines-"Tell, tell, which race has own independence by begging and appealing" was very popular.

158. A. Mishra, *op.cit.*, p. 10; S.K. Das, *op.cit.*

159. Interview—Udayanath Sarangi, Advaitaballav Ray.

160. H.N. Mitra (ed.), Indian Quarterly Register, Vol.-I, January-March, No. 1, Calcutta, 1924. p. 22.

door. Collection of rice in this way was very common. Sympathisers of the Congress kept pots in their homes to drop one fistful of rice daily which was ultimately collected by the volunteers at the weekend. Small girls became experts in this activity. The pots were called as *'Muthi Handi'*.[161]

Many Gandhians started *Ashrams* and tried to become self-sufficient as the Ashramites produced daily-use materials in their own small industries. It helped them not to be dependent on others. They spun clothes, cultivated rice and vegetables inside the campus, and even supplied *khaddr dhotis* and sarees to the Gandhians for marriage ceremonies in their own houses, thus, collecting money to use it for the betterment of the *Ashrams*. But during the time of acute financial shortage *'Ashramites'* did go to nearly villages to collect funds.[162]

To arrange DCC and other local-level meetings, very often, the district leaders had to borrow money to meet the expenditure. But as the local people gradually became enthusiastic—whenever the Congress meetings were conveyed and big leaders were invited to address the meetings, local influential and rich people were also invited to attend the meetings. They contributed some help in either way. Rice, vegetables and other materials were collected or donated by the local people and other expenditures like pendal work, arrangement of vehicles, flowers, etc. had to be met by DCC leaders.[163]

'Utkal Swaraj Fund' was created during the Non-Co-Operation Movement to meet the monthly expenditure of *'Swaraj Ashram'* at Cuttack. At least four to five thousand rupees had to be collected[164] the *Marvari* and *Gujrati* businessmen of Cuttack also very often helped the PCC

161. Interview—Rajkrushna Bose, *Samaj*, 12th February, 1921.
162. Interview—Udayanath Sarangi; G.N. Mohanty, *op.cit.*
163. *Utkal* Dipika, 2nd June, 1928.
164. *Samaj*, 12th February, 1921.

financially,[165] but their contributions were not adequate. In spite of such financial trouble, the PCC could be able to run the movement successfully by its sheer determination. Though faced with acute financial strain, with forbearance, the Gandhians endured pain and strain of the movement to make it continuous in nature.

During this time a satirical article was writen by Laxmikant Mohapatra entitled *"Asahayogira Atmakatha"* (Autobiography of a Non-co-operator). It was beautifully written indicating the weaknesses of the activities of the Congress organisation in the province. Laxmikant Mohapatra was a great support of the cause of the unification of Oriya-speaking areas and the author of the famous song `*Bande, Utkaljanani*' (I salute you, the Mother *Utkal*) which became the national song of modern Oriya nationalism. His critical views regarding the Non-Co-Operation are interesting. The theme of the article in its actual flavour is given below from which the apprehension and doubts of the old guards of Oriya interests regarding the Congress workers can be well visualised.

He wrote thus,

> "During the Non-Co-Operation Movement the Congress declared to abolish the schools, government, railway, motor, watch and cycle etc. The people will be taught in *toles* and *Pathasalas*. The *Satyayug* will come again.... who left home and stayed in *Ashram* became a Gandhian. In newspaper the name of the non-co-operators are published prominently.... In *Ashramas* there are two types of workers. One group is active for *Swarajya* while the other is busy for the propagation of *Khadi* and mass-education. A few are also busy in begging. People give a little. These beggars, in different ways, use to say to help them for the death anniversary of Tilak, for the birthday of Gandhi or their leader has been arrested, a meeting is

165. *Ibid.*

to be held, a procession will start from a particular ground, a national school is to be established, wheel and *Khadar* will be purchased for such and such villages etc.....

The name of Gandhi has mesmerised the people so magically that when the people, who normally hardly help other, knowing that Gandhi's men have come, also search for their own pockets to pretend themselves as great givers. The leaders having highly fertile brains have also been engaged to spread rumours on Gandhi like—a man was snake bitten, but was cured when uttered Gandhi's name thrice, one was ploughing on the day of Gandhi's hartal suddenly fainted. He uttered Gandhi's name and stood straight. The house of a man caught fire. In the night Lord *Mahadev* came to his dream and warned him that he had violated Gandhi's norms. Very soon *'Gandhi Bhagwan', 'Gandhi Devati', 'Gandhi Mukti', 'Gandhi Hukum', 'Gandhi Avtar', 'Gandhi Mela'* such and such became popular.

Women naturally helps a lot. They believe that bad omen will visit their home if they disobey Gandhi. The adult Gandhians use to send small lovable boys who can be easily more appealing. They use to ask the women in soft voices to help them. During picketing the non-co-operators request the customers to return from the shops of foreign articles and intoxicants. The shop-keepers scold them. Here helps come in plenty as the shopkeepers will like to give alms by which the non-co-operators will leave his shop soon. The Gandhians propagated that all are equal, but many are reluctant to mix with the so-called untouchables.

They form *Panchayats* and became king-makers. As the followers of Gandhi, many of them became leaders of the *Panchayat* and create lots of litigations and conflicts. Nobody cares for others. Untouchables do care a little for *Brahmins*. Younger do not respect the elder. So nothing has been done by the *panchayats*.

The Gandhians use to sing a song like this,

> The Gandhi *Avtar* has come,
> He is the saviour of fallen,
> the cause of hapiness of the Universe,
> the holder of wheel, the destroyer of poverty,
> the holder of compassion'.[166]

III

GANDHIANS AND THE YEARS AFTER THE NON-CO-OPERATION MOVEMENT

Political Activities

By 1922 AD almost all the Congress workers of Orissa were put behind the bars, which caused a great setback to the movement. When the movement was suspended party work slackened considerably and the provincial organisation became weak. Some leaders formed *Utkal Swaraj* Party and fought elections, but rest of the workers joined Gandhians constructive programmes and other activities upto 1930 AD—either as full-timers of part-timers.

PCC decided to enter the Zilla Boards and Local Boards participating in the elections. These Boards were created by the government to educate people in the line of local self government. These were 'monopolised'[167] by some selfish moneyed-people and Zamindars. There was no difference between a government office and a Board office where nepotism, discrimination and exploitation were rampart.

When the PCC entered the fray, it chosed its own candidates from different districts. Workers campaigned

166. L.K. Mohapatra, "Ashayogira Atma Katha" (O), *op.cit.*, pp. 1-25.

167. H.K. Mahtab, *op.cit.*, p. 100.

for them. They won the elections in number and top district leaders became the office bearers of the Boards of Cuttack, Puri and Balasore districts. During the election the workers came into closer contacts with the people through campaigning. They highlighted local difficulties and when their leaders came to the office, tried to solve many of their immediate problems.[168]

When new office bearers came to the Boards people felt the difference. The leaders supervised different development works taken by the Boards and saw that every rupee of the Public Fund be utilised. Leaders travelled through the areas and asked the Boards to take immediate steps. Even the presidents and vice-presidents of the Boards went to villages repeatedly to supervise the works.[169] Relief works and medicines for Malaria were distributed. In this work school teachers took prominent role.[170] New Schools and hospitals were opened and roads and lanes were developed. The Local Boards propagated *Swadeshi* for which these became platforms of the propagation of political views. In spite of the governmental hostility attempts were made to hoist the *Swaraj* Flag atop Municipal buildings and employees were advised to use *Khadi*.[171] Steps were taken to make spinning compulsory in primary schools.[172] But occasionally reports were being published regarding the non-committant member of District Boards for whom honest and good were not nominated as the Congress candidates, so had failed to get scope to do something satisfactory for the people.[173]

Upto the year 1930 AD, the Gandhians—whether they

168. *Utkal* Dipika, 5th June, 1926; Interview—Rajkrushna Bose.
169. *Utkal* Dipika, 23rd January, 1926; Interview—Rajkrushna Bose, G.N. Mohanty *op.cit.*, p. 82.
170. *Utkal* Dipika, 5th September, 1925.
171. Interview—Rajkrushna Bose, Udayanath Sarangi and Advaitballav Ray.
172. *Ibid.*
173. *Utkal* Dipika, 11th June, 1927.

were staying in *Ashrams*, District Offices or in villages, observed different National Days regularly to maintain the continuity of the movement. Occasional *hartals* were observed. Meetings of PCC were held at the headquarters of different DCCs. Funds were collected from the people.[174] *Hartals* were observed and village markets were closed. As the Government hiked Salt Tax twice, a protest meeting was held at Puri attended by three thousand men.[175] The activities of DCCs could be ascertained from the Resolutions of a DCC. The Ganjan DCC, in its proposals at its annual session, took following programmes :

(*i*) Revival of Congress Committee this year.

(*ii*) Programmes for the removal of the practice of untouchability.

(*iii*) Appeal to the District Board for the construction of roads.

(*iv*) To select candidates for the Congress for the forthcoming District Board elections.

(*v*) To propagate against the practice of child-marriage.

(*vi*) To work hard for the unification of Oriya-speaking people.

(*vii*) To appeal to the Government to start a new train from Ganjam to Puri.

It is found that almost all the members of the DCC were from *Brahmin* or *Karana* castes.[176] The activities of Gandhians could also be assertained from another example-Dhamanagar *Thana Sammilani*, where seven thousands of people joined it. Following proposals were taken up for that year—

174. *Samaj*, 10th March, 1923.

175. *Ibid.*, 24th March, 1923 & 14th April, 1923.

176. *Utkal* Dipika, 30th June, 1928.

(*i*) Condolence for Gopabandhu Das, who died in 1928AD.

(*ii*) Drinking water problem to be taken up.

(*iii*) To tackle the flood problem of Vaitarani.

(*iv*) To demand for the reduction of revenue.

(*v*) To collect donations.[177]

During Simon Commission's visit, entire provincial Congress was demonstrating against it. Though, there were reports that some sections of the PCC were planning to welcome the Commission to appeal its conscience to look at the cause of the amalgamation, there were demonstrations in different towns of the then Orissa against the Commission. Even the daily labourers did not go to work on the day of *hartal*. The photographs of Gandhi were worshipped and pots full of water were placed in front of the houses as symbol of the success of the hartal. Students joined the movement in number.[178] The City of Cuttack became calm on the day of *hartal* against Simon Commission. The song which was sung by the young volunteers became popular, is mentioned thus,

"Go back Simon,
Indian *Swaraj* is the birth-right of the Indians,
It lies in their hands and you are not worthy to get the affection of the Indians."[179]

Sometimes symbolic occupations of the Congress Offices and Government buildings became the pride for the Gandhians in these years. Cuttack *Swaraj Ashram* witnessed this type of activities very often. As police occupied the Congress offices repeatedly, it provided the Gandhians—the scope to resist the police. In Sambalpur,

177. *Ibid.*, 14th June, 1928.

178. *Samaj*, 24th March, 1923 & 18th January, 1924; For Simon Commission, *Samaj*, 8th February, 1928.

179. *Samaj*, 8th February, 1928.

in 1927 AD, *Harijans* took up their abode in the old palace of the royal family of Sambalpur, which was regarded as the symbol of authority. The non-co-operators hoisted the Congress flags on top of the old palace and used fire crackers when occupied it.[180]

For Annual ACC meetings at different parts of India, the PCC had sent its delegates regularly. When Gandhi visited Orissa in 1927AD, a Reception Committee was being formed under the presidentship of Madhusudan Biswal having Banchhanidhi Mohanty and Raghunath Mohanty as members. It collected volunteers. The students of Cuttack were requested not to waste this golden opportunity to serve a great leader like Gandhi.[181] An interesting latter was addressed to Gandhi through *Utkal Dipika* which was written thus,

> "As compared to other regions of *Bharat Varsha* our strength is weak, objectives of our life is also very limited too. Once upon a time that peasant-militia which had conquered the areas from Himalayas to Kanyakumari, their offsprings are still living here in numbers. But that blood of our great forefathers has been frozen like dew.... We are poor both in mind and wealth".[182]

Very often the office-bearers of the DCCs had to borrow money from the influential people of the locality to arrange the meetings. The collection of member fees was very inadequate. Provisions were made to sale *Khadar* articles at the meetings. But the expenditure was always more than the collection.[183]

As late as 1929 AD also, *Swadeshi* movement was still popular in Orissa, but not as strong as in 1921-22 AD. In

180. O.S.A., Home (Political), Confidential File No. 1, 1927 (Office of the Deputy Commissioner, Sambalpur).
181. *Utkal* Dipika, 10th December, 1927.
182. *Ibid.*, 16th December, 1927.
183. *Ibid.*, 2nd June, 1928.

the areas of Jaleswar of Balasore district, a Ẓamindar was ostracised socially. His foreign made bangles and glasses were destroyed.Clothes were set on fire.[184] But these were some rarer incidents where the Gandhians were just trying to keep the movement alive.The political temperature of the movement was at its lowest ebb.Around one thousand common Gandhians were working as full-time activists even including those of constructive workers.

The unification of Oriya-speaking tracts was still a cry of the Gandhians and they tried to utilise Congress platforms to make the cause very strong. Gandhi's moral support made their task much easier.Throughout the decade the leaders raised this questions at different platforms.Congress Committees of different districts in their annual sessions discussed this problem seriously. On 30th June,1924 the Conference of *'Utkal Samillani'*was held at Cuttack,which was arranged by the Congress workers under the leadership of Sarla Devi. At Berhampur,in *Utkal Ashram*, a meeting was held under the presidentship of Biswanath Das, in which Niranjan Pattnaik was entitled to prepare a book to support the cause of Oriya unification.[185]

The people of outlaying Oriya speaking districts were active and continuously highlighted the issue. In 1925 AD at Berhampur, the DCC of Ganjan tried to enlighten the government as well as public about the history and the boundary of Ganjan district.[186] When the provincial Congress became more concerned for national movement and did not take the case of unification seriouly, the DCC of Sambalpur severed its link with the PCC with disgust. The Gandhians here saw the provincial leaders trying to highlight some lesser issues like capturing Local and District Boards. So they influenced their leaders to

184. A. Mishra, *op.cit.*, p. 13.

185. *Utkal* Dipika, 9th May, 1925.

186. *Op.cit.*

threaten the PCC leaders in this way.[187] Even in the Singhbhum area, the common workers of the provincial Congress became frustrated because of the lenient attitude of the PCC towards their cause of amalgamation. Ananta Mishra, who was deputed to look after the organisation there, even warned that if proper step was not taken in time, the PCC had to lose the area for ever.[188]

Constructive Works

Since the launching of the Non-Co-Operation Movement total Gandhian force in Orissa got engaged in different constructive programmes. When the PCC was formed, despite its limited number of workers, it operated the relief works in the famine affected areas. Even paid workers were employed as an additional burden.[189] When the number of active workers grew they worked for prohibition of intoxicants, removal of untouchability and upliftment of women. Picketings were conducted in front of liquor and Ganja shops. Use of *Khadar* was encouraged during the movement.

After the suspension of the movement in 1922 AD, the PCC tried to utilise its entire strength in constructive programmes. Development of *Khadi* and village Industries took prominent figure in this domain. In this time, the Secretary of Indian *Khadi* Board, Sankar Lal Banker had visited Orissa to audit the financial transactions of Orissa Khadi Board. He had submitted his report to Gandhi in which he had mentioned about the pitiable condition of Khadi Programme in Orissa. He had reported that in 1922 AD, the province had alloted Rs. 60,000/- and fifty training centres were opened. But nobody had any knowledge about *Khadi*. Most of the workers were irregular. There were no discipline and responsibility. It was believed that

187. NMML, Andhra—*Utkal* Boundary Disputes, File No. 16/64/1925.

188. *Samaj*, 28th February, 1925.

189. CWMG, Vol-XVIII, *op.cit.*, p. 294.

one or two fellows had misappropriated the amount for which the centers were abolished.[190] But the provincial workers became determined to make *Khadi* a grand success in the coming year.

As the muslims were few, the Gandhian force here was free from the communal germs, as found in other provinces. Thus, they could save lot of time and energy to use it in other constructive programmes. The few muslims of Cuttack were supporters of Gandhi.[191]

To popularise cotton cultivation and spinning young workers spread over the region and persuaded the people to take the programme in a big way. The PCC collected cotton seeds for other provinces.[192] In Satyabadi P.S. of Puri district some youths went to the villagers to pursuade them to cultivate cotton.[193] Cotton seeds were distributed among the cultivators and centres of distribution were opened by the DCC. The Ashramites, very often, went to nearby villages to train the prople to spin. As spinning was a traditional household affair, and as the people had wheels in their homes, women, particularly, expressed their desire to use these. The interested women called for the Ashram's trainers regularly to be trained how to prepare threads better.[194] In Jajpur of Koraput district, the volunteers influenced the rich people to buy 100 to 200 *Charakhas* at a time to distribute these among the people.[195] The Gandhians also went to villages to demonstrate their skill.[196] In Balasore district the volunteers distributed cotton seeds among the people. In Sambalpur, the students of National School prepared handmade clothes and sold these in the nearby villages. Traditional weavers

190. *Samaj*, 7th March, 1925.
191. *Ibid.*, 22nd August, 1925.
192. *Ibid.*, 2nd July, 1921.
193. *Ibid.*, 15th January, 1921.
194. Interview—Udayanath Sarangi.
195. *Samaj*, 5th March, 1921.
196. *Ibid.*, 12th March, 1921.

who constituted a major chunk of the population were trained with modern techniques. Many *Harijans* gave up liquor.[197]

Special volunteers were enrolled and trained as *Khadi* workers. To popularise Khadi, poet Krushnaprasad Basu wrote thus,

"I will wear *Khadi*, how much coarse it may be,
My country is very beautiful,
I will buy *Khadi* how costly it may be,
I can dare."[198]

When the volunteers of the PCC were busy to popularise *Swadeshi*, some greedy businessmen used Gandhi an a trademark and medium of the advertisement for their products. They used Gandhi's photographs on *bidi*, cigarate, match box, clothes as lebels and people did buy it thinking these as the product of *Ashrams*. They were vehemently condemned by the workers.[199]

Khadi Kendras were opened at Berhampur, Kodala, Bairani (Ganjam), Bolgarh (Puri). District organisations looked after these centres.[200] The PCC had formed *Khadi* Board and All India *Khadi Sangha* had promised to send 1.5 Lakhs of rupees. From the instalment of Rs. 30,000/-, as loan Ganjam DCC got Rs. 6,000/-, Balasore Rs. 6,000/-, Cuttack Rs. 7,000/-, Puri Rs. 6,000/-, Sambalpur Rs. 2,300/- Singhbhum Rs.2,000/-, as reported by Gopabandhu Chaudhury, the member of Provincial *Khadi Sangha*.[201]

In 1924AD, All India *Khadi* Board meeting was held in Bombay and Delhi. The committee decided to strengthen Provincial *Khadi* Board financially and the workers who would be working would get atleast

197. A. Maharana, *op.cit.*, Vol. 43, No. 1, BBSR, 1986, p. 4.
198. A. Mishra, *op.cit.*, p. 9.
199. *Samaj*, 19th March, 1921.
200. H.N. Mitra (ed), *op.cit.*, No.-2, p. 7; S.N. Pattnaik, *op.cit.*,. p. 57.
201. *Samaj*, 10th March, 1923.

employment for two years. Rules as to the qualifications, allowances and conditions of the service were formed in each province quickly.[202] In Orissa Provincial *Khadi* Board and the PCC together tried to popularise *Khadi* and small scale industries. They organised exhibitions at the leading centres of Orissa.[203] Gopabandhu Chaudhury and Niranjan Pattanaik were in charge of this programme.[204] Gandhi wanted *Khadi* Boards to provide employment to non-co-operators with small remuneration. It also encouraged the Gandhians to join the programmes.

In 1924 AD., five groups of workers were trained continuously for ten days. The workers were getting seven to ten rupees per month as allowances.[205] Though they were rudiculed by the opponents of the Congress as *'dasa tankia karmi'* and the *Khadi* Board was criticised repeatedly, still they displayed a determination of high order. Around one thousand volunteers of different training centres, *Khadi* centres and Ashrams were engaged in these works. The PCC strictly asked the DCCs to collect at least 100 [206] *Khadi* workers for their respective areas otherwise their centres would be abolished. By-laws were circulated to enlist members of the *Charakha Sangha* in which it was mentioned that the first class member would deposit atleast one thousand yard of thread a month, the second class member two thousand yard and all would wear *Khadar*.[207] Even the *Sanyasis* were persuaded to wear *Khadar*. Some temples began the practice of using hand-made clothes and threads.

For a special mission to propagate *Khadi*, [208] Gandhi,

202. H.N. Mitra (ed.), *op.cit.*

203. Asha, 20th June, 1924.

204. *Samaj*, 10th March, 1923.

205. *Utkal* Dipika, 26th July, 1924.

206. *Samaj*, 24th January, 1925, Utkal Dipika, 26th July, 1924.

207. *Utkal* Dipika, 5th December, 1925.

208. *Ibid.*, Publication Division, *op.cit.*, pp. 4-10.

as already mentioned, came to Orissa in 1925 AD. and 1927 AD. Exhibitions were organised and Gandhi was satisfied with the progress.[209] Provincial *Khadi* Committee got 1.5 lakhs of rupees from the All India *Khadi* Board and this amount was distributed among different districts.[210] *Khadi* clothes were produced in large quantity. But due to the non-availability of the buyers,* because of their poverty, the *Khadi* Board faced financial trouble. There were reports in the newspapers that some office bearers of the *Khadi* Board mismanaged the affair and the PCC faced total loss of money it invested.[211] The leaders faced lots of criticism. Even during PCC session, a member was accused of being a *bidi* trader than a *Khadi* worker.[212]

The Cultivation of Cotton was not properly encouraged. During the non-cooperation time, in few places of *Moghulbadi*, Cotton cultivation was begun. But because of lack of interest cotton cultivation had been stopped in the province. The DCCs were requested to supply cotton seeds to their respective areas.[213] In the PCC meeting of 1925AD, proposals were introduced to encourage *Khadi* cultivation. Bhagirathi Mohapatra was deputed to collect the credit lying on different *Khadi* centres amounting Rs. 41,000/-. It was also decided that half of the amount, when collected, would be given to Spinning Training Schools. Arrangements were made to collect workers for *Khadi* programme. Total five groups consisting of ten members in each would get training and each one would received Rs. 71/- a day as stipend.[214] It was the availability of few workers, inadequate financial

209. K.C. Acharya (ed.), Agrani Sangrami Niranjan Pattnaik (O), Berhampur, 1980, p. 2.
210. K.C. Acharya (ed.), *op.cit.*
* Who usually used very limited number of clothes and as they themselves were producing it.
211. *Samaj*, 7th March, 1925.
212. S.K. Mahtab, *op.cit.*, p. 88.
213. *Samaj*, 10th January, 1925.
214. *Ibid.*, 24th January, 1925.

help, shortage of cotton and poverty, all contributed for its failure [215] so far as the question of profit and loss was concerned. But the workers, though handful in number, worked hard to popularise and propagate the spinning of *Khadar* in Orissa.

Besides using *Khadi*, Gandhi also asked the workers to uplift the *Harijans*. The members of the Congress, who entered the District Boards, were advised by the people through newspapers to do something noteworthy in this regard. In *Alkashram* students of untouchable castes were enrolled.[216] It is also reported that the untouchables were not properly represented in District Boards.[217] But the workers in their respective spheres of activities tried to remove the practice of untouchability. It is seen that most of the Gandhians were of upper castes—mostly from *Brahmins* and *Karans*. So when fought to remove untouchability, they faced stiff opposition from their own society.[218] As number of Gandhians from the untouchable classes was very few, this social movement of Gandhi was a movement from the above than from the below so far as the province of Orissa was concerned.

As a whole, total Gandhian force was behind this struggle. While working in the streets of untouchables the high caste Gandhians were ostracised by their caste people. Their relatives were harassed and even those Gandhians were forced to undergo some customs for their purification. Those members of the Congress who were not in favour of the war against untouchability were asked by the district committees not to work for the Congress and leave the organisation immediately.[219]

Some *Sanyasis* also became Gandhians and fought

215. *Utkal* Dipika, 16th August, 1924.
216. *Ibid.*, 2nd June, 1923 & 23rd August, 1924.
217. *Ibid.*, 26th January, 1927.
218. S. Mohanty, Andha........., *op.cit.*, p. 329.
219. *Utkal* Dipika, 26th July, 1924.

against untouchability. As for example, Purnananda Brahmachari of Madhab of Cuttack district, opened a school for untouchable boys in his *Ashram*.[220] Some common Gandhians also opened such schools or *Pathasalas* in their own villages. Gauranga Charan Das of Bagalpur in Cuttack district helped the untouchables to be united against the oppression by the *Karana* landlords. He organised them to non-co-operate the landlords during the harvest and asked them to migrate to other safe places. Gauranga Charan Das opened a school for them.[221]

The flood situation in Orissa was quite severe in 1928 AD. Gopabandhu Das, even ill severely, had tried to collect volunteers for Flood Committee, but failed. Only tweo men came. Das was disheartened and had called for school students to help him in this time and they would be provided with some money for daily expenditure.[222] But the sudden and tragic death of Gopabandhu dumbfounded everybody in Orissa. The Congress organisation of the province became standstill.

But afterwards the PCC and DCCs had arranged condolence meetings. Top leaders of Congress attended such meetings in different corners of the province. Gopabandhu's death created a great vaccum in the field of leadership. Intra-party conflicts and groupism disturbed the provincial organisation of the Congress. The organisational activities became low. The workers became inactive.

During such critical time of Orissa, the PCC also selected delegates for the AICC meeting. As the delegates were to be elected by the members of the DCCs, it became very difficult to select delegates. Almost all the members of the DCCs wanted to be the delegates where the voters became scarse. So the PCC asked the members who

220. *Samaj*, 7th February, 1925.

221. Souvenir, Gauranga Charan Das, *op.cit.*

222. *Utkal* Dipika, 17th March, 1928.

wanted to be delegates to collect atleast three hundred members each.[223]

In 1929 AD., the annual PCC meeting was held at Balasore. Alongwith the conference of Primary Teachers, Youth and Women conferences were also held simultaneously which marked the growing popularity of Congress in this year.[224] In 1st June, the DCC of Cuttack held its meeting at Kendrapara, where women and youth also participated in numbers.[225] All these were due to the growth of young groups within the Congress. There were few places in Orissa, where the staunch Gandhian were still active. Pandit Nehru's rise to fame, his style of leadership and his open declaration of commitment to the concept of social equality mesmerised some young people of Orissa.

IV

COMPOSITION OF THE GANDHIANS AND THEIR DEGREE OF CONVICTION IN GANDHISM

Composition

In January, 1922, the primary membership of the provincial Congress organisation was 52,000. But after the suspension of the Non-Co-Operation Movement, their number decreased because the lack of enthusiasms among the people. During the movement, the full-time activists were very few as compared to the number of primary members and the population. They were around three thousands in number as already roughly calculated. Many members also worked for the movement living in villages. They were part-time activists. Their number was larger than the full-timers. Both full-timers and part-time *Karmis* formed the class of Gandhians-freedom-fighters of Orissa during the decade.

223. *Ibid.*, 21st July, 1928.

224. *Ibid.*, 6th March, 1929.

225. *Ibid.*, 1st June, 1929.

The number of full-time activists also decreased considerably after the sudden suspension of the movement. Some of them stayed in different *Ashrams* and Congress offices. Rest went to villages but were linked with different constructive works alongwith those part-timers. Active women Gandhians were very less in number. They were around one hundred. Most of them were relatives or wives of leading and common Gandhians. Full-timers kept constant touch with the leaders and whenever necessary, came to the local Congress offices to take part in any work sponsored by the provincial Congress. But as workers of the *Khadi* Board very few joined it. However, during Local and District Board elections all the Gandhians were active to make the Congress victorious.

Teachers and school drop-out village youths formed the backbone of the group of full-time activists. Most of them had primary *or* incomplete secondary education [226] with them. Some common villagers having political awareness joined this group. Ganerally they were from nearby villages of the Congress offices and *Ashrams*. Some College students also joined them.[227] The part-timers were village youths and adults who were just literates or illiterates having some sort of political awareness.

Castewise, the Gandhians of the decade were of higher castes generally. The full-time Gandhians were mostly *Brahmans* of Puri and Sambalpur and *Karanas* of Cuttack and Balasore. Some *Khandayats* also joined them. Other caste people were vary negligible in this group. The princes or members of royal families were conspicuously absent. There were very few active Gandhians from untouchable caste. The part-timers were from all castes of Orissa, but even this group was also dominated by all higher castes. The participation of common untouchable was meagre. Some domiciled Bengalis also worked as

226. *Samaj*, 29th January, 1921 & 23rd April, 1921.
227. *Ibid.*, 29th January, 1921.

common Gandhians in Orissa.[228]

But the leadership of the district even of *thana* level organisations were held by influencial high caste Hindus among the Gandhians.[229] They were land-owners. But rest of the Gandhians were mostly from lower-middle and landless labourer class of agrarian Orissa where life pattern was more or less identical.

Cuttack, Puri, Balasore, Ganjam and Sambalpur contributed most of the Gandhians of the decade. Very few from different *Garhjats* joined the movement as the political temperature in these areas was very less.[230]

Degree of Conviction of the Gandhians in Different Gandhian Ideas

During the decade, the true nationalists and honest men joined Gandhi as his followers. Their main objective was to organise and mobilise the people against their oppressors. Their had with them the traditional values of agrarian Orissa. It is true that non-violence and different Gandhian techniques suited them physically and materially, but their respect to Gandhism was very high. All those active members worked hard in different programmes of Gandhian movement throghout the decade, which prepared a strong base for Gandhism in Orissa. Part-timers also respected different ideas of Gandhi. Many of them regarded him as a Godly man and even the 'God-incarnate' and supported many social works initiated by the active workers. With great enthusiasm all the Gandhians worked tirelessly having deep respect for almost all the ideas of Gandhi. In their personal lives, most of them followed Gandhi as an example as far as possible. They became idols for rest of the population who esteemed them with great admiration. It was due to their purposeful personal lives many

228. Interview—Rajkrushna Bose, Ghanashyam Pati, Udayanath Sarangi and Advaitballav Ray.
229. *Ibid.*, *Utkal* Dipika, 5th May, 1928, 14th July, 1928.

commoners followed them as their open supporters. They led very simple, dedicated and straighforward lives which was realised by the people. Non-violence was their creed, social services was their profession. Basically they were not hypocrites.[230]

The opponents criticised the Gandhians but failed to check their popularity among the people. Groupism within the provincial Congress organisation was not threateningly present. The movement was not influenced by class or caste feelings. Strong criticism against the Co-Gandhians was absent unlike in later decades. Even those ingonrant people who joined as Gandhian freedom fighters of the decade gradually became educated in Gandhian ideas. Both as creeds and as techniques Gandhi's ideas were followed, in great extent, by his entire co-workers of Orissa of this decade.[231]

Hyprocrites* and bogus Gandhians were negligible in number. Power politicians were not conspicuous in their presence even after the participation of the Congress in different elections of District or Local Boards. Though the supporters of Gandhi were ridiculed as foolished non-co-operators, ignorant or even novice, or even criticised as beggars of *Swaraj*, the popularity of Gandhi in the masses and particularly the Gandhians among the old and women can not be side lined. Their dedication was clearly felt by the people and the profession of 'social service' was taken by many because of strong influence of Gandhian atmosphere.

V

Throughout the decade the soil of Orissa witnessed the activities of these Gandhians in different programmes of

230. Interview—*op.cit.*

231. *Ibid.*, Udayanath Sarangi.

* Few Gandhians of higher castes were conservatives in their outlook so far as the concept of women liberation and anti-untouchability was concerned.

Gandhi. Non-Co-Operation Movement inaugurated the spell of Gandhism in Orissa and by 1930AD, Gandhi became the most well-known personality of the region. The Gandhians became the only group of active political and social warriors. They made their presence felt among the people. Their experience in different ideas, methods of Gandhi and in their feasibility made them more convinced. In spite of sudden demise of Gopabandhu Das in 1928 AD at the age of 53, these Gandhians never lost their heart. It was their tireless work throughout the decade made the province of Orissa a leading Gandhian region of the country by 1930AD. This decade marked a revolutionary change in politics in the province. This change was reflected both in values and works that encouraged the community and the participants. Never before in history these people has engaged in an active political struggle and at the same time were being told to preserve their humanitarian values. Gandhi did come for them not as a system breaker rather a propagator of tradition, a system maintainer attacking only what was wrong in it. This era in Orissa also attracted wider support for nationalist feelings more than the previous language agitation by earlier leaders.

3

Mass-Based Congress Movement : Activities of the Gandhians in Orissa (1930—36 AD)

In December, 1929AD at Lahore Session of the Indian National Congress, the newly elected president, Jawaharlal Nehru, declaring *'Purna Swaraj'* as the main objective of the Congress, thus pronounced, "I must frankly confess that I am a socialist and a republican, am no believer in kings and princes, or in the order which produces the modern kings of industry".[1] This pronouncement marked the presence of a strong group of Congress workers with deep socialistic bent of mind. Many active workers of the Congress wanted to widen the scope of Gandhian movement in which class interest of the common people would be reflected in a clearer manner.

Congress mouth-piece in Orissa, the *Samaj* reported this event in this manner, "The new President Nehru wanted complete Independence for India. To achieve this, peaceful movements and silent penance are required".[2] It also reported that the nation was enslaved for its own faults. But the freedom could be achieved. If a weak Nation determined to break the chains the dominance of any powerful Master could be short-lived like a bubble of

1. Dorothy Norman, Nehru : The First Sixty Years, Vol. I, London, 1965, p. 204.
2. *Samaj*, 1st January, 1930.

water.[3] The PCC wanted the workers to be ready for a great agitation in near future as asked by J. Nehru. 26th January was observed as the Independence Day by the PCC. It was reported that in his efforts Nehru was also supported by Gandhi himself.[4]

The Gandhians, though few in number, observed the Independence Day on 26th January. Gopabandhu Chaudhury, Atala Behari Acharya, *Raja*krushna Bose, Jadumani Mangaraj, Banchhanidhi Mohanty celebrated the Day at the PCC Headquaters in *Swaraj Ashram* in Cuttack. Lingaraj Mishra, Krupasindhu Mishra, Acharya Harihar Das, Radhanath Rath & Mohan Das at Puri also observed the Day. National Songs were recited unfurling the Congress Flag amidst *Sankirtan* at different *taluk* headquarters.[5]

But Gandhi was thinking otherwise. He was preparing himself to start a fresh movement of different nature which would be also a complete mass-based one. It put the government in an alarming situation when it intended to strike the very root of the British authority in India—by attacking its revenue and taxation policies—the symbols of British *Raj*.

The participation of the common people was much wider than of the earlier time. By highlighting the illegal nature of British taxation policy, particularly Salt Law, Gandhi gave the common people a clear vision of their class interest to join his movement. When he started his famous 'Dandi March' on 13th March, 1930AD to break the Salt Law, India became surcharged with excitement and patriotism. Thus, the Civil Dis-obedience Movement was launched and also the real mass-based era of Gandhian movement began. The movement established massive mass support for Gandhi as well as the Indian

3. *Ibid.*
4. *Ibid.*, 8th January, 1930.
5. *Ibid.*, 29th January, 1930.

National Congress for decades to come. The Salt Movement was followed by other movements which got their strong basis from that immense mass popularity of Gandhi and the Congress.

When Gandhi marched to Dandi of Gujrat and broke the illegal Salt Law, it marked the peak of his political influence. It also brought his claims to the attention of a world-wide audience. The Gandhians of Orissa also started the movement following the footstep of their leader. The participation of the masses was so immense that it became a grand success and Orissa of this time got the exalted honour of one of the leading areas of Gandhian movement in India. The Gandhians of the province became very successful in mobilising the people in breaking in Salt Law. Being a coastal region, here the people, who were deeply hurt by this law, joined the movement and in large numbers became active participants. All the participants took Gandhi as their spiritual guide during this great upsurge.

In the previous year, the activities of provincial Congress force was at its lowest ebb. The PCC had faced acute financial strain[6] and few full-time workers were available for organisational works. The number of total primary members was only 6945.[7] The cause of this situation was the financial condition of the PCC. It was reported that the Congress workers might not be provided with the allowances according to their eligibility, but they must get atleast two square meals a day to live and work for the nation. The people could be social workers within their limits. They could not do more than of their endurance for a long period as most of the social workers in Orissa were very poor. It is also said that they were very few in number. Out of these handfuls few were Gandhians. Rest were busy in their own interests. The

6. *Ibid.*, 5th February, 1930.
7. CWMG, Vol. XLI, Delhi, 1968, p.p. 537-38 (Orissa had only 6,945 primary members in the year 1929).

poors were to join the movement otherwise independence would be impossible. The minimum expenditure must be provided to them to get their participation. Poucity of fund in *Utkal* had created hindrance for the work of the Congress. The *Samaj* expressed following views:

> "But who will provide the fund for this work? Orissa is a poor state. Hundreds of people are dying everyday. Rest are migrating to neighbouring states to find livelihood leaving behind their helpless women folks and children in villages. But they should donate as far as possible for the cause of the nation. It may be difficult to get doners, who could donate thousands at a time. But there are one crore of people in Orissa, who can donate a pie per head. There are twenty lakhs families in Orissa and it is calculated that if each family donates only a pie per year, the entire collection would be Rs. 30,000/- a year. In this way, the financial restrain of the PCC will be met".[8]

But in spite of such shortcomings the movement quickly became very widespread when the elder Gandhians who were residing in villages, became active again. Most of those three thousand full-timers of Non-Co-Operation Movement who were adults by 1930AD came out with full vigour. Their rank and file grew when many young school children, Part-time activists and illiterate common people joined them. This time, both villages and urban areas equally shared the political temperature of the time. As urban areas were few, the activities in villages of entire coastal region dominated that scene. It continued throughout the period under study when this movement was followed by other mass-based agitations.

I

CIVIL DISOBEDIENCE MOVEMENT IN ORISSA

The PCC took adequate preparations to make the

8. *Samaj, op.cit.*

movement successful. PCC president Harekrushna Mahtab asked the common youths to join the movement as active participants. He published an article in which he wrote, "Many youths are living in luxury and want to get luxurious life. Many village youths are sitting idle. They should join this movement of *Swaraj*".[9] Because of its sudden nature, the PCC could not get time to make special effort to increase primary membership of the Congress. But the common people came out spontaneously to join the movement, though, to become the primary member of the Congress was not necessarily important by that time. The leaders advised the standing Gandhians or the *Karmies* to organise the new activists in proper ways. In Orissa almost all the population were habituated with taking cold watered-rice called *`Pakhal'*, as for the poor people it was a staple food. This was the traditional way in Orissa to preserve the boiled rice for the next meal. A bit of salt was also necessary to take cold rice. As salt was to be bought from the market—which the people felt as an unnecessary burden—their spontaneous support to the Salt Movement was natural. Many in India as well as in Orissa took up `salt' as a symbol of the movement. But to the common people and most of the common Gandhians of Orissa, their movement was to express deep anguish against the British Salt Law, particularly

The DCCs took special care to enlist more and more volunteers for the movement. The Civil Disobedience Movement very quickly raised the political temperature of the region. Even those men-particularly the educated, who were unable to be active, were advised by the leaders to develop awareness in the village people quickly about the movement.[10] The provincial leaders took charge of different coastal districts of Orissa and organised the workers efficiently. This time

9. *Ibid.*, 19th February, 1930.

10. *Ibid.*, 5th March, 1930.

women participants also increased their number.

PCC meeting was convened on 28th February, 1930AD under the presidentship of Gopabandhu Chaudhury and discussed the matter of selecting the places of sea-shore where Salt Law was to be broken. Puri, Ganjam, Balasore and Cuttack district Congress officials were directed to collect funds and volunteers.[11] It was also decided that when the marches would be in their ways, in towns, picketing would also be continued at the same time. Large number of Gandhians from different districts congregated at *'Swaraj Ashram'*[12] of Cuttack and also in other district headquarters of Orissa for this purpose. The school students joined the movement in numbers and were called as *Banara Sena* as christened by Gandhi. Gopabandhu Chaudhury was in charge of the office of the PCC at Cuttack. Provincial Congress Committee was under the guidance of Nilamani Pradhan. The responsibility of Puri district was given to Lingaraj Mishra, Krupasindhu Hota and Bholanath Shah. Balasore was given to Charuchandra Ray and Nanda Kishore Das. The PCC president himself would go to Ganjam to depute the local Gandhians for this purpose. Rajkrushna Bose was deputed to collect the Volunteers. It was decided that more than two thousand members would be collected from Balasore, five thousand from Cuttack and three thousand from Puri district.[13]

The *'Swaraj Ashram'* kept around one hundred[14] regular volunteers for Cuttack town and directed others to join different marches. Many of them were used as

11. *Ibid*.
12. P.T. Singh, Swadhinata Sangramare Banara Sena(o), Part-I, Cuttack, 1986, p. 6.
13. *Samaj*, 5th March, 1930.
14. P.T. Singh, *op.cit.*, p. 3. (The Daily Expenditure for Fooding of a worker was Six Paise and the total expenditure of *Swaraj Ashram* was Rs. 5/- per day, so nearly One Hundred Regular Gandhians were Staying there.)

messengers for the Gandhians of other localities by the PCC. From towns and headquarters of different districts, the common Gandhians under their leaders marched to coastal places to break the Salt Law. The Gandhians of many villages in the routes welcomed and joined the marches. The local Gandhians of the areas, where Salt Law was to be broken, prepared the field for the marching Gandhians by informing and collecting local people in large number. The volunteers of the districts formed different groups and took different routes through villages to reach the seashore. Many marches were started at a time from different places. Mostly the adult Gandhians were selected by the leaders for these marches because of their discipline and experience. But new volunteers of other localities also joined them when the marches started and entered through the villages.

The Gandhians, who became volunteers of the marches, were directed to take pledge in the name of God that they would follow the rules furnished by the PCC. The were asked to be prepared to go to jails and were told not to ask for any type of financial help from the PCC for their families during their internment. They were directed to take few articles of daily-use with them. They were also not given any guarantee of fooding during the movement.[15]

As different places of coastal Orissa, the Salt Law was broken. Rambha and Huma of Ganjam, Astarang and Kakatpur of Puri, Kujang and Balikuda of Cuttack were such places which became famous.[16] In other places of coastal Orissa also contraband salt was prepared by the local Gandhians with the help of people.

But the PCC chose Inchudi of Balasore coast after lots of discussion. This place was unsuitable to the boot-

---

15. *Samaj*, 2nd April, 1930.
16. *Utkal* Dipika, 17th May, 1930.: 31st May, 1930 & 7th June, 1930.

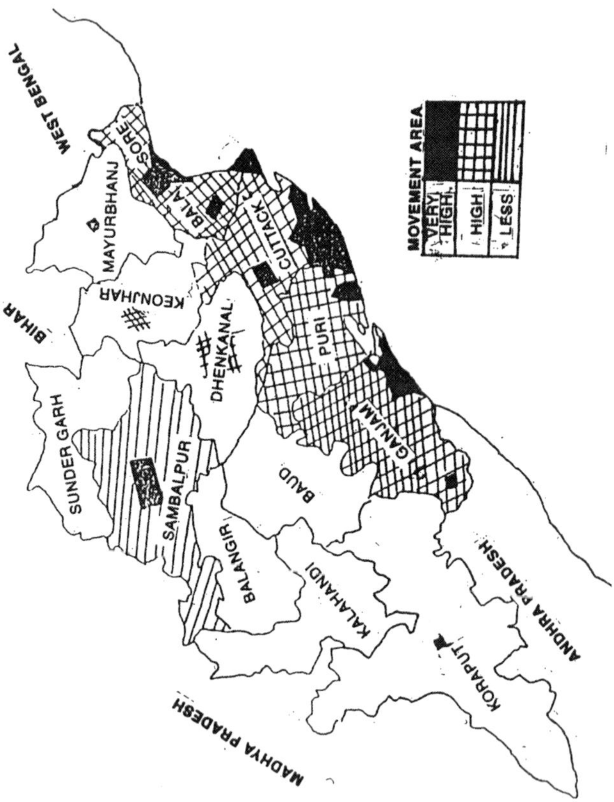

MAP NO. 2
AREAS INFLUENCED BY CIVIL DISOBEDIENCE
MOVEMENT, 1930-33

wearing police because it was marshy and muddy.[17*] But it was helpful for the bare-footed activists. A forward army of volunteers was prepared to march before the real one to inform the people on their way about their motives.[18] Volunteers from different districts came to Cuttack town to join the marches. Five groups of volunteers went from Cuttack for Inchudi one after another.[19] Even the districts of Koraput and Mayurbhanj sent volunteers. Some volunteers also came from Bihar.[20]

A batch of selected volunteers, under the leadership of Gopabandhu Chaudhury and Acharya Harihar Das started for Inchudi from the *'Swaraj Asram'*. When Gopabandhu Chaudhury was arrested Acharya Harihar Das took the lead. The next batch also started its journey after a few days. These batches took different routes to put the police and the officials in a difficult situation and to make the mission successful anyhow. It also helped them to mix with the people of different areas of the coastal districts and to enlighten them. If a particular batch was arrested, another batch would fulfill the target.

17. S.S. Das, *Utkalara* Labana Tirtha Inchudi Ba Biplabini Inchudi(o), Balasore, 1980, p. 19.

* Inchudi was a place near the sea-shore where the communication system was very bad. Muddy and marshy, this place was full of bushes, which was protected by two small rivers from both sides-Kantiachira and Dhobagandi. The place was very unsuitable to the boot-wearing police, but was easier for bare-footed volunteers to run quickly. The volunteers mostly being choosen from the areas were aware of this condition and they, thus, proved successful in the mission.

18. S.N. Pattnaik, Odisare Swadhinata Andolana (O), Cuttack, 1972, p. 73; Interview-Sarat Chandra Maharana.

19. *Samaj*, 2nd, April, 1930; *Utkal* Dipika, 12th April, 1930 and 19th April, 1930.

20. *Samaj*, 16th April, 1930; Sudhakar Das, Swadhinata Sangramara Bhumi Eram(o), 1988, p. 9; H.K. Mahtab (ed.), History of Freedom Movement in Orissa, 1911-30, Vol.III, 1957, p. 88.

While marching, the groups entered the villages and stayed there at nights. Villagers gathered around to listen to them. They received the volunteers and provided them with food and shelter defying the strong warning of the authorities. The volunteers, who were not of coastal areas, were taught how to prepare salt from the sea water. When the march was going on trained volunteers were singing patriotic songs.

At Inchudi, the local Gandhians under Surendranath Das had assembled to receive the procession. The volunteers were divided into two branches. One *Krishak Bahini* who would prepare the salt, and another was *Shanti Sena* to look to the discipline of the volunteers.[21] A strategy was planned to save the prepared salt from police and sent it to other places of Orissa for sale. Local people gathered in numbers in spite of police threat. The Salt Law was broken and the leaders and volunteers were arrested. Police released atrocities over the people who were mostly from nearby villages.[22]

Ramadevi and Malati Chaudhury travelled the areas of Balikuda, Kujang and Paradeep of Cuttack district and gathered many women volunteers. *Rani* of Paradeep with her daughter joined the movement. Seeing such a large number of women, the police became dumbfounded.[23]

Side by side, some old Gandhians with newly recruited volunteers, assembled in different urban areas of Orissa and started picketings to put the authority in a difficult position. *'Utkal Satyagrahi Sena'* was formed and 131 members were recruited by April.[24] In a meeting the PCC leader & asked the *Satyagrahi's* "to clap when clap

---

21. *Samaj*, 30th April, 1930.
22. Interview—Sarat Chandra Maharana; S.S. Das, *op.cit.*, pp. 20-21.
23. H.K. Mahtab, *op.cit*,. p. 89; *Samaj*, 23rd April, 1930; B. Kanungo; Labana *Satyagraha* O Orissa (O), BBSR, 1986, p. 10.
24. *Samaj*, 2nd April, 1930.

around you".[25] In Cuttack town, the volunteers congregated at *'Swaraj Ashram'* and were directed to start picketing in front of foreign cloth and liquor shops. Every morning Nilamani Pradhan, Sahdev Das and Golok Maharana, who were in charge of the *Ashram*, enlisted the volunteers for different types of works at different streets of Cuttack town.[26] Groups under some dictators were sent to start picketing at different place. New volunteers were trained by the older groups how to protect themselves from police *lathi*. They were also directed by their guides not to gather at a particular place to avoid mass scale arrest. They were trained to lie down quickly keeping their heads in others groins to save the heads from police action. When the boys were arrested the *Ashram* received the information quickly by the special messenger among the volunteers and did send another batch to start picketing. Fresh volunteers were coming regularly.[27] Only in Cuttack town, they were hundred in number and most of them were high school students. During the movement many young volunteers from different districts and nearby areas of Cuttack town came to join the movement. Students of Cuttack town joined the movement[28] regularly being influenced by the activities of different voluntary groups in the town. In urban areas young volunteers outnumbered [29] the adult Gandhians. Most of the old Gandhians remained busy in their own localities.

In different district headquarters like Sambalpur, Puri, Berhampur and Balasore towns, these types of activities became frequent. In Sambalpur the students boycotted the schools. Huge gatherings were organised defying the ban order of the authority.[30] In Puri the agitators started

25. *Ibid.*, 9th April, 1930 & 9th March, 1930.
26. P.T. Singh, *op.cit.*, p. 2.
27. *Ibid.*, p. 6.
28. Interview—Sarat Chandra Maharana, Nilamani Mohanty, Bauribandhu Patra and Shyamakanta Mohapatra.
29. Souvenir, Struggle For Freedom in Orissa, BBSR, 1989, p. 89.
30. C.R. Mishra, Freedom Movement in Sambalpur, Delhi, 1986, p. 238.

picketing. The contraband salts were sent to these urban areas from the sea shore of sale. Police arrested the Gandhians who sold it.[31]

The influence of Salt *Satyagraha* was felt in Kanika Zamindari and also in the *Garhjats*. The people of Kanika under local Gandhian workers went to sea shore to prepare contraband salt. King's force resisted and attacked them brutally which made the *Satygarahis* violent. They attacked the police who fled away from the spot.[32]

The Salt Movement continued in the next year also. Salt Law was broken in Puri and Balasore. A *Satyagraha* camp was opened at Puri. It started its journing to the seashore via. Gop.[33] The volunteers of Balasore used a French area nearby to flee after breaking the Salt Law to avoid arrest, though, these Gandhians were directed by Gandhi not to avoid it. This French enclave, Pharashidinga, became asylum of the Balasore district Congress.[34]

The volunteers started picketing in towns and sold small banners of the Congress. Copies of 'Manifesto of Independence' were circulated in towns.[35] The Gandhians observed Independence Day on 26th of January, hoisting National Flag. As *'Swaraj Ashram'* was under the police custody, the *'Congressias'* hoisted flag on Pipal tree nearby. Even volunteers pasted posters on the walls of the officials who were loyal to the British.[36] To honour Motilal Nehru on his death contraband salt was manufactured in some places.[37] Different groups were sent to the sea-shore to

31. *Utkal* Dipika, 2th May, 1930.
32. G.D. Behera, Kanika Biplaba(o), Balasore, 1987, p. 126; *Samaj*, 3rd. December, 1930.
33. *Samaj*, 14th January, 1931.
34. *Ibid*., 21st January, 1931.
35. *Ibid*., 4th February, 1931.
36. *Ibid*., 14th January, 1931 & 4th February, 1931.
37. *Ibid*., 25th February, 1931, 4th March, 1931 & 11th March, 1931.

prepare salt and were arrested. Even a volunteer in disguise of a madman went in night to unfurl the tricolour on the collectorate building of Puri, but surprisingly, he had taken a knife[38] to protect himself—an act against the directive of Gandhi. Very often, except a few, other Gandhians also resisted the police while intervened in preparing salt. The workers in villages were provided with pamphlets-hand—writen or cyclostyled and these were circulated among the villagers.[39]

Gandhi-Irwin pact was concluded in March, 1931AD, it had the dampening effect on the rank and file of the Congress organisation in Orissa.[40] The death of Bhagat Singh and his friends, saddened[41] the Gandhians in Orissa. But in spite of all these events, in many places, the Salt Movement continued. Many volunteer groupsrepeatedly violated the Salt Law in different coastel areas.[42] It was only when the rainy season came the activities of the workers became standstill because of heavy rain and flood in coastal Orissa.

Methods of Propaganda of the Gandhians

The experience of the Gandhians in the previous years helped them immensely to propagate efficiently the cause of Salt Movement. Besides, popular poems of Banchhanidhi Mohanty and Birakishorc Das awakened the students. They advised them to leave their studies for the country's sake. Birakishore Das, composed a poem thus,

> "Don't advice me to read books during the struggle,
> my blood boils when I hear the wardrum;
> which book will I read, solution of which sum will be calculated,

38. Raj Guru, Agnipatha (O), Cuttack, 1985, p. 8.
39. S.N. Pattnaik, *op.cit.*, p. 81; Interview—Shyamakanta Mohapatra and Sarat Chandra Maharana.
40. *Samaj*, 2nd, April, 1931 and 27th April, 1931.
41. *Ibid.*, 1st April, 1931.
42. J.M. Brown, Gandhi and Civil Disobedience, 1928-34, London, 1977, p. 115.

should be I a selfish youngman,........
when I see my country suffering".[43]

His *'Ranaveri'*, *'Rana Nimantrana'*, *'Rastriya Taranga'* and the bulletins like *'Bidrohi'* and *'Biplabi'* of[44] the PCC enthrilled the students.

As the literature of Orissa had been influenced by Rabindranath Tagore, the poets of Orissa, 'made the poetic sensibility more personal, more prone to imagination and more responsive to change of emotions'[45] and were called as 'escapists'. So, in order to incite the contemporary poets Birakishore Das advised them to be realistic. He wrote,

"Oh! poet!
stop writing this worthless poem,
engrip the pen as a canon,
blow the counch of new life only once,
the young will come out-
to encircle you with a great joy".[46]

To awaken the women of Orissa, Banchhanidhi Mohanty, also wrote many poems. A few of the lines run as follow :

"Shouldn't you awake now!
Oh! The daughters of Utkal,
awake! awake! awake!
don't be inert".[47]

Boys and girls sang these inspiring songs. Baikunthanath Mohanty went to Gandhi's *Ashram* to learn *Garba* and *Dandia*. When came back he with Advaitballav Ray and Niranjan Ghosh, prepared a music party and trained the boys and girls. The songs were mostly composed by Birakishore Das and Banchhanidhi Mohanty.[48]

43. Quoted in B. Kanungo, Daria Dakhal (O), Cuttack, 1983, p. 23.
44. P.T. Singh, *op.cit.*, p. 1.
45. J.N. Mohanty, There Where Trees Flower; Wssay on Modern Oriya Literature, BBSR, 1980, p. 7.
46. Souvenir, Jatiya Kavi Abhinandan(O), Cuttack, 1973, p. 15.
47. *Ibid.*, p. 20.

Meetings were organised in big villages of importance where there were supporters of Gandhians. People performing *Sankirtan* composed patriotic songs and received well the visiting leaders or the workers.[49] The workers kept the litho machines safe from the police eye. In some places the Gandhians kept these under the seat of the deities of the temples.[50] Before the meetings, even the high caste Hindu Gandhians beat drums to inform the people about the gathering.[51] The drum-beating known locally as *'Dhengura'* was the traditional way to convey the people some important message. Generally it was done by the village drumer belonging to untouchable class. Beating the drums, the high caste Gandhians, thus, broke the age-old feeling that this work was unclean and should be done by untouchable people only. Sometimes they used tin drums to attract the people towards them.

Very often, they held meetings in the areas where police atrocities were severe to lessen the fear from the people. Important places were selected to hoist flags. The Gandhians went to different fairs and festivals of the villages where they held meetings.[52] In Sambalpur, inflamatory leaflets were published in Revolutionary Bulleting Press and were circulated in the town. During village fairs youngmen organised meetings to awaken the people.[53] In certain areas the sellers of grass and mango and girls of dormatories were used to circulate

48. Interview—Sarat Chandra Maharana, Advaitaballav Ray; Questionnaire-Baikunthanath Mohanty.
49. S. Mohanty, Andha Diganata (O), Cuttack, 1964, p.50; G.N. Mohanty, Mati Matal (O), Cuttack, 1977, p.177; Interview—Gokulamohan Raychudan/mani.
50. Souvenir, Biplabi, Biswanath, Kanasha, Puri, 1983, p. 8.
51. Questionnaire—Mukunda Prasad Majumdar.
52. Interview—Nilamani Mohanty, Udayanath Sarangi; Questionnaire—Nrusingha Charan Samal and Mukundaprasad Majumdar.
53. OSA, Home (pol.), Confidential File No.4, 1932 (Office of the Deputy Commissioner, Sambalpur).

revolutionary bulletins.[54]

II

OTHER POLITICAL ACTIVITIES

Salt Movement had aroused the people so much that they became fearless in their activities. In some areas of Balasore people refused to pay *chaukidari* tax. The tax was collected from the people by the government to pay the salary of the *Chaukidars* and *Dafadars,* who were appointed in the villages to inform the authority about the activities of the people alongwith reporting about the robbery, burglary, death or birth. Usually the supporters of the government were chosen by the authority for these posts. This was an unnecessary burden on the people. Very often, these texes were collected forcibly. The government had engaged these men in the villages who were working as the paid agents.[55]

When people started refusing to pay the tax, the police called for. The police force that had taken rest after their tireless duties during the Salt Movement, exhibited their atrocities severely.

Congress volunteers poured into the area and organised the people effectively.[56] People followed non-violent method of Non-Co-Operation. When properties were forfeited and were auctioned nobody came forward to purchase them. When the police arrived to collect the tax, women were directed to blow counch in a peculiar manner to inform the villagers, who subsequently came forward collectively under the guidance of the Gandhians to persuade the police to return. Influencial people of the villages were also persuaded by the workers to support the movement. When some people resorted to violence

54. S.N. Pattnaik, *op.cit.*, p. 104.
55. A. Maharana, 'Kusuma Parase....', *Utkal* Prasanga (O), Vol.47, No.1, August, 1986, pp. 11-12.
56. *Ibid.*

these Gandhians prevented them doing so.[57] At Srijang, police atrocities reached the maximum. Women were also not spared. Government imposed Punitive tax. Gradually the movement was subsided as the provincial Congress leaders were not serious enough to be involved in this type of local movements.[58]

In 1931 AD the AICC decided to hold its next annual session in Orissa which gave a great boost to the PCC's enthusiasm. The *karmis* of the Congress became very active to make the session successful which was supposed to be a great honour to the people of Orissa.[59] But the PCC became faction-ridden by this time. Gopabandhu Chaudhury was preparing himself to indulge totally in constructive activities. Nilakantha Das and his group were trying to enter into the Legislative Council and he got elected as an independent candidate. Nabakrushna Chaudhury was accumulating his energy to start socialist movement in a big way.[60] Even in jails when the Gandhians were arrested during the Civil Disobedience Movement, leaders were trying to influence the common Gandhians to support them in the forthcoming party election. Infighting started in the Congress at the provincial level. Rumours were spread to tarnish the images of different leaders by their rival groups.[61] This internal dissensions continued even when the Gandhians were released. There arose a competition among the leaders of the different districts to hold the AICC session at their district headquarters. Nilakantha Das and his Puri followers wanted Puri town to be the venu of the session when Gopabandhu Chaudhury and his group wanted

57. *Ibid.*, p. 12.
58. *Ibid.*
59. Interview—Annapurna Maharana; *Utkal* Sevak, 23rd. December, 1931.
60. Interview—Annapurna Maharana.
61. H.K. Mahtab, Sadhanara Pathe (O), Cuttack, 1972, pp. 137-43.

Cuttack city. The *Karanas* of Cuttack and the *Brahmans* of Puri district Congress committees supported their respective leaders while Harekrushna Mahtab of Balasore remained neutral. At last Puri was selected as the venue of the forthcoming AICC session.[62]

Total Gandhian force of the province started their preparation to make the session successful forgetting groupism for time being. Volunteers were collected, special training was given to both male and female workers. While the workers were coming from different corners of Orissa to Puri, they got the news that the government had declared the Congress illegal after the failure of Second Round Table Conference. So the AICC session could not be held that year.[63]

The internal strife of the PCC became more intense then. The organisation could not function well. By 1933AD, some Gandhians became socialists to champion the cause of peasants and agricultural labourers. They became known as Socialist Gandhians. People knew them as the followers of Gandhi because many of them behaved as Gandhians and were *Khadar*-clad. The orthodox Gandhians, on the other hand, entirely devoted their life to work for the upliftment of the weaker sections of the society by engaging themselves in various constructive works and avoided power politics sincerely. The Political scene of Orissa started witnessing new emerging forces working in different specialised fields of Gandhi's national programmes. Peopls of *Garhjats* were also deeply influenced by the temperature of Salt *Satyagraha* and other agitations in coastal Orissa.

Police Action

The authorities declared the Congress illegal, prohibited

62. N.K. Das, Nilakantha Granthabali, Cuttack, 1963, p. 105; Interview—Harekrushna Biswal.
63. C.R. Mishra, *op.cit.*, pp. 236-37; Interview—Harekrushna Biswal.

the publication and circulation of certain books written in nationalist tone and[64] also nationalist newspapers. *Satyagrahis* were arrested and were sentenced to various terms of imprisonment. They were sent to distant places like Patna, Hazaribag, Vellore, etc. Common people, in some places, did not dare to help the *Satyagrahis* in day time. After arresting the picketing Gandhians, very often, police tied them with ropes and abused them with filthy words. They were beaten up one after another and were told, "Now pray your Gandhi Bopa". Even young boys were taken from the places of demonstration to the jungles. Many of the volunteers, who broke Salt Law, were arrested and sent to jails. Many common people turned activitists were imprisoned. Restaurants and hotel owners of urban and semi-urban areas were also directed by the authority not to provide food to the demonstrators.[65] Anybody-from whose house a *Charakha* was found, was beaten up black and blue.[66]

The police officials ridiculed the volunteers through songs of filthy words. They arranged folk dancers to sing these songs openly to frighten the people. While the volunteers were singing song like, "Brothers come, come, if you want independence break the Salt Law",[67] in the same style and tune the police asked the folk dancers to sing thus, "If your back is irritating then go to break the Salt Law".[68] The Gandhians after their release from the lock-up and jails were kept under strong vigil by the police.[69]

The police brought false allegations against the Gandhians for kindnapping children to enroll them as

64. H.K.Mahtab, History of Freedom......, *op.cit.*, p. 89.
65. P.T. Singh, *op.cit.*, pp. 1-8.
66. S.S. Das, *op.cit.*, p. 33.
67. A. Maharana, *op.cit.*, p. 8; Interview—Advaitaballav Ray.
68. *Ibid.*
69. S.S. Das, *op.cit.*

'Congressia'.[70] Police even used *Bichhuati* to thrash the small volunteers.[71] Congress offices were taken into custody. *Ashrams* were frequently raided. On the other hand to envoke the conscience of the police the trained singers sang appealing couplets. It made the public sympathetic to the cause for which the small children were suffering. One line of such a poem runs thus,

> "You can beat us as much you like,
> Oh! brothers!
> but we had already sacrificed our,
> lives for the nation,
> you can't tame us"[72]

In spite of their oppressive attitude, many police personnels, particularly, the lower class employees, were not so cruel. Some of them were sympathetic to the movement. Sometimes the police beat the *Satyagrahi* only[73] for the sake of their duty. Some *chaukidars, dafadars,* Union Presidents* and police constables—who were the representatives of British administration in villages, in many cases supported the Gandhians in camera and used to give information about the steps to be taken by the police against the Gandhians.[74] Only the officers were very oppressive as they wanted to satisfy their superiors go get promotion.

Cause of Unification and Formation of Orissa Province

In 1931AD, at the *Utkal* Provincial Congress meeting held at Balasore, Congressmen under the presidentship of Nilakantha Das, passed a resolution urging the AICC to

70. *Samaj*, 7th January, 1931.
71. *Ibid.*, 7th April, 1931.
72. Interview—Advaitaballav Ray.
73. Questionnaire-Narayan Birabar Samant.
* Each Thana was divided into some Unions having nominated Presidents who used to inform the authorities about the law and order of the area.
74. Questionnaire—Govinda Chandra Mohanty.

expediate the formation of a separate Orissa province. It expressed regret for the disregard, apathy and negligence shown by the Indian national Congress towards the Oriya movement.[75] An all Party Conference was convened at Cuttack on 2nd May, 1931AD under the chairmanship of Acharya Harihar Das to urge all the party workers to work unitedly.[76] But Harekrushna Mahtab gave emphasis on the National Movement and Independence. He said, "Attainment of the country's independence would be followed by the redressal of the Oriya grievances".[77] No doubt, this factional attitude between different leaders affected the activities of the Congress in Orissa. The Gandhians of Sambalpur helped the O' Donell Committee and claimed complete merger of the district with Orissa. But when the Committee failed recommending merger of the entire Oriya speaking areas the Gandhians of this district started an agitation. In Ganjam, Niranjan Pattnaik with the support of his Gandhian force met Gandhi at Karachi session of the Congress and asked him to take the question of Oriya unification to the Second Round Table Conference.[78] The PCC also deputed Radhakrushna Biswasray and Sashibhusan Rath to open Congress offices in Jajpur of Koraput district.[79] Congress workers were sent to Medinipur to dissuade large number of Oriya population form changing their titles to be identified as Bengalis. Godavarish Mohapatra wrote a very fiery poem entitled *'Utha Kankala'* to invoke those Oriyas of Medinipur to help fighting for the cause of the Oriya movement.[80]

Common Gandhians of Orissa, irrespective of their

75. *Asha*, 16th March, 1931.
76. *Samaj*, 2nd May, 1931.
77. P*Raja*tantra, 23rd November, 1931.
78. Questionnaire—Rushi Behera.
79. *Samaj*, 6th May, 1931.
80. B.C. Acharya, Godavarish Mohapatra Parikrama (O), Cuttack, 1969, p. 40.

different group identities, were great supporters of the cause of unification of Oriyas-particularly of the outlying Oriya speaking tracts. In these areas the cause of unification was very strong among the Gandhians where was in coastal region the cause was not so immediate. In spite of the step-motherly behaviour of the committees appointed by the government and the loss of some tracts where Oriyas were in majority, an unified Orissa Province became possible on 1st April, 1936AD. The Gandhians of the province rejoiced the event halfheartedly.

III

ACTIVITIES OF GANDHIANS IN OTHER MASS-BASED AGITATIONS

Constructive Programmes

When Civil Dis-Obedience Movement was pushed into the background and Gandhi declared the movement suspended in May, 1934AD, many Gandhians of Orissa engaged themselves in different constructive programmes. It also helped them to continue the tempo of the movement among the masses. Though entire Gandhian force was not actively engaged in these programmes and many preferred other fields, still they had also strong support and sympathy for these constructive workers.[81] In the previous decade the Gandhians had induced the people to support the programmes, but this time people's participation was spontaneous.[82] As educated people grew in number and as people became more conscious than before, they themselves came forward to co-operate. As before, Gandhians opened different spinning centres to train the people as well as the students.[83] In Kuhudi, the school students started wearing *Khadi* dress.[84] In Ballikhala

81. Interview—Sarat Chandra Maharana and Udayanath Sarangi.
82. A. Maharana, *op.cit.*, p. 1.
83. Interview—Sarat Chandra Maharana and Annapurna Maharana.
84. R.C. Ram, Sangrami (O), Cuttack, 1986, p. 8.

one untouchable school was run by the local educated people since 1930AD. Students of all castes got education there. High-Caste Hindus, provided rooms for these schools.[85] In Banki, cotton cultivation and spinning became more popular.[86] In Bagalpur, a school for the untouchables was run by Gauranga Charan Das, [87] who, in spite of persuasions did not discontinue it. Some Gandhians went to Wardha, even to Svagram to learn and to be trained in Basic education.[88] Women training camps were opened to train the women workers.[89]

Gandhi too pin-pointed the practice of untouchability in his constructive programmes. He organised All India Anti-Untouchability League in September, 1932AD and started also the Weekly *'Harijan'* later, in January, 1933AD. He had asked his co-workers to observe the Week, following the end of his fast unto-death in August, 1932AD after the communal award, which was observed in Orissa. A branch of *'Harijan Sevak Sangha'*[90] was organised at Cuttack by Balunkeswar Acharya, and Ramadevi being one of its distinguished secretaries. Nilakantha Das was active in Puri and Mukunda Prasad Das was in Balasore.[91] Nrusingha Guru of Sambalpur championed the cause of the untouchables.[92]

Before 1931AD, the Gandhians of Orissa under Pandit Nilakantha Das tried the entry of the Harijans into the temples. He tried to rouse the public opinion of Puri in favour of the entry of the untouchables into the temple of Lord Jagannath. This move was strongly opposed by the

85. *Samaj*, 1st January 1930.
86. *Ibid.*, 19th February, 1930.
87. *Ibid.*, 5th March, 1930.
88. Nirupama Das (ed.), Souvenir, Rajendra Verma, p. 36.
89. Souvenir, Sachi jena, 1987.
90. *Utkal* Dipika, 20th May, 1933; Souvenir, Struggle for freedom in Orissa, BBSR, 1989, p. 100.
91. Souvenir, Struggle for....., *op.cit.*, pp. 100-01.
92. *Ibid.*

orthodox upper caste Hindus. *Raja* of Puri, *Mahantas* of different *Mathas* and members of *Sanatana Dharma Raskhini Sabha* totally opposed the entry. Local intelligentsia also could not support it.[93]

But in other areas some upper caste Hindus opened temples for the untouchables. Mahtab opened temples of his village for the untouchables[94] and Narayan Birabar Samant[95] did the same in Paradeep. These were few instances when the Gandhians opened the temples for untouchables. These Gandhians were landlords and leaders of the PCC and were very influential, so their attempts were not opposed militantly by the local people. And as also some of these leaders opened their own temples, they also did not face stiff opposition from the orthodox society. But the common Gandhians could not dare to do so in their own villages. Temple-entry movement in Orissa wasn't, in all, successful in spite of the efforts by the Gandhians. It lacked the needed sharpness and intensity.

In the district of Sambalpur, Gandhians in 1933AD observed *Harijan* Day. They arranged *Kirtans* and processions, cleaned *Harijan* quarters, held public meetings and even opened wells for the untouchables. There were more such instances when wells, roads and other common places were opened to them. But these wells were not opened for the untouchables for a long time.[96] It was the high political temperature and the effort of the Gandhians made this possible in some fewer cases and for a temporary period only.

Birakishore Das wrote against the system of

93. A.C. Pradhan, "Temple Entry Movement in Puri (1932-34)", Proc. IHC, 1983, 44th session, Delhi, 1984, pp. 473-74.
94. H.K. Mahtab, Sadhanara Pathe....., *op.cit.*, p. 154.
95. Questionnaire—Narayan Birabar Samant.
96. C.R. Mishra, *op.cit.*, pp. 237-40; Interview— Harekrushna Biswal, Advait Ballav Ray.

untouchability to invoke the conscience of the caste Hindus. When by 'appealing to the conscience' of the British Might the Gandhians could lessen the brutal police attack, failed to strike the conscience of orthodox Hindu society. Birababu, as he was called by his friends, wrote,

> "Please eradicate the greatest sin
> *i.e.* untouchability,
> No evidence is given in any scripture
> in favour of it...............
> you don't see your own brothers equally,
> how you claim the same from the foreigners?"[97]

Caste system was severe and rigid in Orissa. The Gandhians of *Brahmin* caste opined that though there was untouchability, there was also presence of fellow-feeling among the people of different castes. But some *Karana* Gandhians informed that they were also looked down upon by the *Brahmins*.[98] Even a high caste Hindu of non-*Brahmin* origin was not allowed to take food, from or enter a *Brahmin's* house.[99] The untouchable students were not allowed to take scholarships from the upper caste teachers because of their lower caste origin.[100]

Banchhanidhi Mohanty composed heart-touching couplets denouncing such practice. He wrote,

> "The practice of untouchability;
> Determination of people's status-
> on the basis of caste,
> these are being propagated by the orthodox
> supporters of the society,
> to meet their selfish desire.

97. Chandrasekhar Mohapatra (ed), Silver Jubilee, National Independence, Cuttack 1971.
98. Questionnaire—Govind Chandra Tripathy, Jagannath Tripathy, Mukund Prasad Mazumdar, Interview—Shyamakant Mohapatra and Advait Ballav Ray.
99. *Ibid.*
100. Questionnaire—Biswambar Behera.

> They do weight the sin and bliss and
> concept of caste-
> on the basis of wealth".[101]

In 1934AD, Gandhi came to Orissa to generate awakening against the practice of untouchability and started his famous *'Padayatra'*. Gandhi went on foot through the interior of Orissa and the Congress force in Orissa worked tirelessly to make the *'Padayatra'* successful. Alongwith the top leaders, the local workers were very busy in arranging meetings and in looking after the workers who had come with Gandhi.[102] Gandhi became very happy with the arrangements and praised thus,

> "You have laboured with rare devotion and never complained of overwork. Your have laboured night and day in order to make the pilgrimage a success .... I would ask you to continue the work so well begun in the villages. I leave *Utkal* with happy memories of association with you".[103]

Women Gandhians under the leadership of Ramadevi and Haimavati Devi tried to improve literacy among the *Harijans*. Kokila Devi, Godavari Devi, Tulasi Devi, Sushila Devi, Manika Devi, Annapurna Maharana, Sobhabati Panda, Ansumali Ray, Amiya Ghosh, Mangala Sen all worked hard. They particularly went to the untouchable people and mixed with their women folk and tried to educate them. They were supported by Anti-Untouchability Board of Orissa Branch.[104] Admiring their zeal Gandhi praised them, "I congratulate these sisters of Cuttack on their devotion to the cause of much desired reform".[105] Even Night Schools were opened to educate

---

101. Souvenir, Jatiya kavi Abhinandan(o), *op.cit.*, p. 43.
102. Publication Division, Gandhi in Orissa, Cuttack, 1970 pp. 13-26.
103. *Ibid.*
104. Interview—Annapurna Maharana.
105. Souvenir—Struggle for Freedom, *op.cit.*, p.102.

the *Harijans* who were working as agricultural labourers at day time.[106]

These women became trained in different camps held by the PCC for special occasions. When, as already mentioned, the AICC session was scheduled to be held in Puri, a camp was opened before the session to train the volunteers adequately there to make the session successful. Under the supervision of *'Hindusthani Seva Dal'* this camp was organised. Before it, Malati Chaudhury had trained the women volunteers at Cuttack. They learnt Hindi from Ramananda Sharma. Many girls like Amiya, Namita, Bijan, Premamala, Sobhabati, Annapurna, Sati, Hasi, Khusi, Tapasi, Nila and many others joined the programme. Many of them were daughters of eminent Gandhians and some of them were of Bengali Origin.[107] In Puri camp both men and women were selected to be trained in different works. They taught how to work as volunteers at the meetings, how to control the mob, how to watch the tents in the night. The leaders also taught the volunteers in history, music, *Satyagruha* movement and Gandhism. Even it was surprising to find that women were taught how to use knife to protect themselves.

The camp had nearly 88 female trainees and much more male volunteers. They were selected from different districts. Most of them were wives and daughters and relatives of leaders as well as common Congress workers. Almost all of them except, two or three, were from Cuttack, Puri, Balasore and Ganjam district. It their caste would be considered, most of them were from *Brahmins* and *Karanas*. Some of them were also from the stock of domiciled Bengalis.[108]

---

106. Interview—Annapurna Maharana.
107. Interview—Annapurna Maharana; *Samaj*, 9th September, 1931.
108. Interview—Annapurna Maharana; S.N. Pattnaik, *op.cit.*, pp. 95-97.

The volunteers were divided into many groups and sub-groups, under a leader. Committees of water supply, light supply, exhibition, publication, volunteers, health and heygine were formed. Though the session was not held, the training the volunteers received, became very useful in later years.[109] Harekrushna Mahtab observed that in every district under the jurisdiction of the PCC such training centres were opened. Many women of non-Gandhians households joined these camps.[110]

The volunteers, very often, targeted the shops of intoxicants in the towns. But in villages, as mostly the untouchables were adept to different intoxicants, the Gandhians in their programme to fight against untouchability, tried to persuade them not to use it. In Sambalpur the volunteers picketed in front of Ganja or liquor shops and were arrested. Here the untouchables also became conscious of their conditions.[111] The *dhobas* or washermen in certain places promised to leave the practice of taking liquor altogether.[112] *Panas* of Bari also decided to leave beef-eating as well as taking country-liquor.[113] The *Satyagrahis* cut down many *Khajuri* trees from which *tadi* was made. They, in many areas, destroyed *'Tadi Thekis'* or the pot containing liquor on the trees.[114]

The Gandhians were also engaged in different relief works at different places which were affected by flood in 1933AD, 1934AD and 1935AD. Cyclone destroyed some sub-divisions of coastal districts in 1936AD. Consequently Diarrhoea, Malaria and other epidemics killed many

---

109. *Samaj*, 28th January 1931.
110. H.K. Mahtab, *op.cit.*, p. 5; S.N. Pattnaik, *op.cit.*, p. 98; Interview—Annapurna Maharana.
111. C.R. Mishra, *op.cit.*, pp. 237-40.
112. *Samaj*, 15th April, 1931.
113. *Ibid.*
114. B.Kanungo, Daria Dakhal (o), *op.cit.*, p. 25; Questionnaire—Nrusingha Charan Samal.

people.[115] The Gandhians went to the affected areas and helped the helpless people.[116] They opened relief centres in many villages and with the help of local villagers conducted the relief works efficiently.[117]

But these constructive workers were gradually alienating themselves from the mainstream of provincial Congress. They were identified more as social workers than political activists. They lived in *Ashrams* and engaged themselves completely in elevating the common exploited people from their backwardness.

In the year of 1936AD the PCC observed Golden Jubilee of the formation of the Congress. Meetings were held and *Sankirtans* were recited in villages of each districts. Mass dinners were arranged by local Gandhians. Dramas were held to commemorate the occassion. Exhibition of indigenious handicraft were helf in many places.[118]

Growth of The Socialist Gandhians

Although from 1934AD a group of young Gandhians in Orissa became socialists, as back as 1930AD the awareness in the line of socialism had already present among the educated people of Orissa. They *Samaj* in February, 1930AD had publishcd about the formation of peasant organisations in Madras presidency and so wanted the Oriyas to take step for such organisation in Orissa. It reported, "In other provinces the *ryots* were organised to start the agitation. There should be an organisation of the peasants of the entire *Utkal* province. Non-Co-Operators, co-operators, supporters of complete independence or

115. M. Ahmed (ed), Census of India—Orissa, Vol. 1, 1951, Cuttack, 1953, p. 8; Vol. IX, pp. 36-40, 54.
116. A. Maharana, *op.cit.*, Sucharita, May, 1987, 12th year, No. 10, pp. 34-36; Interview—Shyamakanta Mohapatra.
117. Interview—Shyamakanta Mohapatra, Ghanashyam Pati, Harekrushna Biswal.
118. *Samaj*, 22nd January, 1936.

dominion status all may join it".[119] The cause of the peasants, industrial labourers and agricultural workers assumed added importance in these years. In Orissa lack of industrial facilities had not allowed for the growth of a working class movement. As the state was totally agrarian and the condition of the peasants and landless agricultural labourers was very precarious, it attracted the attention of emerging socialists within the provincial Congress organisation. Working with the Congress they devoted their time in organising the peasants against the exploitation.

Surendranath Pattnaik, a noted Gandhian freedom fighter, was of opinion that though many Gandhians joined the soialist group, felt isolated quickly. The could not discontinue their relationship with other Gandhian brethern. Some also felt that they should not isolate themselves from many ideas of Gandhi. When peasant organisations grew,[120] mostly the Gandhians in villages helped the socialists to strengthen the peasant movement. So in many respect, the Gandhians who believed in many ideas of Gandhi and even non-violence and followed many of these in their personal lives, became socialists and active peasant activitists. These socialists, though differed from Gandhi in certain ways and doubted the repeated applicability of non-violance in a movement, yet acknowledged him as their leader. They also followed many ideas and techniques of Gandhi.* They respected

119. *Ibid.*, 5th February, 1930.

120. S.N. Pattnaik, *op.cit.*, pp. 134-35.

* Writing about the closer relationship of the socialists of Orissa with Gandhism, N.G. Ranga had said on Nabakrushna & Malati Chaudhury, the pioneers of the socialist movement of Orissa that, "Nabakrushna and Malati loved villages, villagers and specially the tribal people, they settle down in rural area..... Though they appeared as communists, they promoted the cottage industries and peasant proprietorship in the trully Gandhian manner". Quoted in "Shradhanjali, Nabakrushna Chaudhury", S.N. Dwivedi (ed.), Rourkela, 1984, p. 20.

Gandhi because for him only the common people were awakened.[121] Gandhi was a great lover of the poor and all of his ideas and techniques were meant ultimately for the poor class. They opined that Gandhi's commitment to non-violence restricted his vision. Gandhi was, a socialist, but a socialist of his own understanding. His over-emphasis on the moral life of man lessened his importance on the material life. But he also championed the growth of small scale industries and made the Congress an organisation of the poor peasants and labourers.[122]

Some common Gandhians of Orissa expressed the view that Gandhi never vehemently opposed to the activities of socialists which he could have done easily. So, perhaps, he was aware of the development of the time and silently allowed this force of socialism to grow.

The socialists, influenced by Marx and his ideas defied religion and God. Surendranath Dwivedi discarded his sacred thread. Malati Chaudhury donated her ornaments to start a magazine of the Oriya Socialists, '*Sarathi*'. When the socialists started marchings in Cuttack city, the people who were acquainted with the cries of '*Mahatma Gandhi ki Jai*', became surprised seeing these socialist volunteers urging the workers to unite. But the Marwaris of Cuttack called them '*Ardh-Pugala*'.

At the primary stage some Congress workers became enemies of these socialists. They started spreading rumours that socialists would collect the wealths of rich and would distribute among the people. Nobody would be allowed to keep any wealth with him or her. Food would be prepared at a particular place and would be served with the help of a lady once only, irrespective of people's appetite. Even women would be common property.[123]

---

121. Interview—Gokulamohan Raychudamani.
122. *Ibid*.
123. S.N. Dwivedi, Mo Jivana Sangram (o), Cuttack, 1984, pp. 27-50 and 58.

But gradually hostilities of these Gandhians disappeared when they realised the importance of the activities of the socialists in mobilising the poor peasants of Orissa. Nabakrushna Chaudhury, being the leader of the socialists could become the secretary of PCC. So the common Gandhians supported the socialists and helped them without any reservation to widen the influence of Gandhi among the people.

Peasant organisations on socialistic pattern were formed in villages. The socialists worked as relief workers during the flood and opened relief centres in villages. They opposed to the excesses of zamindars and even quarrelled with such men who were also members of provincial Congress organisation. Even some of them did not hesitate to man-handle zamindars who assulted common men. The socialists travelled different districts and arranged meetings with the help of local Gandhians. To infuse self-confidence in the peasants, very often, in the meetings, the socialists requested the ignorant and illiterate peasants to express their anguish and experience in their own language.[124]

Although few orthodox Gandhians have adverse remarks on the socialist movement in Orissa and criticised the socialists, they praised them at the same time. Some constructive Gandhians remarked that the socialists were impatient workers. They also could not leave the Congress because without it, they could not find their existence. They opined that remaining in the Congress, the socialists used the platform and popularity of Gandhi for their own cause.[125] But the Gandhians also did not find any harm in the growing activities of socialists, rather they felt that fighting for the cause of the peasants they socialists strengthened the stability of the Congress among the people. The socialists fought for the peasants under the

---

124. *Ibid.*, pp. 58 and 75.

125. Interview and Questionnaire—Harekrushna Biswal.

Congress banner and the credit of their achievements went to the Congress and ultimately to Gandhi.

Harekrushna Mahtab lamented that the growth of socialist movement in Orissa divided the Gandhians into factions and weakened the Congress organisation in the province.[126] Some other Gandhians also apprehended that it might weaken the Congress[127] as independence was the primary objective of the national movement. But they denied to acknowledge those socialist Congress workers as a clearly separate group having no link with other Gandhians and Gandhian programmes because what they did was nothing new to the Gandhian ideas.[128]

The opponents of the socialists called them hypocrites. Even *'Utkal Dipika'* published a letter which had ridiculed these socialists in the following way, "It is very easy to become a socialist by distributing one's land in *benami* among one's relatives."[129] However, these workers really widened the vision of the people. And they also proved better than those communists in Orissa so far as organising the peasants and working as a pressure group within the Congress was concerned.

The socialists were mostly educated. They used the strength of the peasants through organisations for which they became active in villages. Very often they came across the staunch Gandhians in the localities and took their help to organise the peasants. These socialists like Mohan Das, Gatikrushna Swain, Surendra Nath Dwivedi, Gokulamohan Ray Chudamani, Prananath Pattnaik etc. under the leadership of Nabakrushna Chaudhury and Malati Devi did praiseworthy works and created traditional based for the socialist movements in Orissa for decades to come. Rabindranath Das in Balasore,

126. H.K. Mahtab, *op.cit.*, p. 166.
127. Interview—Ghanashyam Pati.
128. *Ibid.*, Nilamani Mohanty and Shyamakanta Mohapatra.
129. *Utkal* Dipika, 18th March, 1934.

Gatikrushna Swain in Kakatpur, Mohan Das in Nimapada, Prananath Pattnaik in Khurda created their own followers and areas of influence to challenge the dominance of the Congress leaders in the province. Many of the socialists were elected as the convenor of Congress organisation of their localities.[130]

Relationship Between Gandhian and the Communists of Orissa

With the growth of the socialist movement in Orissa, a group of young communists also became active under the leadership of Bhagabati Charan Panigrahi. But as compared to the Gandhians and socialists they were very few in number and their activities became confined, at the initial stage, within some urban areas. They defied the authority of *Guru*, Guardian and Government. Some young poets like Sachidananda Routray, Manmohan Mishra and Ananta Pattnaik joind them. They formed a branch of All India Students Federation in Orissa.[131]

When Gandhians were asked about the communists they expressed that the influence of Gandhi was so strong that no other organisation except the Congress, could grow here. Socialists were recognised by the people because they fought non behalf of the Congress and Congress was synonymous with the name of Gandhi for the village people. So whoever fought for the people were called as *'Congressia'* by the people. Some communists were identified as Congress workers, though, they did not wear *Khadar*.[132] They were staying in the Congress Offices.

The communists alleged that many of the Gandhians were hypocrites and were not really aware of the intentions of Gandhism. According to them Gandhians tried to misguide the people against the communists lest their monopoly and dominance over the people could be

130. *Samaj*, 17th June, 1936.
131. R.C. Ram, *op.cit.*, p. 10.
132. Raj Guru, *op.cit.*, p. 28.

endangered because of the growing popularity of the communists. They said that these '*Congressilok*' spread rumours that if communists came to power they would kill the old-men by bullets.[133] It was found that some workers of the Congress were deputed by the leaders to keep constant touch with the students in schools, colleges and hostels lest they might be influenced or polluted by the communists.[134]

Gandhians preferred the socialists to the communists because, they felt that the attitudes of the former were on the basis of Indian environment, whereas the latter were alien in nature.[135] Because the socialists, in many respects, respected Gandhi and his ideas and never opposed him vehemently what the communists did.

In spite of the growth of socialists, communists and the conflict within the provincial Congress force, the dominance of Gandhism still remained in the region. The Gandhians having commitment to the ideas of Gandhi as well as to the cause of people were still dominating in these years.

IV

COMPOSITION AND CONVICTION OF GANDHIANS IN GANDHISM

Composition

In these years, thc number of Gandhians increased because of the involvement of large number of volunteers in Salt Movement and also in later years when mass-based peasant agitations were organised by the socialist Gandhians and constructive works were taken up seriously by others. Except those Gandhians of earlier years, many new volunteers were involved in Salt agitation who were mostly high school dorp-outs and peasant

133. *Ibid*., p. 46.

134. Interview—Shyamakanta Mohapatra.

135. Questionnaire—Gourachandra Mohapatra.

youths. Many of them also remained active as Gandhians for succeeding years. The elder Gandhians were adults by the year and were experienced enough to guide the new volunteers. Participation of women was much more than that of the previous years. Few of them remained within the Congress as Gandhians, though, they were more in number than before.[136]

In rural areas mostly adult Gandhians who had joined the Congress in the previous decade, formed the local leadership of the movement. Illiterate and school-drop-outs formed the rank and file. But in urban areas the availability of the adult[137] Gandhians was less. It was the school students who formed the majority of the common Gandhian volunteers. Adults joined the marches and arranged the common people to break Salt Law in their own areas.[138] But young boys and girls became picketers in towns.

After the suspension of the movement, many staunch Gandhians who were orthodox believers in Gandhism, became constructive workers. Some educated youths formed the socialist group of the Gandhians for the cause of the peasants. Many Gandhians who were living in villages, but were not totally involved in constructive works, helped these socialists. Educated rural youths and adults formed the rank and file of these organisations. So, unlike the previous decade, when only one type of Gandhians was present in provincial Congress organisation, during this time, two types of Gandhians emerged on the basis of their nature of work and conviction. They were constructive workers and socialists. As the Salt Movement continued for longer period and

136. Interview—Sarat Chandra Maharana, Udayanath Sarangi and Shyamakanta Mohapatra.

137. Souvenir, Struggle for..... *op.cit.*, p. 89.

138. Interview—Gunanidhi Patra, Bauribandhu Patra, Ghanashyam Pati, Sarat Chandra Maharana, Udayanath Sarangi, Rajkrishna Bose.

retained the political temperature for considerable time, the Gandhians in Orissa had to remain busy and active throughout. The socialist agitation and successive constructive works required the active and direct participation of the common workers for longer period because of the mass-based nature of these movements. Though both full-time and part time activists were existed, their involvement was much deeper and more frequent than of previous decade.

Castewise, the Gandhians of these years emerged from all castes. Though the number of *Harijan* workers increased, it was very few as compared to their population. So far as the class structure was concerned, the workers from the lower middle class peasant households formed the backbone of the group of Gandhians. Even the student participants were also mostly from these classes.

As the Salt Movement was intense in coastal area, naturally the Gandhians of the coastal districts formed the majority. Even after the suspension of the movement, these Gandhians spearheaded the peasant agitations in the coastal areas during the period. From among them the number of educated Gandhians grew alongwith the number of illiterate or semi-illiterate Gandhians. Thus, the younger sections gradually outnumbered the adults and the village level Gandhians totally dominated the Congress provincial Gandhian force.[139]

Conviction

The Gandhians of the previous decade mostly had strong belief in different ideas as well as techniques of Gandhi. In the subsequent years, many constructive workers emerged from this matured group. But unlike the previous years, as the number of the Gandhians grew considerably, the conviction in different ideas of Gandhi varied from person to person and from group to group.

139. *Ibid.*

Unlike the previous years, when the Gandhians totally acknowledged, respected and followed Gandhian ideas to a great extent as far as possible, the socialists who were carved out of the Congress, questioned or expressed their inability to believe certain ideas of Gandhi. But they used Gandhian techniques of *Satyagraha,* marches and *hartals* to induce the common people to join the movement. They were aware of Gandhi's sway over the masses and so respected him as a great political strategist and a real mass leader. The unwanted elements could not be able to pose a threat to Gandhism, and despite the inclusion of the socialists, the dominance of Gandhism remained intact within the Congress organisation in Orissa.

Among the orthodox Gandhians who were constructive workers and were staunch believers, the degree of conviction also varied. Some expressed inability to follow almost all the ideas of Gandhi in their personal lives.[140] They paid respect to these ideas and followed many in their own lives. They became Constructive workers to guide the social front of the movement and they had great faith in its fertility. They were trying to be true Gandhians in the strict sense of the term. It was Gandhi's personality and dedication in different fields of activity throughout the year that induced most of them to join him.[141] But, however, feasibility of Gandhian techniques allowed the younger generation to join Gandhian movement in large numbers in which will for social service, patriotism and political awarness could be displayed easily than by becoming supporters of other non-Gandhian agitations.

So far as the concept of *Khadi* and spinning was concerned the Gandhians in general expressed comfort in using the dress, and also believed that spinning would help the poorer class financially. Use of *Khadar* made them

140. Questionnaire—Haricharan Berma.

141. *Ibid.*

branded among the people as *'Chellahs* of Gandhi *Maharaj'*, which was a symbol of great respect in contemporary society. Though they succeeded a little in their mission to remove untouchability, all of the Gandhians, even who were not active like the branded constructive workers, worked in their personal level or within Gandhian programmes against the evil practice. In spite of the reservation among a few Gandhians about untouchability, no Gandhian dared or thought it proper to raise any issue against the movement.[142] Many Gandhians were free from the use of any intoxicants. But some were adept to milder intoxicants like battle, *gudakhu* and *bidi*.

These Gandhians of Orissa formed the first batch of full-time social workers of the province in the previous decade. In this decade also, they were the only group who were engaged in such social works. They all were involved in the movement for a cause—which was the reflection of their class interest, *i.e.* agrarian lower middle class and landless labourer class, irrespective of caste status. So, when they dreamed of an Independent India, it was the eradication of agrarian exploitation that came into their mind. Two full meals a day, a shelter and dignified life they desired in an independent but democratic India. There should be no death by starvation and women would not be dishonoured—what they cherished.[143]

As the total Gandhian force of Orissa had deep faith in Gandhi as a great political strategist, irrespective of their group identities, the Gandhians never doubted Gandhi's attempts of sudden start and unexpected withdrawls of the political movements which created controversies within the Congress organisation in other provinces.

142. Interview—Udayanath Sarangi, Sarat Chandra Maharana, Questionnaire—Suresh Chandra Mishra, Mukund Prasad Majumdar, Akrura Jena, Jagannath Tripathy.

143. Questionnaire—Sarat Chandra Maharana, Annapurna Maharana, Udayanath Sarangi, Narayan Birabar Samant, Biswakeshan Dalua, Baikunthanath Mohanty.

Though these steps of Gandhi had sometimes dampening effect on the rank and file of Gandhians, they had the belief that '*Satyagraha* had no defeat'. Nobody could yet have victory over a true '*Satyagrahi*'. Many of the Gandhians believed that Gandhi was well aware of their abilities and limitations. So he was right and justified when he started and suspended any movement.[144]

But at the end of the period, when a separate Orissa province was formed and the provincial Congress had to join the electoral battle for state legislation, in 1936AD, many unwanted elements entered the Congress to get power and influence. Even some opponents of the Congress joined as primary members and as Gandhians. Regarding this development within the Congress organisation in Orissa, B. *Raja*sundar Das had reported,

> "I am not a bonafide Congress worker...., But I follow many ideals of Congress with love and respect which are meant for the betterment of the Indians and these are products of basic Indian Morals. The Congress workers have been nourished by the donation of lakhs of poor and simple Indians. They are vocal supporters of red-tapism and corruption now. The countryment should recognise them who have been devouring the fruits of British maladministration".[145]

They used *Khadar* and talked high like Gandhi.[146] But the dominance of true Gandhian was still intact there. The social workers, who saw the feasibility of the Gandhian movement and believed Gandhi more as strategist than an idealist, gradually joined the movement more and more. Believers of Gandhism as a creed and ideals in personal life were found less in number among the new

---

144. Questionnaire—Gaurachandra Mohapatra.
145. *Samaj*, 16th June, 1936.
146. Questionnaire—Nityananda Mohapatra, Interview—Advaitaballav Ray.

entrants. But nearly all of them were committed to peoples' cause except those hypocites to entered the Congress organisation recently.

V

LIFE STYLE OF THE GANDHIANS

Village Life

The Gandhians except those who were in *Ashrams* or in different Congress offices, stayed in villages. They were known as social workers or '*Samajsebi*' in their localities. They arranged meetings in village fairs, *yatras* and markets and propagated Gandhism among the people. They looked after their cultivation casually due to their frequent involvement in different programmes of the Gandhian movement. They helped the constructive workers as well as peasant organisations to strengthen their sway over the people. Some of them made their own houses as *Ashrams* and opened *Pathasalas* to teach the village children. They conducted relief camps during natural calamities.

The young Gandhians could not continue their studies. They remained in villages but were also not regular in cultivation as they had to be engaged in different Congress works. They formed rank and file of the peasant and constructive movements in villages.[147]

Many bachelor Gandhians got subsequently married against certain social objections as they were branded as 'worthless' men. Some did not marry at all. A few maintained married life only after independence in their early forties also.[148]

The Gandhians who were not from joint families, faced lot of trouble. As they did not look after their fields

147. Interview—Shyamakanta Mohapatra, Bibhutibhusan Acharya, Harekrushna Biswal, Gunanidhi Patra and Bauribandhu Patra; Souvenir—Ramachandra Mohapatra, Jharapada, Govindpur, 1975.

148. Interview—Harekrushna Biswal.

their financial condition deteriorated to a miserable extent. Their family members suffered a lot. Moreover, the small patches of lands of these Gandhians were auctioned to meet the government demand. Their children passed through miserable childhood and were neglected in their studies. The henchmen of British, in villages, very often, harassed them. Their caste people could not come out to help them in distress as they had worked for the removal of untouchability. Whenever the Gandhians were imprisoned, their families faced the worst type of mental and financial sufferings.[149]

In spite of such difficulties, these Gandhians bore the strains of their lives. Whoever live in villages, they could not sit idle. Spinning was their hobby. They constantly travelled the nearby villages and kept intimate touch with the villagers. Their presence also created hope among the people. They were aware of the fact that the poor, ignorant people of villages were very much afraid of the authorities. Even they were frightened seeing a man of the urban areas. So these Gandhians tried to eradicate the ghost fear from the people. [150]

The couples—husbands and wives, who joined the movement, did not face much trouble in their personal lives. Their life style became example for others in their localities. They were seen busy always in different programmes and their houses were used as local Congress offices, where the local Gandhians could gather to chalk-

149. Most of the Gandhians have expressed such opinions; S. Mohanty, Andha Diganta (o), *op.cit.*, (In this novel, Surendra Mohanty himself a Gandhian has described vividly such examples).

150. K.C. Panigrahi, Luhar Manisha (o), Cuttack, 1971. (In this novel, the novelist, who himself a believer of Gandhian ideas whose younger brother was a ranked communist leader and founder of Communist movement in Orissa, Bhagabati Panigrahi, has mentioned about such feelings and conditions among the people during the Gandhian movement in Orissa).

out plans. They also brought-up their children in this atmosphere.

The Gandhians had very cordial relations with their leaders. Though the provincial Congress leaders were men of repute, still they personally knew almost all the common Gandhians of their respective districts. The leaders whenever visited the villages stayed in the houses of the Gandhians.[151]

The involvement of these Gandhian workers in different constructive works, their fight against any type of exploitation and their personal life also, made them popular among the villagers. Very often their daring activities became subject of admiration of the masses. Even those who became members of Local and District Boards became busy in different developmental works. Young Gandhians tried to be examples for other following the footsteps of the adults. Their influence was so strong that whenever they called for the villagers they joined the meetings and marches. [152]

Ashram Life of the Gandhians in Orissa

Many Gandhians of Orissa also stayed in different *Ashrams* which were situated in different comers of Orissa. Some new *Ashrams* were also opened these years. These *Ashrams* were under the supervision of eminent Gandhians and all these were meant for the popularisation of different constructive programmes among the people. Harekrushna Mahtab had opened *'Karma Mandira'* in Balasore, Krupasindhu Hota opened an *Ashram* in Berboi of Delang. There were *Ashrams* in Bhandaripokhari, Jhadapitala,

151. Interview—Sarat Chandra Maharana, Annapurna Maharana.

152. Questionnaire—Sarat Chandra Maharana, Annapurna Maharana, Udayanath Sarangi, Rajkrushna Bose; Questionnaire—Raghunath Singh Samant, Gaurachandra Mohapatra, Jagannath Tripathy, Mukunda Prasad Majumdar.

Chatia, Bhapur, Berhampur, Puri and also in the district of Koraput. *Alakashram* was still running, but in 1934AD, Gopabandhu Chaudhury shifted the *Ashram* to Bari and opened a training centre for basic education.[153]

The life in these *Ashrams* was very strict and purposive. Both men and women; boys and girls stayed there. Some common Gandhians sent their children to get education in these *Ashram*. There were competent teachers who taught the students spinning and other techniques of handicrafts. The daily life of the works as well as the teachers was divided according to different kinds of works regularly and systematically.[154]

In Bari *Ashram*, more than two hundreds of Gandhians were staying. The Ashramites constructed the houses in their own hands and by 1935AD, the work was completed. There was a small factory in the *Ashram* to produce *Khadi* and other articles. The Ashramites produced vegetables and sold them in the villages. They bought high yielding milch cows and brought up bulls of high quality breed.[155]

There were many women Ashramites in different *Ashrams*. In Bari *Ashram*, the women were staying under the guidance of Ramadevi. Some girls were also staying there. Many Gandhians also sent their sons and daughters to get education in this *Ashram*. In the nearby village of Malliaghai, Surendranath Pattnaik also had opened an *Ashram* where he was mostly engaged in eradication of untouchability.[156]

The relation between the Ashramites and the villagers was very cordial. Mostly, many workers of the *Ashrams* were from the nearby villages. Very often people provided needed help to the Ashramites and donated according to

---

153. G.N. Mohanty, Dhuli Matira Santha (o), Cuttack-1985, pp. 62-65, 70-80, 95-115 and 149.

154. *Ibid*., pp. 145-49.

155. *Ibid*. Interview—Annapurna Maharana.

156. R.D. Chaudhury, *op.cit*., pp. 116-118.

their capacity. The *Ashrams* became a matter of great pride for them. Very often the women Ashramites went to these villages, mixed with the women folk and taught them how to spin and also trained them in different handicrafts.[157] The volunteers of the *Ashrams* used to collect rice called *'Panchubarni'*.[158]

Every Ashramite was directed to use *Khadar* dress produced from the *Ashram*. They were strictly vegetarians. The workers sat in a room irrespective of caste and took their meals at a time. Both male and female stayed there under strong discipline and dedication. The women of the *Ashrams* of the *Ashrams* opened the eyes of the orthodox people who were supporters of the *purdah* system. Women by doing different kinds of work proved themselves equally capable with men.[159] The morale life of the Ashramites was quite high, though, in fewer cases, opponents of the Congress questioned the cordial relationship of Ashramites of both sexes.[160] Sarat Chandra Maharana praised the good relationship between the males and females.[161] Annapurna Maharana was of opinion that as the number of females was more than males in the Bari *Ashram*, the women did not face any trouble.[162] Though the opponents of the *Ashrams* did spread malafide rumours, nobody listened to them.[163]

Harekrushna Mahtab opined, "An intimate relation grew over the years among the Ashramites due to the hardship and struggle they had gone through"[164] The *Ashram* became shelter for the destitutes —particularly the

157. *Ibid.*, p. 119.
158. Questionnaire—Gaurachandra Mohapatra.
159. Interview—Annapurna Maharana, Harekrushna Biswal.
160. Surendra Mohanty, *op.cit.*, pp. 320-29.
161. Questionnaire—Sarat Chandra Maharana.
162. *Ibid.*, Annapurna Maharana.
163. *Ibid.*, Birabar Rath.
164. H.K. Mahtab, *op.cit.*, p. 54.

helpless women. Once a woman of high caste named Sushila came to Ramadevi. She was a widow, but was aware of Gandhi's ideas which appealed her most. When she wanted to join the movement her mother-in-law and other family members abused her severely. Because it was taken as a great shame for the family where women stepped out of their houses. In spite of strict vigil over her, when she left the home and straight came to Ramadevi, the latter gave her consolation and sent her to Cuttack '*Swaraj Ashram*'. She got a new name and was called Jatadhari Sushila. She circulated pamphlets, went to bustees of untouchables of Cuttack town, took care of the untouchable children and taught them the alphabets. This became her routine work in daily life. She lived in the *Ashram* for a long period.[165]

There was no caste feeling among the Ashramites. In Bari *Ashram*, both touchables and untouchables were staying. Even during the ceremonies and marriages in *Ashram*, all were enjoying collectively.[166] In later years inter-caste marriages were preferred. A *Harijan* girl married a Brahman boy in 1940AD and in spite of strong opposition from the local people, the marriage got materialised. Even Annapurna, daughter of Ramadevi, married Sarat Chandra Maharana. White the bride was *Karana* by caste, the groom was of *Astalohakarmi*.[167]

In the *Ashram* of Ramachandi Sahi of Puri, the volunteers went to the nearby bazar to collect donation. They sang songs and within two hours they used to collect atleast 20 to 25 seers of rice, sufficient vegetables, salt and edible oil. The shop-keepers helped the volunteers without hesitation. In the *Ashram* at Berboi under the guidance of Krupasindhu Hota women associates were leading very disciplined life on Gandhian ideas.[168]

165. C.S. Mohapatra (ed.), Souvenir, Jatiya Kabi Avinandan, *op.cit.*, p. 24.
166. Questionnaire—Akrura Jena.
167. Interview—Sarat Chandra Maharana.
168. Questionnaire—Suresh Chandra Mishra.

Many Gandhians in different places also opened *Ashrams*. It is found that *Ashrams* were established in Sukinda, Kendrapara, Patakura, Tirtol, Kendupatna, Jajpur.[69] Some common Gandhians also opened *Ashrams* in small thatched houses of their localities. They used to assemble there to plan out strategies to continue the movement in their locality. [170]

There were no financial help to the Gandhians of Orissa to spend for the *Ashrams*. Except the *'Swaraj Ashram'*, the Headquarters of the PCC, other *Ashrams* were running by the Gandhians on their own efforts. Mostly the *Ashrams* were run on the donation of the common people. Sometimes *'Gandhi Seva Sangha'* helped the *Ashrams*,[171] Sometimes the local rich and influential people also donated. But all the Ashramites tried to be self-sufficient, laboured hard, produced their own clothings and food and constructed their own shelters.[172]

Except the *'Swaraj Ashram'* —where some leaders and workers lived permanently and congregated in the time of crisis to discuss about the movement, other *Ashrams*, mostly, were meant to spread and popularise constructive programmes. But their role in the political field was also noteworthy. Many Gandhians denied the fact that these *Ashrams* were meant for the leaders to chalk out strategies secretly. Sarat chandra Maharana opined that the activities of Alaka and Bari *Ashrams* were wide open to the public. There was nothing secret. As the movement was not violent and the authorities were clearly aware of the role of the Ashramites, there was nothing for them to be panicked.[173] Of course, in these *Ashrams* the leaders did congregate at the crucial junctures and discussed their

169. *Ibid.*, Mathurananda Nath.
170. *Ibid.*, Hari Charan Berma.
171. *Ibid.*, Godavari Devi.
172. *Ibid.*, Mukunda Prasad Majumdar.
173. Interview and Questionnaire—Sarat Chandra Maharana.

future plans and programmes. The personal *Ashrams*, in villages, too, were used by the local workers to congregate in critical periods. The *Ashrams*, big or small, helped immensely in shaping the attitude and belief of these social workers as well as the local people. Many people of the localities where the influence of the movement was very strong because of the activities of the *Ashrams*, joined the Congress.

Life in Jail

Jail-going was a common feature of the Gandhian movement. In spite of the fear of social ostracisation, the Gandhians of Orissa went to jails without hesitation. In the previous decade, many Gandhians were arrested and interned. Rajkrushna Bose was the first Gandhian of India who became a political prisoner. [174] The people who became Congress workers were aware of the fact that they might be arrested and could be in jails. When the leading Gandhians went to jail nobody talked about social boycott after their return. Because most of them were living in towns and were very educated and extremely influential people. On the other side, the village level workers faced difficulties in their villages. Even most of the higher caste Gandhians were threatened to be ostracised by their dominating caste brethern.* But as they were branded as jail-going Gandhians, the fear of being ostracised no longer became effective.

---

174. Interview—Rajkrushna Bose, *Samaj*, 25th June, 1921.

* During these years people ostracised the persons who were in jail, because there was a strong belief in the society that in jails one caste-fellow had to live with untouchables. Muslim prepared the food and prisoners did unclean work in jails. So generally people were afraid of jail, because it was very difficult for the persons who returned from the jail, to be accepted in the society. He had to go through many purifying ceremonies which were also costly. Poor people had to face difficulties to satisfy their own caste people as well as of other higher castes. The grip of social ostracism was so powerful that no one could be escaped from it.

When the Gandhians were arrested, they were behaved as criminals instead of being treated as political prisoners. The accomodation in jails was inadequate and the authorities faced difficulty to keep such a large number of prisoners. At that time, the condition of the jails in Orissa was quite precarious. Except one or two jails, other jails were of thatched houses. Sanitary condition was very bad. As the jails were meant for the criminals the colonial authorities need not pay importance to these jails. The atmosphere inside the jails was unsuitable to improve anybody's morale.[175] There was the system of classification among the prisoners according to their crime, and status or nature of punishment. They were divided into A,B and C classes. The common Gandhians became 'C' class prisoners. Some also felt honoured when they became 'B' class prisoners.[176] They tried to classify themselves superior among the lower ranks of the Congress organisation. [177]

Due to the unexpected number, the jail authorities failed to provide the minimum facilities to the prisoners. Even the small cells, meant for one man, were alloted to two or three prisoners. The condition of the latrines, dress, food was filthy and unheygenic.[178] Almost all of the Gandhians who spent years in jail said that the food which they got was like cattle-food. The rice was mixed with small stones, the *dal* was just like water and somctimes no vegetable was given. Even the leaves of *saru*,[179] which nobody took as food, was supplied. The individual dress was two sleeveless shirts, a small napkin, an underwear,

175. Interview—Ghanashyam Pati, Sarat Chandra Maharana, Harekrushna Biswal.
176. Interview—Advaitballav Ray, Ghanashyam Pati.
177. S. Mohanty, *op.cit.*, p. 74.
178. H.K. Mahtab, *op.cit.*, pp. 74-85; Nirupama Das (ed.), *op.cit.*, Surendra Mohanty, *op.cit.*, p. 73; Interview— Gokulmohan Raychudamani.
179. *Ibid.*

a blanket and a bead around the neck with a number. [180]

Nilakantha Das remarked that the atmosphere in jail was very bad.[181] However, the jail life of the leaders was not a quite difficult one. When the expenditure for 'A' class prisoner was three rupees per day, for 'B' class prisoner it was only Seventyfive paise and 'C' class prisoner, thirty seven paise. So, a 'C' classes prisoner was getting facilities nearly one eight of 'A' class prisoner. Sometimes leaders, on their own accord, made themselves 'C' class prisoners to live with their common co-workers. Each prisoner had to prepare *'atta'* from wheat provided to him.[182]

When all the prisoners of the then movement talked about the miserable life in the jails, some also spoke that it was very pleasant to be a 'C' grade prisoner. It was interesting because one could find himself among his co-workers. So the feeling of isolation could not be found. [183]

In the jails, the workers, while got time, discussed important matters with their leaders. Very often debates were held on burning issues of national and international fields. It developed the awareness among the workers.[184] When the prisoners were kept in Bihar or Bengal jails, they got chance to mix with the prisoners of neighbouring provinces and exchanged views among themselves.[185]

Very often, the Gandhians collectively protested against the behaviour of the officials as well as the quality of the food supplied to them. They also, in certain cases, succeeded in their mission. The Gandhians observed

180. H.K. Mahtab, *op.cit.*, p. 75; Questionnaire—Baikunthanath Mohanty.

181. Nilakantha Das, *op.cit.*, p. 100.

182. Questionnaire—Suresh Chandra Mishra.

183. Interview—Advaitballav Ray.

184. Questionnaire—Suresh Chandra Mishra, Biswakashan Dalua.

185. *Ibid.*

National Days and Weeks in jails in spite of warnings from the authorities. Their hoisting of National flags forced the authorities to use brute force on them. [186]

The increase of female prisoners created trouble for the jail authorities. There were separate wards for male and female prisoners. The females among the Gandhians were living separately. Talking about women prisoners, Annapurna Maharana opined thus,

> "Many women had left their home coming under the spell of Gandhi. Some of them also had joined the movement only being persuaded by other workers. So to educate them in the line of patriotism and about different ideas of Gandhi and their applicability in the society, adult women Gandhians were deputed to teach these women. These women got adequate knowledge in history and got training in music by competent Gandhian trainers."[187]

When male prisoners had to face lot of social difficulties in their villages the condition of female prisoners could be well understood. The women Gandhians who were wives and relatives of many leading Gandhians did not face such trouble as the village level women Gandhians of non-Gandhian households.[188]

186. Interview—Advaitaballav Ray.

187. Interview—Annapurna Maharana. (Among these women Kiranabala Sen, Mangala Sen, Jahnabi Devi, Kokila Devi, Subhadra Mahtab, Kumudini Devi, Ambika Devi, Tulasi Devi, Kshetramani Devi, Kausalya Devi, Sakhi Devi, Ahalya Devi, Suka Devi, Kusuma Kumari Devi, Bimala Dutta, Ashalata Acharya, Karuna Acharya, Annapurna Maharana, Sarala Devi, Rama Devi, Malati Chaudhury, Sobhabati Panda, Hemalata Devi, Krishna Kamini Devi, Mohini Devi, Radhamani Devi, Nishamani Devi, Kadambini Devi, Annapurna Ratha, Sunamani Devi, Gunamanjari Devi, Haramani Behera, Jhumpei Devi, Manika Devi, Sushila Ghose, Sundarmanichau Pattnaik, Nirupama Devi, Charubala Ray etc. were also arrested and got imprisonment.)

188. Souvenir, Jatiya Kabi....., *op.cit.*, p. 26.

Though the number of these women was few, still their joining the Congress and even imprisonment were dare devil steps at that time. Sushila Devi a veteran female Gandhian, was imprisoned and when released, her family did not accept her. She came back and stayed in Cuttack *'Swaraj Ashram'*.[189]

There was also a separate ward for juvenile prisoners. The boys who were jailed during the movement, stayed here. The jail authorities oppressed these boys because they protested very much any illegal practice in the jail. The boys were, therefore, asked to do manual labour twice a day. They had to prepare flour from wheat. Very often they were supplied with single meal a day. But the boys were looked after by other adult Gandhians who were allowed to meet the boys everyday for some limited time.[190] They inspired the boys to maintain their spirit. They spoke about the achievements of revolutionaries of different countries of the world. They also made these boys aware of the fact that the Britishers got India by dividing the nation.

The Gandhians were helped by Indian lower-level servants in the jails. They were sympathetic to these Congress workers. Those lower-level workers of jail used to provide informations about outside developments.[191] But the officials were not so.

VI

To sum up, the participation of common people was spontaneous during the Salt Movement. Salt identified itself with the interest of the poor Oriyas including those

189. C.S. Mohapatra (ed), *op.cit.*, p. 26, Interview - Harekrushna Biswal.

190. Souvenir, Orissa State Freedom Fighters Association, BBSR, 1986, pp. 21-22; Interview—Advaitballav Ray; Questionnaire—Jagannath Tripathy, Mukunda Prasad Majumdar.

191. H.K. Mahtab, *op.cit.*, p. 82; Interview—Harekrushna Biswal.

common Gandhians. Unlike the previous decade, the people's direct participation made the movement intense and wide-spread. After the movement, the people became very much aware of nationalism and consciousness grew among them to a great extent. Confidence of the people in them increased tremendously and the fear for British might gradually evaporated. It was the most satisfactory feature of Indian National Movement. Gradually the peasants and agricultural labourers, clearly discovered their class interest in the objectives of the *Congresswallas* in villages. Thus, Gandhi declared [192] the Congress as an organisation of the peasants. The PCC leaders including those socialists also tried their level best to make the Congress as the sole representative of such class of people. Gandhian force became diversified, and Gandhi, as a political strategist, became more clearer and prominent. Though Gandhi's dominance on the mind of Gandhians was still too strong, the growth of educated people and also consciousness in the illiterate mass gradually made Gandhi's different ideas more feasible political techniques in the political struggle. Practicability of Gandhism became clearer among the common masses.

This time, unlike the previous movement, the political temperature of the time was equally shared by the villages with urban areas. The political activities in the villages dominated scenes of the years. Different constructive programmes, *Ashrams*, peasant agitations — all found their place in rural areas where Gandhi's influence was strong in spite of the presence of new elements within the Congress. The participation of women had increased tremendously. It is found that only in Paradeep and Kujang, around 500[193] women joined Ramadevi to prepare contraband salt. The number of

192. CWMG, V. XX, Publication Division, Ministry of Information and Broadcasting, Delhi, 1970. (Young India, 13.8.31).

193. P*Raja*tantra, Saptahiki, June,18-24, 1989, pp. 34-35.

political prisoners increased alongwith that of women. Mostly students and adult Gandhians formed the local leadership of the Congress and the peasants and labourers became active supporters. The political temperature of Orissa remained strong throughout these six years because of various and continuous political activities which was absent in the previous decade. The Gandhians, this time, were found being engaged in different mass-based agitations. The Congress actually deserved the credit of dominating these years with its mass-based movements because Gandhism became clearer as a feasible political weapon to most of the people.

4

Congress Ministry in Orissa : The Gandhians and the Power Politics (1936—39 AD)

In 1936AD, the British Government declared to hold election for the Provincial Assemblies and the Congress agreed to participate in it. The election took place in 1937AD. The newly formed Orissa as the first province of India went to polls. The election went clearly in favour of the Congress. The Congress formed Ministry and remained in office upto October 1939, when it resigned in protest against the British war policy and antipathy to Indian sentiment. During their time in office the Congress ministry in Orissa under the Prime Ministership of Biswanath Das heralded many healthy parliamentary conventions and functioned on the principle of collective responsibility as far as possible. It introduced certain pro-people measures and widened the popularity of Congress among the masses. But the election and victory of the Congress in 1937AD and its tenure in office witnessed the growth of intense power politics within the provincial Congress organisation. Unwanted non-committed elements entered the party to capture the power and sabotage the fruit of the hardship of the true committed Gandhians. Power politics became naked and power-brokers were increased in number. Full-time Politics as a career was taken by many people in the Congress without any respect for Gandhism or peoples' cause. The entry of these heretics destroyed the sanctity of the Congress organisation.

I

ELECTION AND THE FORMATION OF MINISTRY

It was a matter of great responsibility and prestige for the entire provincial Congress force to prove itself the sole representative of the aspirations of the masses and to win the forthcoming election by a clear majority. It has to fight with the pro-British elements of the society. The influence of Muslim League or other Depressed Class Associations was literally absent in Orissa, but there was no dearth of political parties having the support of the Government. *Rajas*, Zamindars, big land-owners and pro-British influential people formed parties to put their candidates against the Congress. This election saw a tussle between the traditional pro-British elites versus the group of progressive and modern political activists who had clear commitment for the betterment of the masses. This was the last chance for those pro-British and orthodox elements of the society to adopt their inhuman tactics, money and position to sustain their hegemony over the people. It was also a first chance to those advanced modern elites to prove their capability as the real leaders of the masses.

According to a common Congress worker named Nrusingha Charan Samal, "This election inaugurated the real political life of the Congress Party. For the first time the Congress asked the people to elect its candidates. They came out victorious. The 1937 election thus laid the solid foundation of the Congress power politics for the decades to come".[1]

There were 5,20,584 voters in the province consisting of six districts such as Cuttack, Puri, Balasore, Ganjam, Koraput and Sambalpur. 80,487 were women voters; 19,453 were Scheduled Castes and 7,928 were Muslims.[2] The eligibility to vote was 12 annas of *chaukidari* tax for a year in case of higher castes and 6 annas in case of

1. Questionnaire—Nrusingh Charan Samal.
2. J.N. Mohapatra, Orissa, 1936-37 to 1938-39, Cuttack, 1941, p. 7.

Scheduled Castes. The men having more than matriculation as their educational qualification were also eligible to vote.

There were 60 assembly seats including 20 reserved, and the provincial Congress put only 40 candidates opened for general election. The Congress had a glorious past of selfless struggle for independence with it whereas its opponents had bad reputation because of their anti-people activities. It was mostly the tax-paying peasants of both upper and lower castes who were enlisted as voters. Most of the electorates were high caste Hindus and if the condition of the peasant society at the time would be considered, majority of the tax-paying peasants were from *Khandayats, Karans* and *Brahmin* Castes. The educational qualification of the voters allowed lower middle class and middle class agraian society to get a major share in the list as by the year 1937AD many educated men from these two classes already existed. Popularity of Gandhi and the Congress was very strong among the *Harijans*. The lower middle class Oriyas extended a clear support to the Congress and the standing army of the Gandhian force belonging mostly to this class made easier the victory of the party. As most of the students formed the backbone of the Congress political movement, the lower-middle and middle class students had a natural support for the Congress.

The Congress was the most dominating political organisation and the common Gandhians were the only group of available full-time political workers in the countryside. Moreover, after the Lucknow session, the socialist [3] Gandhians became very active in mobilising the peasants of the province which helped to widen the popularity of the Congress. The popularity of Gandhi among the people was still very strong. In spite of the internal strife, the Gandhians of the province worked as a team of elect their candidates with a clear mandate.

3. *Samaj*, 22nd April, 1936.

The candidates were selected by the PCC in collaboration with different district committees. The Congress candidates were, it was told, selected, keeping in view the general feelings of the local Gandhian worker.[4] But if one would see the list of the candidates selected. Most of the top provincial leaders who had dominated the political scenes in the last decades and who had large followers in their respective districts were the Congress candidates. Even the leaders among the Scheduled Castes were selected. The poor, semi-literate or not so highly literate Gandhian workers were never considered for.[5] The monopoly of hegemony of the PCC members also remained intact in legislative fields besides in organisational activities. One common worker of the organisation opined, "When bigwigs were fighting among themselves nobody cared us".[6] Many workers who had good reputation as honest Gandhians were denied the chance. Top leaders used their influence to enlist some unwanted candidates in the Congress list. Even a Zamindar who was an enemy of the Gandhian movement earlier, became a Congress candidate by the blessings of a reputed member of the PCC.[7] There were rebel candidates and it affected the lower-level organisations. It was also alleged that in some places local Congress organisers were instigated to propagate and work against the party candidates.[8] These created bad precedents in the organisation.

The socialist wing of the provincial Congress forced the leaders to accept many socialistic and pro-people ideas in the Party manifesto, which helped the campaigners to beg the people for the votes confidently. Abolition of

---

4. Interview—Harekrushna Biswal.
5. Satya Samachar, 25th November, 1936.
6. Interview—Nilamani Mohanty.
7. N.M. Routray, Smruti O Anubhuti (O), Cuttack, 1986, p. 82; Interview—Sarat Chandra Maharana.
8. *Lokamata*, 17th February, 1937.

Zamindari System, reduction of illegal taxes and revenues, ownership over lands were included in the Manifesto.[9] Soon after the selection of the candidates, electoral rolls were distributed among the workers area-wise. The Candidates with the help of area leaders collected the workers—both active full-timers and part-timers and sympathisers, who were directed to keep watchful eyes on the voters to keep them away from any temptations. This was a time of great test. The Gandhians had to prove their ability as able organisers and as real local leaders of the people.[10] It is true that many of the Congress candidates were well-to-do people, but they did not use their own money illegally to win over the voters. Massive popularity of Gandhi and the Congress and of the leaders, most of whom were also candidates, did not require such expenditure. The common Gandhians were so well alert and organised and worked so enthusiastically that within a very few days the victory of the Congress seemed clear. The opponents used money illegally and adopted many tactics which violated the code of campaign. But Congressmen penetrated into almost every village. Meetings, processions and slogans kept the atmosphere surcharged with enthusiasm and emotion.[11] And 'amidst everything one name acted like magic in drawing the voters to the polling booths to exercise their votes. It was of Gandhi'.[12] The formation of peasant organisations also widened the area of the Congress support considerably.

The government directed the district officials not to hesitate to use peons of the Revenue or other departments to assist the police in controlling the voters. The *thanas*

9. Interview—Gokulmohan Raichudamani; J.K. Samal, "Politics & Government in the Province of Orissa, 1936-39", *OHRJ*, Vol.-XXVII, NO. 1 to 4, p. 13.
10. Interview—Harekrushna Biswal, Gokulamohan Raichudamani; Questionnaire—Haricharan Berma.
11. J.N. Mohapatra, *op.cit.*, pp. 9-16.
12. M.N. Das (ed), A Century History of the Indian National Congress, 1935-37, Vol-III, Delhi, 1985, p. 12.

were selected as polling centres.[13] All these were meant for the disadvantage of the Congress candidates as the revenue or other personnels were not pro-people and the *thanas* were symbols of British tyranny and atrocity. Surprisingly the officials were expecting a keenly contested election.

The Congress launched its campaign by holding its first meeting at Cuttack Town Hall. In the meeting, Dinabandhu Sahu, a well-known Congress supporter while appealing the people to vote for the Congress candidates narrated their sacrifice and works for the people.[15] The common workers composed songs. known as 'Vote *Giti*' and with the help of *Kirtan Mandalis* toured the villages. Both socialists and other Gandhians worked as a team in their own localities leaving aside their differences. They carried on intensive propaganda against the Zamindars. Leaflets, Posters, exhibition of portraits of eminent leaders, *Kirtans*, eulogising candidates, condemning the rivals and explaining the clauses of Manifesto among the peasants the Gandhians gave the toiling lower-middle and middle class Oriyas the hope of a bright tomorrow.[16] In spite of the money-power used by the anti-Congress force and pressurisation using religious and emotional points, they could not influence the voters. The zamindars tried to insist the Beheras of the Scheduled Castes but they did not support the non-Congress candidates.[17]

The candidates held their meetings at different places

---

13. OSA, Home (Pol.), Confidencial, File No.-6, 1937 (Police arrangement for the election to Legislative Assembly, From Office of the Collector, Ganjam, 4th January, 1937).
14. *Ibid.*, (Letter to Chief Secretary, Government of Orissa, 5th September, 1937).
15. *Samaj*, 16th September, 1936.
16. J.N. Mohapatra, *op.cit.*, Interview—Rajkrushna Bose, Harekrushna Biswal, Ghanashyam Pati; J.K. Samal, *op.cit.*, p. 19.
17. R.C. Ram, Sangrami (O), Cuttack, 1986, p. 8; Satya Samachar, 13th January, 1937.

of their constituencies. But openly criticising the misdeeds of the opponents in the past, the candidates tried to make the voters brave and open. The absolute enthusiasm displayed by the common people created some sort of psychological pressure on the countable local voters. The songs and music party of *Jatiyakabi* Birakishore Das created nostalgic scenes of national movement in the countryside.[18] The *Chaukidars, Dafadars* and Union Presidents tried their level best to check the activities of the Gandhian campaigners. They openly scolded the Congress and the candidates in filthy words.[19]

But it was not possible to check the people to support the Congress. To avoid the watchful eye of the henchmen of anti-Congress candidates, the Gandhians, very often, preferred campaigning in the night and, thus, came out successful. The Gandhians also approached their relatives—who were voters, to elect the Congress candidates. They travelled in the villages on foot and used to stay there in the nights,[20] and informed their outside co-workers about the developments in the villages through the messengers.

In some places the opponents physically attacked the Congress candidates and mostly *Harijan* workers. The opponents, who held meetings, scolded and maligned the Congress, were not successful because of very poor public attendance and antipathy of the people. On the other hand, in many places the audience asked such questions which embarrassed the anti-Congress candidates. In some cases the zamindars ordered the boatmen to frustrate the Congress campaigners.[21]

Some living Gandhians expressed that it was pleasant

---

18. Interview—Ghanashyam Pati.
19. Interview—Shyamakanta Mohapatra; Satya Samachar, 6th January, 1937.
20. Interview—Harekrushna Biswal.
21. Questionnaire—Biswambar Behera; Satya Samachar, 20th January, 1937 and 13th January, 1937; *Lokamata*, 6th January, 1937.

to work for the Congress during their campaign. Few of them also described how some voters behaved indifferently at the day time but well-comed them in the night and expressed their clear support for the Congress. School boys[22] campaigned for the Congress candidates. They wore yellow caps symbolising the colour of the Congress boxes in the election. Manifesto in Oriya was cyclostyled in different colours and were distributed. In some places the opponents also circulated such types of leaflets having similar [23] colour in order to confuse the voters. Nevertheless, all classes of people in the villages wanted victory of the Congress. They were also very restless to see an independent India.[24]

Even some pro-government people entered the Congress organisation and informed the opponents about the activities of Congress workers.[25] The PCC cautioned the people not to be waved by these elements. Pranakrushna Padhihary, a PCC member wrote,

> "To defeat the Congress in the coming election, not only the Zamindars, lawyers and their henchmen are trying, there are also some people within the Congress in the attire of *Khadar*, who are also working to defeat the Congress. It is wrong to think them as Congressmen who pay four *annas* a year and wear *Khadar.....*".[26]

Some rebel candidates also used the name of the Congress openly and used Congress banner. They condemned the Congress workers as worthless semi-literate dogs.[27] Even they asked the voters to elect them

22. R.C. Ram, *op.cit.*, Interview—Advaitballav Ray, Questionnaire—Godavari Devi.
23. Satya Samachar, 13th January, 1937.
24. Questionnaire—Gokulamohan Raichudamani; R.C. Ram, *op.cit.*, p. 7.
25. Questionnaire—Gaurahari Prusti.
26. *Lokamata*, 6th January, 1937.
27. *Ibid.*

and they would provide them with cultivable lands, contracts, jobs etc. *'Satya Samachar'* ridiculed their attempts and thus wrote, "Where were these Samaritans? Why today so much love"![28] The PCC again and again published its directives for the voters not to select the rebels. Mohan Das was the Congress Candidate for Puri who faced a rebel live Banamali Das. The *Mahanta* of Emar *Matha* of Puri was also the candidate. Prananath Pattnaik was a candidate for Khurdha region. These socialists becoming candidates of the Congress took active part in the new era of power politics to check the complete monopoly of power brokers with the Congress.[29]

Even there were instances where the PCC did not produce necessary documents for its candidates. Govinda Chandra Mishra was selected as a candidate for Barchana constituency, but no leader went to his area to campaign. He was not provided with Congress Manifesto. So, the local workers demanded explanations from the PCC Secretary Bhagirathi Mohapatra in this regard.[30]

The district organisations also condemned the rebel candidates and asked the people to defeat them. The newspapers condemned an anti-Congress candidate in Banpur who tried to get the support of the dominating *Khandayat-kshyatriya*[31] caste people. As the voters had to cover at least ten to fifteen miles[32] to cast their votes at their *thana* offices, the candidates opened their offices in the nearby places, but the pro-government candidates hung skinned goats in front of their tents to attract the voters. *Mahaprasad* was distributed among the voters. In spite of these, the people took hearty meals from them but cast their votes in the yellow box.[33]

28. Satya Samachar, 20th January, 1937.
29. *Lokamata*, 6th January, 1937.
30. *Ibid.*, 17th February, 1937.
31. Asha, 10th January, 1937; Satya Samachar, 5th February, 1937.
32. Satya Samachar, 21st January, 1937.
33. Interview—Harekrushna Biswal.

The election ended with a thumping success to the Congress. It secured 36 seats out of its 40 candidates in the fray. But the Congress refused to form the ministry as it wanted an assurance from the Governor not to interfere in the works of the ministry. When the Governor of Orissa did not listen, the Congress gave a call to the people to observe *hartal* throughout the province. The *hartal* with full success, was observed in every corner of the province. After a few months, the Congress formed ministry. The local workers gave overwhelming receptions to their leaders.[34]

II

Growth of Power Politics and Factionalism in Provincial Congress Organisation

But the hidden intra-party conflict became surfaced. The faction-war got intensified when Nilakantha Das was not selected as the Prime Minister of Orissa. The Congress organisation in Orissa was already suffering from factionalism since 1936AD. A strong resentment had been originated against Nilakantha Das's style of functioning by his opponents. His opponents were Pranakrushna Padhiari, Harekrushna Mahtab, Binod Kanungo, Bhagirathi Mohapatra, etc. [35] The cause of this conflict was the clash of egoes among the leaders alongwith the question of morality in politics. Nilakantha Das was not a staunch Gandhian though he was the closest associate of Gopabandhu Das. Where Mahtab was famous for his organisational ability due to his shrewd maneavours. After the election the rebel candidates and their supporters were expelled from the Congress which intensified conflict within different district organisations of the Congress. The Congress was no longer a revolutionary organisation; it had assumed the role of a political party.

34. OSA, Home (Pol.), Confidential, File No. 5, 1937 (Orissa Police Abstract of Intelligence, 3rd April, 1937).
35. *Samaj*, 29th January, 1936.

Harekrushna Mahtab played the game well and tactically he deprived Nilakantha Das of the opportunity by selecting Biswanath Das from Ganjam District as the first Congress Prime Minister of Orissa.[36] The fiery Nilakantha Das with the help of his Puri District Congress force and his supporters in Ganjam and Sambalpur became a strong critic of the PCC and Ministry. A great-man like him who was the closest associate of Pandit Gopabandhu Das, and the Headmaster of National Schools of Satyabadi and Sambalpur, failed to retain his influence over the provincial Congress and indulged in intra-party fractional conflict.

Nilakantha Das published a newspaper *'Lokamata'* and reported, in detail, against Harekrushna Mahtab and the Biswanath Das Ministry. His reports based on facts because the Gandhians of contemporary and later years never doubted his honesty and integrity as an editor. By doing so he was trying to check the growth of hypocricy and bogus members of the organisation under the shadow of power politicians of the provincial Congress. He even formed a strong group of rebel members in the PCC and different DCCs and ran a parallel Congress organisation in the province. Expressing about this conflict, a devoted constructive Gandhian, Gopabandhu Chaudhury, later regretted that there were individual differences and rancours among Congress workers.[37] *'Lokamata'* published, "The Congress won the election by selling the name of Gandhi ..... zamindars (Some Congress ministers) got poor peoples' vote". [38] It also criticised Biswanath Das for taking Birakishore Ray as Advocate General who was a candidate against the Congress. It published in detail how Mr. Ray had attacked the Congress candidate, the party and its constructive programmes in filthy words by circulating

36. *Lokamata*, 17th February, 1937.

37. *Samaj*, 18th January, 1937, N.N. Mitra, Annual Register, 1938, Vol. I, January-June, Calcutta, 1938, p. 409.

38. *Lokamata*, 30th June, 1937.

leaflets. Though a reputed lawyer he had condemned the programmes like an illiterate, orthodox and unprogressive man. The content of the leaflet revealed thus,

> "The *Congressias* are liars, irreligious. The women are now behaving independently. They will now claim half of the property and will take *ghaita* on their own choice. The *Congressias* have misguided the women of the house taking them out of it and allowing them to mix freely with the males. People should be careful of these *Congressias*".[39]

The ministry, in spite of its many limitations, did some praiseworthy works and people felt the difference between it and the British administration. A newspaper however reported that after the assumption of the ministry the exploitation by the bureaucracy had increased.[40] It was also reported that some people taking the opportunity of their relationship with the Congress leaders were involved in some dubious activities.[41]

III

FRACTIONAL CONFLICT IN THE PCC AND ITS INFLUENCE ON THE DISTRICT CONGRESS COMMITTEES

The PCC had its members represented from different districts who were elected by the respective primary members of the primary committees. The DCC selected the candidates for Local and Districts Boards and municipalities. So the members of the DCC had a great say in the party affairs. Even the members who would represent the province at different conferences of the Congress outside Orissa were to be selected by the DCCs. But due to the growth of factionalism intensely, the six district Congress organisation were badly affected.

39. *Ibid.*, 25th August, 1937.
40. Desakatha, 28th September, 1937.
41. *Lokamata*, 25th August, 1937.

Regularly annual elections were held for the purpose of thorough democratisation of the party. But, pollution overcast the atmosphere when different factions fought among themselves to dominate the district organisations to influence the provincial Congress and the PCC ultimately.[42]

When the new PCC was formed, Nilakantha Das and his group expressed unhappiness.[43] To maintain his dominance over district organisation throughout Puri district, Nilakantha Das toured different places and instigated his supporters to form local Congress committees. Political conferences of different political groups were held at district level as well as at provincial level. Very often Congress workers of the districts of both the factions congregated to discuss position of the party and the national movement. Even constructive programmes and peasants' causes were highlighted.[44] But all these activities failed to provide any cementing force to different warring groups.

Every district organisation of the Congress had some active peasant activists who were working tirelessly to organise and agitate the cultivators and agricultural workers.[45] But seeing the growth of numerous peasant organisations at the grass-root level some anti-socialists within the Congress and others condemned their activities and expressed deep concern over the growing dominance of the peasant activists at the cost of national independence the main objective of the Congress movement. Even at some conferences the peasant organisers and other elements made[46] allegations against each other. Even Nilakantha Das, himself a champion of the peasants,

42. Newspapers like *Lokamata, Samaj,* Asha, Satya Samachar, Desakatha, etc. regularly published on these matters.
43. *Lokamata*, 3rd March, 1937.
44. *Ibid.*, 2nd June, 1937 and 14th March, 1938.
45. *Ibid.*, 30th July, 1937.
46. Satya Samachar, 9th June, 1937.

because of his dislike for the hypocrites and differences with Harekrushna Mahtab, criticised the socialists. His allegation was that the Congress workers were becoming more and more involved in peasant organisations disregarding other ideas and objectives of the Congress. He also expressed the fear that the peasant movement was becoming a threat to the Congress because of the independent nature and activities of the Congress socialists. He wanted proper definition of the peasants from the Congress to check the activities of the hypocrites. He asked the workers to take permission from the respective district committees to work for the peasant movement.[47]

The conflict in Ganjam DCC intensified when Dibakar Pattnaik of Nilakantha Das group developed differences with Umakanta Pattnaik, a sympathiser of Harekrushna Mahtab.[48] The PCC in the absence of Nilakantha group, took strong action against Dibakar Pattnaik for the alleged mis-appropriation of Congress fund.[49] This conflict became so open and vulgar that many newspapers condemned it. It was even reported that people were disgusted with these developments. It was thus published in *'Lokamata'*.

> "It is a well-known fact that the PCC has two groups... but whether anyone understands it or not, it is a fact that this deeply hurts the sentiment of those countless workers of the Congress who by their sacrifices, sufferings in and outside the jails have built the Congress provincial force by their flesh and blood. These workers will try to remain outside this disturbance. Rather their duty will be for the amicable settlement of the problem quickly".[50]

47. *Ibid.*, 16th June, 1937; *Lokamata*, 9th June, 1937 and 24th January, 1938.
48. *Samaj*, 12th January, 1938 and 19th January, 1938.
49. *Ibid.*, 19th January, 1938.
50. *Lokamata*, 14th March, 1938.

Even a Congress worker had threatened to go on fast upto death unless these conflicts ended quickly.[51] To settle the group conflict in PCC. Dr. P.C. Ghosh had come to Orissa. But many members left the meeting. Many workers of the Congress anticipated a weak Congress in near future if such types of conflict went on in Orissa Congress. Those left the meeting were mostly from Puri, Ganjam, Kuraput and Cuttack districts. They had formed a parallel Congress Organisation in the province.[52]

Annual elections were held in different districts to constitute the District Congress Committees. The districts were divided into different constituencies and different Congress members put their candidatures. Sometimes as many as four [53] candidates also contested for a single seat. These elections became very competitive. As the influential candidates were trying to be elected they recruited many more men into the Congress organisations as members of the primary Congress Committees. This was also a great factor for the growth of primary committees these days. Even in the district of Koraput, where the influence of the PCC was not very strong, numerous primary committees were formed. The offices of DCCs became more busy than before.[54]

In Berhampur Municipality election, the DCC elected its own candidates where some rebel candidates also contested the elcction.[55] The DCC became a big structure of small groups loyal to different leaders. Very often the DCCs interfered in the works and affairs of Local and District Boards, and even in the Municipal offices where the Congressmen were office-bearers. In 1939AD, the DCC selected its own candidates for three Local Boards in

51. Asha, 27th December, 1937.
52. *Samaj*, 19th January, 1938.
53. *Lokamata*, 4th April, 1938.
54. Interview—Ghanashyam Pati, Udayanath Sarangi; *Lokamata*, 27th June, 1938; Desakatha, 16th July, 1939.
55. *Samaj*, 23rd February, 1938.

Cuttack district.[56] Allegations were raised against the misappropriation of public money by some Congress members. The DCC was cautioned to select honest candidates for the election. Even some candidates, selected by the DCC, were ridiculed as grocers and doubts were raised about their honesty in office.[57]

It was also alleged that sometimes honest and straight forward candidates were not selected and occasionally workers of grassroots-level were considered for contest the elections. Those who were loyal to the leaders could get this opportunity. This attempt created a group of petty power-brokers within the organisation who got involved increasingly in factionalism to dominate the local Congress organisations. They were more busy to capture power than in devoting for national emancipation. Perhaps they became aware of the forthcoming opportunities within the Congress. This type of men gradually formed a strong and influential group within the Congress.[58]

The DCCs had three types of Congress workers. One, the constructive workers who were busy in different social programmes of Gandhi and were trying to remain outside the factionalism. Their loyalty to Gandhi and his doctrines were much greater than other groups. The second group was of the socialists. They had acknowledged Gandhi as the leader, used his techniques of movement, had faith, more or less, in constructive programmes, but did not stricity believe in non-violence and did not take part in naked politics. The third group were the power brokers, who used *Khadar*, actively participated in all types of Congress programmes, but in fact, many of them were hypocrites and were opportunists. After the formation of the ministry certainly their dominance in the organisation was felt. Surprisingly, many leaders of the PCC became members of this group. They had their sub-contractors

56. Desakatha, 27th May, 1939.
57. *Ibid.*
58. Interview—Udayanath Sarangi.

among the workers. This group laid the foundation of petty and selfish politics of power grabbing for decades to come. The socialists became vocal against these power-mongers and criticised them as pro-bourgeois in many instances, but could not check them.

These leaders and their camp followers became more careful in keeping the area primary committees under their influence. Even a leader dissuaded the workers from organising the Congress primary committees in his absence lest it would hamper his dominance in the locality. He faced stiff opposition form the members of the DCC who warned him not to interfere in the organisational work as he was elected as a MLA. All these destroyed the intra-party discipline. Nepotism within the Congress local organisation became rampart.[59]

IV

INSTITUTIONS OF LOCAL SELF-GOVERNMENT AND THE GANDHIANS

The common Gandhians in the countryside, irrespective of their loyalties and support to different ideas, participated in different elections held for the institutions of local self government. It is already indicated earlier how it affected the spirit of true nationalists among the workers because of factionalism within the organisation. The constructive workers, socialists and the power politicians—all worked hard to make the Congress successful in these elections. In spite of the selection of unjust candidates in some cases, the humble Gandhians obeyed the official directives to support the selected party candidates and to work for their victory.

During the elections, the constructive Gandhians never criticised or attacked personally any opponent candidates verbally. They tried to maintain a healthy

59. OSA, Home (Pol.), Confidential, File No. 5, *op.cit.* (10th August, 1937).

atmosphere during the campaigning. It was for the constructive Gandhians, the common people donated something regularly for the electoral expenditure. They did not encourage the people to raise derogatory slogans against the opponents.[60] But other Gandhians could not keep themselves in control and abused opponents publicly.

The Congress workers toiled hard to elect their party candidates. But lots of criticism were heard when the elected members assumed offices. Many of the elected Congress members were sometimes indulged in illegal practices and misused their powers. Some members of different Boards collected illegal money and accumulated wealth. These members did not care for Gandhian ideas of selfless social services and were indulged in many immoral acts disregarding public opinion.[61] They behaved themselves as small rulers over their subordinates and exploited the primary teachers and *pathasala* tutors,[62] who were under the supervision of the Boards. Even many were trying to get the blessings of the ministers to be supported as the chairman or office bearers of the Boards and Municipalities.[63] After their victories, these members as pseudo-zamindars tried to maintain false dignity among the people. They even went to the extent of earning quite a good amount of money from their travelling allowances.[64]

---

60. A. Maharana, "Kusuma Parase....", Sucharita (o), 12th year, No. 12, July, BBSR, 1987, p. 36; Questionnaire—Baikunthanath Mohanty.
61. Newspapers started ridiculing the members of these institutions of local-self government. *Desakatha*, published a small play ridiculing the board members in which the father said to the son, "Son, that man of our village is sending Rs. 40 to 50 every month working for the Congress. He has already purchased four to five acres of land but you speak that nobody gets anything if he works for the Congress. Then how he gets so much of money?" *Desakatha*, 23rd March, 1937.
62. *Ibid.*, 14th September, 1937.
63. *Lokamata*, 25th August, 1937 and Desakatha, 21st September, 1937.
64. Desakatha, 29th June, 1939.

The DCC issued directives to the candidates of the party regarding the eligibility and the minimum code of conduct. It highlighted the immediate local needs to woe the voters, and also prepared the Manifesto of the election and took full charge of the total campaigning. The candidates were asked to use *Khadar* regularly and were directed to fight the election in any sub-division of the district. They should not fight the election independently and work against the party's nominee in case they were not selected. The candidates after the election were advised to obey the directives of the DCC.[65] Thus there emerged a direct relationship between the Boards and the Municipalities in one side and the DCCs on the other, in which groupism and nepotism had already existed.

These institutions of local-self government created lots of low-paid job opportunities for the posts of clerks, peons, typists, primary and *pathasala* teachers and contractors for developmental[66] works and construction of buildings. Some people also got these jobs and contracts by the mercy of the Boards and Municipality office bearers.

The DCCs faced many problems within the district organisations.[67] In Cuttack district Harekrushna Mahtab interfered in a case in the selection of candidates and instigated his supporters to contest the election as rebel candidates disregarding the DCC directive.[68] Similarly when the DCC of Ganjam wanted to put the Congress candidates in Board election many people who were not the supporters of the Congress earlier and had tried to ruin the reputation of the Congress workers entered the organisation as candidates.[69] In Puri District, some socialists worked against the Congress candidates for Local or District Board election as they happened to belong

65. *Lokamata*, 19th September, 1938.
66. *Ibid.*, 14th March, 1938.
67. *Lokamata*, 17th January, 1938.
68. *Ibid.*, 14th March, 1938.
69. *Asha*, 29th September, 1937.

to Nilakantha Das's group.[70] These affairs considerably lowered the prestige of the Congress organisation in the eyes of the people. *'Deshakatha'* openly criticised that the members of Zilla Boards or Municipalities were not honest.[71] The selection of the candidates was also not proper. As they supported the leaders and used the names of Gandhi, they could become candidates. Even there were competitions among the elected members to be in supposed to be profitable committees.[72]

V

PRIMARY CONGRESS COMMITTEES AND THE POWER POLITICS

It is already mentioned that after the coming of the Congress Ministry to the power, primary Congress committees got mushroomed. In the six districts of the province almost in every corner there was a primary committee. The old Gandhians and the young *Banara senas* of the Salt Movement were still enthusiastically active.[73] They in collaboration with the socialists collected thousands of people as primary members of the Congress. Both socialist Gandhians and constructive Gandhians alongwith Congress politicians formed numerous peasant organisations. The entire peasantry and middle-class educated groups supported the Congress. Without any fear they came forward to be primary members when they saw the success of the Congress in the election and the emphasis given on peasants' cause by the socialists.[74] Thus by 1938, the Congress was really a party of poor and middle-class people except a very few dominating rich and pro-British elements. Poor and lower middle class

70. *Lokamata*, 17th January, 1938.
71. Desakatha, 29th June, 1939.
72. *Ibid.*, 21st July, 1939.
73. Interview—Harekrushna Biswal, Advaitaballav Ray, Sarat Chandra Maharana; Questionnaire—Haricharan Berma; Desakatha, 12th November, 1937.
74. Interview—Gokulamohan Raichudamani.

Brahmins, Karanas and *Khandayats* with other castes formed the strong supporting base of the organisation. Class interest of these people became prominent in the provincial Congress activity with their participation in various programmes.

To form a primary committee there should be more than fifty members in one or more villages. Atleast two *Khadar*-wearing officials should be ready to devote their whole time for the committee. After three months the DCCs or the PCC would investigate the matter to register it. Then the primary committee would be eligible to spend the collected fees to meet its own expenditure. The DCCs published the codes of conduct and by-laws for the primary members. The members should wear *Khadar* and would fight against untouchability and use of intoxicants. He, atleast, should work only two hours a month for the party. He would not do anything against the PCC or DCC's directives. He should submit the report of the activities to the DCC in every four months.[75]

Both temporary and permanent primary committees were recognised. The committees having more than fifty members were recognised as permanent and those having less than fifty members were called temporary.[76] People in Tirtol areas of Cuttack district became eager to be the members, but could not be because of their inability to pay the annual member-fees of four *annas*.[77] In Parlakhemundi *taluk* of Ganjam district, the workers worked hard to increase the number of the primary members, as there was less influence of the Congress because of the presence of Maha*Raja* Krushnachandra Gajapati Deo.* However, atleast five thousand members could be

75. *Samaj*, 19th January, 1938 and *Lokamata*, 27th June, 1938.
76. *Lokamata* repeatedly reported about the matter in the years 1937-39.
77. Satya Samachar, 29th September, 1937.

* He was the first Prime Minister of Orissa in 1937 when the Congress denied to form Ministry after the election.

enlisted from the said *taluk*.[78]

Gopabandhu Chaudhury in 1993AD, circulated a pamphiet for the incoming primary Congress members. The pamphlet expressed the following views,

> "..... Today the Congress is a big organisation. You should do something for the people and the country through primary committees, you discuss how your village can prosper, please keep your village clean and the atmosphere healthy. Keep the village money inside the village. Don't be misguided by the little pain and be satisfied with your coarse products. Try how to improve the quality of production. Don't be extravagant during marriage ceremonies and anniversaries or festivals. Use your village *panchayats* to settle your disputes amicably. The *panchayat* should be neutral and no coercion should be practised. Don't impose fine or social castigation on anybody. It is not good to be afraid of British injustice. If you are frightened your neighbour will follow you. They all will be encouraged. It will harm your national self-respect and prosperity. So drive out the fear and oppose the injustice with the help of truth and non-violence. Don't be idle. Idleness makes a man violent. He who does not work or produce anything depends on others labour becomes jealous to others. This creates intoxicants. It destroys the rationality and ruins the prosperity. Encourage your fellow villagers to stop taking such things. Every human being has the God *Narayan* in his body. Don't make a man untouchable and so don't insult the God. To save the Hindu religion eradicate the ghost of untouchability. As we have made out own brothers untouchable we are also treated as same by the foreigners. If we do not stop this, the atrocities on us by the foreigners would not stop".[79]

78. *Asha*, 1st August, 1938.
79. A. Maharana, *op.cit*.

From this one can see how emphasis on personal conduct of a Congress member was given. The importance of Gandhian principles on social behaviour for the common workers —who were generally called as *chelahs* of Gandhi *Maharaj*, was emphasised to maintain Gandhian nature of the movement.

There were, 1,96,980 primary Congress members in the province by 21st November, 1938AD [80] against 52,000 in February 1922AD. So from this mammoth number one could well imagine the popularity, stature and hold of the provincial Congress. The number of Common Gandhians grew considerably. The number of constructive workers remained more or less same and their programmes were not felt necessary to be highlighted. The number of peasant activists increased in these days because of the intense activities of the socialists. The anti-feudal and anti-British movements in different *Garhjats* and Zamindaris saw the spread of Gandhi's influence there. Though the activists here did not become primary Congress members except in a few cases, many of them followed many Gandhian ideas and techniques. The constructive Gandhians, socialists and peasant activists as well as some Gandhian activists in *Garhjats* and Zamindaris formed the class of real common Gandhians who were committed to the people.

But these modern educated elites, who took the leadership from the orthodox traditional leaders, could not check the growth of hypocrites in the organisation. The number of those real Gandhians did not grow considerably though the number of primary members grew to a large extent. Respect for Gandhism and aim to be champion of people's cause were absent in many of the new-comer opportunists. Consequently, in spite of the presence of thousands committed social workers and committed

80. *Asha*, 21st November, 1938. (It reported that there were 58,878 members in Cuttack, 27,714 in Puri, 28,292 in Balasore, 23,455 in Ganjam, 50,048 in Koraput and 8, 551 in Sambalpur districts).

Gandhians, the non-believers in peoples' cause gradually increased their influence to prepare their stronghold for the future.

VI

THE SOCIALIST GANDHIANS AND THE MINISTRY

It is already mentioned that the socialists of the provincial Congress became champions of the peasants and agricultural workers and, thus, strengthened the area of the Congress influence further. Though, they differed from many of Gandhi's ideas, accepted his entire techniques. They were supporters of the constructive programmes. But they were a strong group of bitter critics of the Ministry. They forced the Ministry to initiate measures against the zamindars and ably introduced certain bills-pro-people in nature, to be passed in the Assembly. They never criticised Gandhi or constructive workers and were pretty aware of their influence over the masses.[81]

The socialists targeted the zamindars of their attack irrespective of their party loyalities. Even the zamindars among the supporters of the Congress were not spared. They asked people to protest the illegal actions of the zamindars and to stop paying excess exacts and presents.[82] The socialists organised separate conferences to mobilise the common people. A socialist organisation called 'Cuttack District *Krishak Sammilani*' was held on 30th April, 1937 at Anakhia which was attended by five thousand peasants including one hundred school teachers. Here the leaders openly acknowledged the Congress as

81. Interview—Gokulamohan Raychudamani, Udayanath Sarangi; Questionnaire—Lokanath Senapati; *Lokamata*, 10th February, 1937; S.N. Dwivedi, Mo Jivan Sangram O Ardha Satabdira Samajvadi Andolanara Kahani (O), Cuttack, 1984, pp. 81-84; R.C. Ram, *op.cit.*, p. 9, J.K. Samal, *op.cit.*, p. 22.
82. OSA, Home (Pol), Confidential File No.-5, *op.cit.*, (24th May, 1937).

their mother organisation. All India *Krishak* Day was observed at Cuttack which attended by more than ten thousand people.[83]

The socialists tried for the introduction of some reforms in the Assembly by mobilising the peasants. These were really remarkable and beneficial for the peasantry of the province. But it is alleged that these reforms benefitted the middle[84] class peasants at the cost of the zamindars and the poor people could not be benefitted from it. However the province had large number of marginal farmers. Introduction of ownership of land, reduction of different revenues also largely benefited these marginal farmers. They became strong supporters of the Congress. This also created a hope among the poor people.

But factionalism in the provincial Congress organisation did not allow any of the groups to work freely. If one group worked for a cause other highlighted its negative aspects without any concern for the cause for which the former was fighting. Some zamindars were also socialists in Orissa whose dubious activities for the cause of peasants was criticised by the opponents. The workers in a conference at Balanga in Puri district made a resolution to the effect that Congress members who happened to be zamindars should set an example by abolishing in their Zamindaris or *Maqdamis* the land registration fees against which peasants had been struggling. But this resolution was suspected as a move by Nilakantha Das's group to embarass Harekrushna Mahtab who was also a champion of peasants cause and was also a Zamindar.[85] Thus, though different groups openly and repeatedly acknowledged their loyalty to the Indian National Congress, they weakened the organisation in the province and created unhealthy atmosphere. Personal rivalry of the leaders became quite open at the

83. *Ibid.*, (3rd May, 1937).
84. J.K. Samal, *op.cit.*
85. OSA, Home (Pol.), Confidential, *op.cit.*, (24th April, 1937).

cost of peasant's cause. It is even found that common workers of both of the groups worked separately for a single cause. In his mission to criticise the hypocrites Nilakantha Das found himself as the leader of the opponents of the socialists.

The conflict between socialists and their opponents became worse when the workers started abusing each other openly.[86] When socialists in some cases arranged meetings of the peasants they campaigned against their opponents. Parallel peasant organisations and conferences were formed and even on some occasions, the socialists and their opponents indulged in verbal duels. Sometimes, meetings of the peasants turned to meaningless symposiums for the illiterate common peasants.[87]

The opponents declared that the success of the so-called socialists in mobilising the peasants was untrue. Their mouthpiece, *'Lokamata'* described how ignorant villagers gathered in the meetings arranged by the socialists without having any knowledge in socialism, peasants' cause, their rights and equality etc. Reporting about the congregation of more than 10,000 people at Cuttack on the occasion of the 'All India *Krishak Sangha* Day', another newspaper opined that the peasants of the villages had come to attend the meetings not influenced by socialism but for Gandhi's name. They came there wit the idea that the disciples of Gandhi were doing something beneficial for them and so they attended it. The newspaper expressed the view that it was the magic spell of Gandhi on the people that attracted them to attend the meetings of the socialists. The socialists, in fact, according to it, could not succeed in mobilising the people with their own ideologies alone.[88]

86. *Lokamata*, 9th June, 1937 and 17th January, 1938.
87. OSA, Home (Pol.), Confidential, *op.cit.*, (24th April, 1937); Satya Samachar, 24th February, 1937 and 2nd June, 1937.
88. Desakatha, 7th September, 1937 and Satya Samachar, 8th September, 1937.

Even the allegations spread that zamindars who were also socialists and vocal supporters of peasants' cause, collected marriage fees from subjects of their Zamindaris.[89] The socialists of Orissa were also criticised because of their inability to start peasant movements in the Zamindaris of certain influential Congress leaders.[90]

The socialist in the garb of Congress were criticised as hypocrities who gave false assurance to the people before the election and forgot it later. The Congress was branded as the party of the Zamindars. Doubts were raised whether those zamindars would be able to support the Congress where the socialists came out successful in mobilising the peasants against them.[91] They were called as pro-bourgeois who were not really the champion of the peasants. It was also alleged that some became socialists because many of them were zamindars and landlords and wanted to maintain their hegemony over the people and control political temperature and awakening of masses which might turn a threat for them. The *'Lokamata'* thus expressed its views,

> "......The middle class people are always clever.... They can change their colour with the change of time.... The zamindars when realised that Gandhi's movement would destroy British administration and also their own dominance, they, so, wanted to take the power from the government into their hands to rule the people. Many changed their dress, wore loin clothes, talked high about socialism. They told the people that the government is sole responsible for these miseries.... They assured the people that they will make them very prosperous if they voted them to power. They got power, but after this when the *Chasas* started talking against them they said the people to

89. *Ibid.*, 24th August, 1937.
90. *Lokamata*, 7th February, 1938.
91. *Ibid.*, 30th June, 1937.

fight against the government and to drive them out".[92]

The periodical also contained that the selfish socialist leaders instigated the people to fight for the reduction of revenue after which they would listen to them. The paper ridiculed further these socialists in their own language thus,

> "We remember your demand and write it down. If we cannot fulfill your demand our sons and grandsons will fulfill it. You sacrifice more. The difference between us would be settled later......."[93]

The true socialists, through few in number, in fact, fought a great war these years and worked untidily and restlessly for the cause of the peasants in collaboration with other Gandhian workers. Many of them were firebrands and respected figures in the organisation. They even fought with their brethren in the Congress on this issue without hesitation. In spite of the presence of some zamindars among them, they succeeded in mobilising the people to demand for their due rights. However, the peasant movement in Orissa became weak when power-politicians gradually dominated the scene and the ministry gradually avoided the peasants cause. Socialism in Orissa could not thrive in spite of the presence of few ranked leaders, because the young men of the group who had been shouting so loudly became silent gradually.[94] The growth of power-brokers never gave the socialist opportunity to lead the Congress in their own way of thinking, so far as the Orissa Provincial Congress was concerned.

But, the socialist members of various district Organisation formed their respective district level socialist organisation. The Puri district 'Congress *Samyavadi Sangh*' was formed under the presidentship of Mohan Das and Gokul Mohan Ray Chudamani as secretary. It appealed

92. *Ibid.*, 9th June, 1937.
93. *Lokamata*, 9th June, 1937.
94. Desakatha, 27th May, 1939.

the government to take step for the deaths due to starving and exploitations. Other socialist workers became engaged in different pro-peasant programmes.

VII

ANTI-FEUDAL AND ANTI-BRITISH MOVEMENTS IN GARHJATS AND ZAMINDARIES OF ORISSA

Gandhian movement in British Orissa had its repercussion in the *Garhjats* and Zamindaris. The Zamindari of Kanika had already witnessed the growth of a Gandhian way of Non-violence and *Satyagraha* movement against its king. The Salt Movement also had its strong impact in the area. In the years of 1937-39AD. The oppression of the *Raja* of Kanika was at its highest point. Chakradhar Behera, an activist and a Congress candidate got elected defeating kings' candidate, Girish Chandra Ray. So king's people inflicted oppression on the common people. The king used castes against castes to divide the people to weaken the movement. Chakradhar Behera visited his constituency repeatedly and with the help of the Congress ministry pressurised the king to reduce his atrocities. Village organisations were formed and *Charakha* centres were opened. Trained Instructors were invited to teach in these institutions. Gandhians of the area very enthusiastically became active in different developmental work after the formation of the ministry.[95]

The *Garhjats* also felt the warmth of the movement. The local educated and conscious people formed the leadership among the *Garhjat* people who were restless to start an agitation. In these years in many *Garhjats*, people started agitation with open support from the provincial Gandhian leaders and workers, in spite of the reluctance of the Congress. Though the movement was not strictly Gandhian in nature so far as the concept of Non-violence

95. G.D. Behera, Kanika Biplaba (O), Chandabali, Balasore, 1987, p. 122; M.D. Mallick, Biplabi Chakradhar (O), Haladia, Cuttack, 1973, p. 77 and pp. 143-50.

was concerned, in many respects, the people followed Gandhian techniques and used Gandhi's name as the symbol of their agitation. Even many local activists followed Gandhi's ideas personally and were deeply influenced by Gandhi's concern for the poor people. Many of them also claimed themselves Gandhians. They used Gandhi's name to attract the common people and also to infuse confidence in them. *'Mahatma Gandhi Ki Jai'* was their war-cry and they used the techniques of *Satyagrahas,* Non-Co-Operation, marches and realise to express their anguish. Many started Gandhian constructive programmes in their own areas, thus, strengthening Gandhian nature of the movement in the *Garhjats.*

The support of the Congress ministry of Orissa and also of Gandhi in 1938 onwards gave them a moral boost. The socialist Gandhians of Orissa openly supported[96] the people of *Garhjats* in organising and guiding the agitations properly.

In the princely state of Dhenkanal the agitating people were organised in 1938AD. But the movement did not follow non-violence strictly, in spite of the presence of some Gandhians among the activists. Many *Ashrams* were established to recruit volunteers. Some of Gandhi's constructive programmes like *Khadar* spinning and removal of untouchability were adopted. Many *Harijans* also became workers of the movement.[97] Some agitators used *Khadar.* In their personal lives they were against untouchability and called them proudly as *Satyagrahis.*[98]

The followers of Gandhi in Dhenkanal worked hard to organise the people and lead various processions against the king. Around 100 Gandhians including many socialists in different groups entered the state from

96. S.N. Dwivedi, *op.cit.*
97. Questionnaire—Balakrushna Nayak.
98. *Ibid.*, Prabhakar Swain; Souvenir, Mahanti Pradhan, Dhenkanal, 1987, pp. 12-13.

different sides to help the local Gandhians and faced the wrath of the state police alongwith the people. They were arrested and were kept in jails.[99] Some of them were brutally manhandled by king's police.

The Gandhian nature of the Dhenkanal movement during the years of 1938-39AD was very much purposeful. The people enthusiastically took Gandhi's photographs or tricolour with them during the processions.[100] The movement turned violent in many cases, through, the agitators called themselves *Satyagrahis*.[101] Their peaceful activities could not remain Non-violent when the police brutally attacked them.[102] Pabitra Mohan Pradhan, leader of the Talcher movement, did not appreciate the violent retaliation of the *Satyagrahis* of Dhenkanal as it lost the Gandhian nature.[103]

On the other hand the Talcher movement following Gandhi's principles of non-violence gradually realised its momentum and became very famous in India. Pabitra Mohan Pradhan claimed that the movement strictly followed Gandhian principles of non-violence and truth for which it had the blessings of Gandhi. Volunteer groups were formed and around 1400 such workers joined the volunteer camps to be *Satyagrahis*. They faced police atrocities bravely. This Non-Co-Operation and Non-violent Civil Dis-obedience really astonished other Gandhians. When the oppression of the king became intolerable, people around 60,000 in number left the state en-masse to Angul and other British Orissa regions. The refugees were kept in different camps. The constructive Gandhians came to the camps to educate the people in

99. Souvenir, Mahanti Pradhan, *op.cit.*; Samaj, 21st December, 1938.
100. B.K. Dhal, Bhulibu Nahin (O), BBSR, 1980, p. 3.
101. NMML, AISPC, File No.-127/255, No.-35, (18th November, 1938); *Samaj*, 21st December, 1938; S.N. Dwivedi, *op.cit.*
102. B.K. Dhal, *op.cit.*, pp. 36-71 & 82-91; *Samaj*, 26th October, 1938.
103. P.M. Pradhan, Mukti Pathe Sainik (O), Cuttack, 1949, pp. 50-54.

spinning for self-sufficiency. *Satyagrahis* including many Gandhians were arrested. They lost crops of one year. Their families suffered a lot as they were did the targets of the king. But when the Viceroy of India, forced the king, the latter fulfilled many demands of the *Satyagrahis*.[104]

In Nilgiri the *Satyagraha* movement was in full swing. The Congress Ministry supported it. The *Satyagrahis* refused to pay the fines imposed on them. More than 10,000 people gathered at the local car festival to demonstrate against the king. But R.L. Bezellgate, political agent of Orissa *Garhjats*, unleased intolerable atrocities and oppression on them.[105] The *Satyagrahis* rushed to the adjoining *Mughulbandi* areas.[106] Leaflets were circulated. When oppression[107] by the king increased the Congress leaders asked the agitators to discontinue the movement. In Khandapara, the activists with the help of their supporters defied the order of the king and formed primary Congress members.[108] In Keonjhar the police seized two *Charakhas* from a spinning centre incidentally and remarked that it was a heinous crime to possess *Charakha*. *Charakha* was declared as mis-possession. Activists were arrested and were sentenced to imprisonment.[109]

Though the movement in states were claimed as Gandhian in style, in many instances it became violent. The growth of large number of activists also contributed largely for this. The tactics of *Satyagraha* was frequently adopted which was really suitable to the unarmed mob.

---

104. *Ibid.*, pp. 54-92; S.N. Pattnaik, *op.cit.*, pp. 145-46; A. Mishra, Talachera Andolana (O), Talcher, p. 25.
105. Compilation, Nilagiri States Peoples' Movement, Balasore, 1982, pp. 32-34.
106. S.N. Pattnaik, *op.cit.*, p. 147.
107. NMML, AISPC, File No.-127/157 and File No.-127/277.
108. Questionnaire—Reghunath Singh Samant.
109. NMML, AISPC, 127/251 (14th September, 1938); N.M. Mitra, Annual Register, 1938, Vol.-II, July-December, 1938, Calcutta, p. 297.

The illiterate local youths and activists were not able to follow the principle of Non-violence strictly in face of brutal police action. Opponents of the *Garhjat* Movements criticised these as not Gandhian in nature rather these were violent and hence should not be called as *Satyagrahas.*[110] But influence of Gandhi and his ideals could be well found in these movements and there were some activists who were more or less Gandhians. These *Garhjats* were mostly the adjoining areas of coastal areas. The tribals were yet to be agitated openly through Gandhian movement. In these princely states mostly caste Hindus and non-tribals became organised.

VIII

ROLE OF CONSTRUCTIVE GANDHIANS

This group of Gandhians was the most disciplined and well versed in the ideas of Gandhi. Personally they followed many of Gandhi's principles in their lives. They were expert in spinning and were regularly weaving and wearing *Khadar*. They were self-sufficient in their personal lives and most of them were living in different *Ashrams* or in their own houses which were tiny hermitages. They obeyed Gandhi's directives and as obedient primary workers of the party never disobeyed the directives of the PCC or district committees. Their respect within the party and in the power politics of the party and tried their level best to be very far from factionalism. It was this group within the province, that was responsible for the continuity of Gandhi's sway over the common people thorough the constructive programmes.[111]

When Congress ministry was formed in June 1937 Gandhi's emphasis for basic educations was taken into consideration. For *'Nai Talim'* Mahesh Chandra Pradhan, Sarat Chandra Maharana, Raghunath Mohanty on behalf

110. Deshakatha, 27th May, 1939.
111. Interview—Sarat Chandra Maharana, Annapurna Maharana and Udayanath Sarangi; A. Maharana, "Kusuma...", *op.cit.*, pp. 63-65.

of the government of Orissa went to Wardha. A Board of Basic Education was formed under Gopabandhu Chaudhury and Kishore Chandra Panda, Srinivas Mishra, Kanhu Charan Mohanty, Lalatendu Pattnaik, Gouranga Charan Das as its members.[112] Meanwhile, with the growth of the number of primary members the sales of *Khadar* increased, [113], but it was not so much satisfying as compared to the vast number of members. It was alleged that if the members used one *Dhoti* and a napkin the *Khadi* programme would get atleast Rs. 40,000 a year, which was a very healthy figure.

Ramadevi proposed to hold a conference of 'Gandhi *Seva Sangha'* in Orissa. A village was to be selected as the conference was scheduled to be held in rural area. Berboi of Delang (Puri) was selected. Arrangement was made to meet the expenditure of at least one thousand people a day. The Gandhians collected vegetables, coconuts, milk and the nearby *Brahmin* villages (*Sasanas*) gave coconut leaves which were used to thatch the entire area of the conference pandal and exhibition stalls. Women from the nearby villages were invitied to prepare varieties of *pithas* for the guests.[114] The states ministry donated Rs.1,000/- for the conference.[115]

There were around 2000 volunteers at Berboi including sixty women. *'Utkal Gandhi Seva Sangha'* sent 150 volonteers. Local handicraft experts were invited. The Conference was well-attended by village people.[116] Gandhians of other districts were invited. Many spontaneously came to observe these rarer incidents which was inaugurated by Gandhiji himself on 25th March, 1938. School teachers came with their students

112. A. Maharana, "Kusuma Parase....", *op.cit.*
113. Desakatha, 12th November, 1937.
114. A. Maharana, *op.cit.*, pp. 51-53.
115. *Samaj*, 16th February, 1938.
116. *Lokamata*, 4th April, 1938.

to visit the exhibition.[117]

The Secretary of *Utkal Charakha Sangha*, Krupasindhu Panda meanwhile appealed the people of Orissa to support this sacred programme which had deep rooted meanings related to social self-sufficiency and patriotic feelings. He informed that the other provinces of India, variábles articles were being made in *Khadi Kendras* and these had great market in those provinces. In Orissa there were also scope for the development of such indigenous arts. But the educated people of Orissa had the tendency to buy goods made outside in spite of the good quality of indigenous products like *Sambalpuri* Sarees, Berhampur *Patas*, Kendupatna *Masaries*. To meet the demand of cotton in Orissa, cultivation was encouraged by providing quintals of seeds to different districts.[118] Spinning centres were opened in flood-prone areas. The president of the Cuttack district Congress had appealed to *Utkal Charakha Sangha* to open spinning centres at different places. But side by side he demanded relief works for the flood-affected areas immediately like boats, money, temporary huts. He had also demanded thousands of rupees from the government to establish *Khadar Kendras*.[119]

But these constructive workers gradually became more and more isolated from the Congress mainstream in the province because of the growth of intense power politics and naked factionalism. They remained away from it, so could not come to the limelight. Their number was static. Their lives were no longer followed as examples by other new hypocrite Gandhians. Though highly esteemed among the Congress workers and members, their rank and file did not grow substantially as in case of power-mongering Gandhians in these years in spite of the imminent success of the Gandhian Movement. Constructive programmes of Gandhi were

117. Questionnaire—Lokanatha Senapati.
118. Navin, 1st August, 1939.
119. *Ibid.*, 26th September, 1939.

losing their grounds and becoming more and more symbolic in nature. Most of the members of the provincial Congress were interested in factionalism and naked power politics disregarding Gandhian ideas—committed to the common people. To be a Congress member or even a Gandhian, one need not have to follow any Gandhian principles in life. *Khadar* dress was enough to be identified as a Gandhian among the people without any commitment.

The constructive Gandhian along with socialist, in some respects, could retain Gandhian nature of the national movement in Orissa in these years. Real commitments to the people's cause was their objective which was conspicuously absent among the power brokers. But without caring their growing dominance, the constructive Gandhians became engaged in their duties and were eagerly awaiting Gandhi to take any novel step.

IX

CONDITION OF THE GANDHIANS

When the ministry was formed the Common Gandhians had rejoiced the occasion. Subsequently the intra-party factionalism went to its height. Some of the Congress workers taking the opportunity of this conflict benefitted themselves by supporting either of the camps. On the other hand, the ministers did not look at the miserable condition of the common workers. The true Gandhians did not like to approach their leaders for their personal benefit or they did not demand the ministry to do some favour for them in spite of requests made through newspapers. *'Deshakatha'* wrote,

> "The leaders didn't remember those men—who, one day, had suffered a lot. They were mercilessly beaten up by the police. They were dragged by neck on the rough roads. They with the word `Gandhi' on their lips made the Congress in province very powerful. Who propagated the ideas of Gandhi in villages? Our

leaders had fulfilled their financial aspirations by elevating themselves to the height. Where were the leaders in those days when the workers were suffering a lot by the hands of police. Their rice bowls were snatched away or broken. At that time the leaders fled away from the scene and absconded. Many went into the interior of their Zamindaries. Some declared their retirement from politics to avoid police. One or two told that they were going to their father-in-law's house to take rest. If they had come out by that time they had to bear the *lathi* of the police. Their lands could have been mortgaged.... The workers of Orissa and the people of Orissa are really honest but they are always exploited by selfish men who claimed themselves Gandhians. *Mahatma* have called them as third class Gandhians. We see the workers suffer a lot because of their poverty. Being influenced by the leaders and also Gandhi and also out of their impuse they untimely left the study and ruined their future. They had no means to maintain their household life. But the leaders do not see." [120]

'Lokamata' also wrote,

"Due to the Congress workers in Orissa the province has been maintaining a reputed place in the National struggle. During Non-Co-Operation, Salt and *Satyagraha* movement, Oriya Congress workers were not left behind the workers of other provinces. In the last election Orissa made the Congress victorious in its first major electoral battle and it was possible only for these humble workers of the provincial Congress. The leaders with the help of their position in the party had misused the power...."[121]

While the role of true common Gandhians were highly praised, the activities of the bogus Congress members were

120. Desakatha, 12th October, 1937.
121. *Lokamata*, 7th March, 1938.

ridiculed. Criticism on them were rampant in these days and no sympathy was expressed in their favour. It was also alleged that among these two lakhs of primary Congress members only a thousand were true Gandhians. These one thousand Gandhians[122] were the active full-time constructive workers. But there were true Gandhians living in their villages who were working within their capabilities.

In spite of the mammoth membership of the provincial Congress, the achievement of the Congress in Orissa was nothing but the electoral success. Nothing was done for the national movement except collecting primary members[123] and fighting elections in the institutions of local self government. These dummy members were used by the leaders to strengthen their own position. *'Lokamata'* observed,

> "Now-a-days people do not believe in the speeches of the Congress leaders. The Congress which was built on the basis of truth, non-violence and sacrifice now is deeply affected by violence and selfish desire."[124]

Some unemployed men turned Gandhians joining primary committees and collected member fees.* Funds on different occasions were collected regularly[125] in the pretext of different causes, which was also severely criticised by the newspapers. How the members of

122. *Ibid.*, 23rd May, 1938.

123. *Ibid.*

124. *Ibid.*, 5th September, 1938.

* "There is an unemployed Congress leader in Puri. Everyday he rises early and approaches the people to be the members of the Congress contributing 4 Annas. By this way if he gets prey he keeps three annas in lieu of office expenditure and rest, one anna he sends to the DCC. The office expenditure is nothing but his own household expenditure", Desakatha, 29th July, 1939.

125. Desakatha, 19th November, 1939.

Congress primary committees in an area became unruly and man-handled a sub-inspector who had gone to investigate a theft case, was also reported. It marked the presence of unwanted elements within the Congress at lower level who could turn violent disregarding Gandhian principles even during normal time.[126]

X

ACTIVITIES OF GANDHIANS IN OTHER PROGRAMMES

To check the atrocities of the zamindars over their subjects Nilakantha Das, now being the member of the Congress along with Godabarish Mishra, went to Kakarudrapur and Balianta where they organised the meetings of the peasants. Though not a socialist, these leaders awakened the peasants against their exploiters.[127] By that time the Chinese people were going through a great crisis of their history. To help the people of China, some primary Congress committee of villages had gathered funds performing *Sankirtan*.[128] *'China Diwas'* was observed and Japanese aggression was severely condemned and donations were sent to the external affairs office of All India Congress Committee. In spite of the opposition from the local landlords the people formed primary Congress Committees.[129]

In 'Bari, where Constructive Gandhians had established a model Gandhian centre for self-sufficiency, a primary committee was formed making Gopabandhu Chaudhury as president. It is not-able to mention that a top leader line Gopabandhu Chaudhury could be a member of a local Congress primary Committee. This was a rare example of simplicity and belief in equality exemplified by a great leader like Gopababu. The

126. OSA, Home (Pol), Confidential, File No.-6, 3rd June, 1937.
127. *Samaj*, 12th January, 1938.
128. *Ibid*.
129. *Ibid*., 19th January, 1938.

members were 155 and they took oath to work for the general hygiene during natural calamities, to organise the peasants against landlords and prohibition.[130]

On 26th January, 1938, Independence Day was observed by the Gandhians. In all *Ashrams* and District Offices the Day was observed. Oaths [131] were taken and Bye-laws were circulated.

XI

All these allegations were natural because of the sudden growth of the number of the primary Congress members and many of them not being socialised in the ways of the Gandhian movement. It is a fact that increasingly the leaders were criticised and accused and very few workers were also pin-pointed for their dubious activities. But the real common Gandhians of the provincial Congress organisations were never, in general, criticised. They were still working within their own limits to continue the spirit of nationalism. After the death of Pandit Gopabandhu Das, no leader became successful to reach his stature and popularity. It was the guiding spirit of Gandhi and the presence of many true and staunch Gandhians who saved the provincial Congress from its downfall. It was the power politicians including many PCC leaders, who misused the members to dominate the Congress in the province to maintain their hegemony. The presence of petty power brokers was felt this time within the organisation. They gradually captured the party's organisational affairs. Their selfish intentions polluted the Congress atmosphere and unhealthy precedents were created. Honour of the party in the public eye lowered. A frustrated Nilakantha Das was trying to retire from the Congress and he hobnobbed sometimes with Netaji Subhas Chandra Bose and finally had to be expelled from the Congress in spite of his decades long service for the

130. *Ibid.*, 23rd February, 1938.
131. *Ibid.*, 21st February, 1938.

organisation. Constructive Gandhians, through, were working for the Congress, were active in the elections just as obedient workers of the organisation but were not enthusiastic enough. The socialists were gradually becoming frustrated and their silence was the victory of power-brokers within the Congress.

The ministry, in spite of the presence of a group of power-mongers, had done some good things. People felt the difference between the administration of a foreign power and the Congress. The Congress had proved itself as a party of entire lower and middle class agrarian society. Poor working class also were benefited out of the reforms. The states' activists became quite successful in agitating the people. But due to the compromising attitude of the leaders of the provincial Congress they could not achieve their goals in spite of their strong positions. The common Gandhians having commitment to the people's cause were watching the scene eagerly. Gandhi was not so vocal and he had yet to speak anything novel. Though these years were taken as a glaring phase of the Congress movement, it was in fact, the period of the power-brokers, and the 'Third Class Gandhians'—a name given by Gandhi himself.

5

Gandhian Movement in Orissa : The Last Phase (1939—47 AD)

With the outbreak of the Second World War on 3rd September, 1939 the political scenario of India witnessed dramatic changes one after another in quick succession till partition and independence of India on 15th August, 1947. The mass-based Gandhian movement reached its final phase. The Quit India Movement of August 1942 proved Gandhi the most successful mass mobiliser in India. The committed Gandhians, who were restless due to the growth of naked selfish politics within the organisation, felt relieved when Gandhi wanted all his co-workers to engross in this historic political movement which seemed much bolder and clearer than those of previous years. The common Gandhians of Orissa, irrespective of group loyalties, made the movement successful. The British could realise the actual strength of the Gandhian movement so far as the involvement of the masses was consumed. The high political temperature of the Quit India Movement united different sections of Gandhians in Orissa for the time being. Power-politics and groupism were also put aside.

I

EVENTS BEFORE THE OUTBREAK OF QUIT INDIA MOVEMENT : 1940—42 AD

When the Second World War broke out, the British

administrative structure in Orissa also became busy in war efforts. The Gandhians in Orissa were watching the events with interest. The Congress wanted the British to give up her imperial and colonial domination on India and arrange for a reasonable quantum of self-government by the Indians themselves. The British did not accept the demand and offered concessional recommendations which the Congress did not accept.

When the authorities opened military camps in many places of coastal Orissa, the people became frightened and started migrating to nearby urban areas. The authorities banned bonfires, seized boats and cycles and the canals made dry.[1] The rates of daily use commodities rose higher and higher. The Gandhians entered the villages and asked the people to be calm but fearless. The voice of the common people increasingly rose against the government.[2]

Repeated failure of crops widened people's despair. Their pitiable condition worsened when price hike continued and commodities of daily use became dearer. The people became more frightened when the Oriya repatriates from Burma described the horrors of war in the eastern world.[3] The military exploits of Japan against the Allies was seen with a great curiosity and surprise by the common Oriyas who had a strong feeling of invincibility for British might. The Gandhians, who were living in villages, could realise the vulnerable position of the British. The eagerness of the British to get the support of the National Congress was seen by these common Gandhians as the right time to win over the colonialists.[4]

---

1. S.N. Pattnaik, Orissare Swadhinata Andolana (O), Cuttack, 1972, p. 166; Nabin, 24th September, 1940; B.R. Mohanty, August Biplaba (O), Cuttack, 1962, pp. 114-24.
2. A. Maharana "Kusuma Parase....", Sucharita, 13th year, No.5, Bhubaneswar, December, 1987.
3. Nabin, 17th March, 1942; Degar, 4th year No. 9, 1941.
4. Interview—Harekrushna Biswal, Advaitballav Ray, Gunanidhi Patra.

'August Offer' of 1940 AD was rejected by the Congress and Gandhi decided to launch an individual Civil-Disobedience Movement. His primary objectives were to symbolise the Congress protest against participation in war without consultation. Some selected individuals among the Congress workers were to recite in public a set formula of anti-war slogan. From Orissa Gandhi selected twentynine Congressmen as individual *Satyagrahis* and the PCC empowered the DCCs to select workers to launch *Satyagraha* individually in their own localities. Pranakrushna Padhiary was the first Oriya individual *Satyagrahi*. In Koraput district the primary committees were numerous and the tribals were taking active part in different Gandhian programmes. Many common Gandhians offered individual *Satyagraha* in this district.[5]

Those who were selected by the PCC, their biodatas were sent to Gandhi for final selection of *Satyagrahis*. These selected Gandhians went to different places and in the meetings publicly condemned the war policy of the government. They had to stay in any particular place only for twenty-four hours and had to move to another place to offer *Satyagraha*. Generally most of them were arrested at the second meeting.[6]

But the selection of these *Satyagrahis* was not free from controversy. It was reported that the old well-known common Gandhians were not informed or asked to offer *Satyagraha*. They were not provided with the printed format to express their willingness to be *Satyagrahis*. It was also reported that those who were interested to be ministers and presidents of the Unions were enlisted as *Satyagrahis*. As this group did not like some other popular

---

5. S.N. Pattnaik, *op.cit.*, pp. 162-64; N.R. Pattnaik, Swadhinata Andolanare Orissara Adivasi Laxaman Nayak (O), BBSR., 1990, p. 91; G.N. Mohanty, Dhulimatira Santha(O), Cuttack, 1985, p. 243.
6. A. Maharana, *op.cit.*

eminent social workers to challenge their monopoly in these affairs, they cleverly selected the workers from their own camps.[7]

Meanwhile Pandit Nilakantha Das and his friend Dibakar Pattnaik having no faith in this type of movement, interpreted individual *Satyagraha* as a selfish electioneering campaign designed by the leaders of a party which was losing the faith of its adherants. A provincial unit of the Forward Block of Subhash Chandra Bose was constituted for Orissa in March, 1940AD with Dibakar Pattnaik as President. Godavarish Mishra and Nilakantha Das left the Congress to form a coalition government. In 1941 AD some other MLAs of the Congress left the party to support Nilakanths's effort.[8] But in spite of his popularity and dominance in Puri Congress Organisation and the Province also, Nilakantha failed in his mission as he was condemned severely due to his defection from the Congress party. Such a step was not timely and the voice of the public was against this effort which might hinder the Congress interest. Most of the common workers of the Congress remained with the provincial Congress organisation because of their deep faith in Gandhi's leadership. When Nilakantha and his group left Congress other young elements took the charge of the organisational duties of the districts. Management of the DCCs were taken over by them.[9]

While the selected Gandhians were observing individual *Satyagraha* and became successful in some extent in educating the people about the obnoxious was policy of the authority, some other workers became busy in constructive programmes. Rest of the Gandhians were watching the scene. Many of them were busy in the Local

7. Dagar, 4th year, No. 3-4, 1941.
8. H.K. Mahtab, History of the Freedom Movement in Orissa, Vol. IV, Cuttack, 1957, p. 65.
9. N.K. Sahu (ed), Who's Who of Freedom Fighters, Puri District, p. VII, 1967.

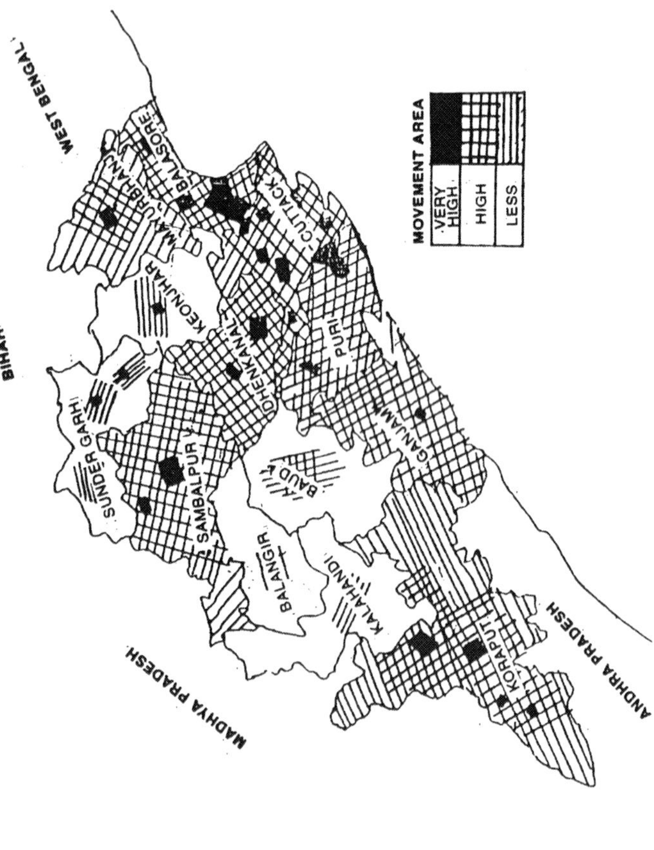

MAP NO. 3
AREA INFLUENCED BY QUIT-INDIA MOVEMENT
1942

and District Boards to which they had been elected. *Satyagraha* camps[10] were opened to train the interested workers. Village welfare organisations were sponsored by local Congress workers. People worshipped Gandhi's photographs on his birth days and workers hoisted tricolour flags on 26th of January, 1940 AD and 1941 AD to observe Independence Day. Death anniversary of Gopabandhu Das[11] was also observed by the workers.

The Congress members of the District Board did not co-operate with the government in its war efforts. After winning the Cuttack District Board election, Nilamani Pradhan was elected as Congress chairman. When the defence authorities wanted the Board to allow the troops to use the roads under its jurisdiction and supervision, Mr. Pradhan did not take any step. Rather he asked his workers, '*Chupse Baitheraho*'. He also ignored authority's directives. Consequently the Board was superseded and Mr. Pradhan was arrested. Doing so he only obeyed the— directive of the Congress to which he owed his loyalty and not to the British.[12]

But these activities of the Congress could not raise the political temperature to the maximum because of very limited number of participants involved in these works. These were only symbolic protests to continue the Congress struggle against the British. But these helped contributing to common Gandhians to be more alert, eager and wise by 1942AD. They were just awaiting Gandhi to give a big breakthrough.

Quit India Movement and the Gandhians

When the provincial Gandhian force was expecting Gandhi to take a major step in this critical juncture, Gandhi in August, 1942, finally asked the British to leave India permanently—a direct dialogue with the colonialists after

10. Nabin, 4th June, 1940 and 25th June, 1940.
11. *Ibid.*, 9th July, 1940.
12. *Samaj*, Death Anniversary special (Gopabandhu Das), July, 1991.

a long era of struggle. The 'Quit India' resolution marked a turning point in the annals of Indian history because Gandhi, using the weakness of the poor Indians as his strength, could mobilise them effectively. He ordered his common soldiers to incite the people to demand independence from the British directly. The participation of the people was so great and their daring activities were so enormous and committed that it proved Gandhi's success in his mission as a propagandist of people's cause for the last two decades. The call 'Do or Die' was simply enough to make the common people brave and fearless which was unprecedented in modern Indian history. In fact, people's gradual socialization through the years of Gandhian movement in line of self-respect and dignity invigorate them to shed fear of the British invincibility.

The Gandhians of Orissa worked hard to make this movement successful. This time the movement was very bold and clear and the call 'Quit India' also have the final touch to the year's long Gandhian movement in Orissa. The Gandhians' expectation was perfectly met by the leader, who, targeted Indian independence as the only goal to achieve. The Gandhians realised it as their last and final battle against the British. After a decade, again, the scenario of the countryside became volatile with patriotic feeling. Entire Gandhian force—both active full-timers and part-timers, as well as sympathisers, became active. All the Gandhians believed that the clarion call was timely and the Congress holding a strong position could bargain with the British. The entire Gandhian force had deep faith in Gandhi and were aware of the world opinion in favour of Indian independence. The Gandhians were really hopeful as Gandhi's generalship was at the best of its perfection.[13]

The active members utilized all of their energy to mobilise the people. The Ashramites of different *Ashrams*

13. Questionnaire—Rabindra Mohan Das, Akrura Jena, Gaurahari Prusti and Lokanath Senapati.

went into the nearby villages and advised the people to form *Panchayats* and live independently and peacefully.[14] Carbon and cyclostyled copies of Congress national songs were distributed. For the time being the game of power politics was postponed and all the members of the Congress became busy in the movement. Knowing that the work 'Quit' would make the British very oppressive, the Gandhians and the common people still braved police brutalities as it was the boldest and direct challenge to British interest in India.

In all the districts of Orissa the workers made their localities filled with revolutionary flavour. The government arrested the leaders quickly and made the movement leaderless and inorganised. Those who were not arrested, tried to continue the movement. Jails were filled up very quickly. The movement turned violent and the people targeted government institutions the symbols of British tyranny. Rest of the Gandhians, in remote villages, went underground and continued the agitation. These Gandhians who had successfully made the previous movements non-violent, now were forced to lead the people in a violent way. The new entrants—mostly students and uneducated or semi-educated youths of agrarian life, were happily engaged in riots by damaging telegraph and telephone lines and setting fire the *thanas* and government offices. The fact that during the Congress ministry days the farmers and middle class land owners who had got many facilities, really wanted to make the Congress successful. Years of movement in *Garhjats* had made the people bold and brave enough. People became daring and self confident—otherwise these people, who were, once, submissive and inert in the face of severe oppression, could not have become so alert and active in this direct war-of-independence. Those poor Oriyas who were physically and mentally so weak, became active

14. B.R. Mohanty, *op.cit.*, p. 119; Questionnaire—Baikuntha Nath Mohanty.

anarchists. The long suppressed anguish of the common people exploded.

The Gandhians could not control the mob fury. They, in some cases, so, tried to excite and incite the people in targeting government institutions. While marching in procession, they were confronted by the police, and, thus, turned the situation violent and bloody. When the Gandhians and the common people heard Gandhi in jail and he was not so hostile to people's violent attitude, they lost control and became indisciplined in their activities. The people set the offices on fire and destroyed telegraph and telephone lines. The public led by Gandhians wanted the police to go back and even, out of sheet excitement, snatched away the arms from them. It was the dare-devil attitude of the people—the product of intense propaganda and series of movements in the past occasions and also the mob psychology—that led to such violent incidents. On the other hand, the panicked police opened fire at mob killing and wounding large number of people.

As already indicated, in Orissa the activists' main targets were Post offices, *thanas* and other offices to set fire. Absence of communal riots made the public fully engaged in this agitation. A few railway lines were destroyed by the mob. Most of the offices were thatched houses, so it was easier for the *Satyagrahis* to burn these. In Ersama of Cuttack district, Gourishyam Nayak, a known Gandhian worker, with three thousand strong mob attacked the local police thana. They forced the police to surrender their arms. Padmanav Ray of Jajpur with many followers set Jajpur *thana* on fire and was arrested. Krushnamohan Routray of Barchana of Cuttack district, burnt down a government office. At Bhandaripolhari of Balsore district, people mobbed the *thana*, but retreated when shot by the police. At Srijang, people forcibly took away rice from the hoarders and burnt the dresses of the *Chaukidars*. The *Satyagrahis*, including many students of Nimpara of Puri district, gheraoed the *thana*. The police opened fire in which one man was killed.[15]

In Puri town, the activists made Nuamatha as their places of secret meetings. They went into the interior villages in the guise of beggars to incite the people. Biswanath Parida, a Gandhian, to avoid the police, hid himself in the store-house of a man, where he remained for many days. Many Gandhian workers with common people started picketings at the liquor and ganja shops. Revolutionary bulletins were circulated.[16]

Police started oppressive measures and arrested the local leaders. Biswambar Parida and Jayram Panda were arrested.[17] The students of Jagatsingpur High School started hartal. The local people quickly supported them. In villages people formed *'Rakta Bahini'* to confront the police openly. The government servants who were hostile to the movement were socially ostracised.[18] Police also started house to house search operation to arrest these Congress activists.

In villages, when the peasants under local Gandhians set on fire the government institutes like *thanas* and post offices and humiliated *chaukidars* and *dafadars*. In towns the activists—mostly from colleges and schools-started rioting. Even many sacretly supported the movement and organised the revolution.[19] The students of Ravenshaw College started picketing and rioting. They set fire to the College office. The college teachers threw their ties into the fire. Meetings were held in many places of the town. Students became very violent. Even the sons and daughters of government officials joined the movement

15. Questionnaire—Gourishyam Nayak; B.R. Mohanty, *op.cit.*, pp. 124-29.
16. Souvenir—Biplabi Biswanath, Kanasha, Puri, 1983, p. 10.
17. *Ibid.*,pp. 54-58.
18. *Ibid.*, pp. 59-63; H.K. Mahtab, *op.cit.*, p. 93.
19. Interview—Advaitaballava Ray; M.R. Das, August 9 (O), Cuttack, 1947, p. 15; A. Maharana, *op.cit.*, Vol. 37, No. 9, April, 1980.

disregarding their parents.[20]

The constructive Gandhians workers rushed to join the agitation. The socialists followed suit and also the communists of Orissa. Boys and young men under Surendranath Dwivedi in Cuttack town, started underground activities. Surendranath Dwivedi circulated revolutionary bulletins instigating the public against the British. Soon young socialists—mostly the Ravenshavians, declared the college free from British control.[21]

Like the previous decades, the district of Balasore took prominent part this time. Many people lost their lives and much more were wounded. The entire district was burning with revolutionary zeal. In Eram and Basudevpur area, people of twenty-six villages, under the local Gandhians, declared independence and named their area after the prominent local revolutionary poet, Banchhanidhi Mohanty. The area was called 'Banchhanidhi *Chakada*'. The workers selected their own president and prime-minister. The office was called as '*Satyagraha* office' having tricolour atop. Entire *Chakada* was divided into eight jones under different officials. The *Chakada* had its own jail, police station, police, army, court and judges. One confidential department was created and the workers were selected to collect information about the progress of the movement within the area for the revolutionary government. For the army, a commander-in-chief and other officials were also selected.[22]

The top leaders of the area were wanted by the police and the police summoned them to meet the police officer immediately. But they frequently changed their dresses to avoid the police. The women of the area collected rice and food and served to those workers who were—hiding

20. M.R. Das, *op.cit.*, p. 49, S. Mohanty, Krushnachuda O Annanya Galpa (Pataka Uttolana) (O), Cuttack, 1965, pp. 60-65.
21. S.N. Pattnaik, *op.cit.*, pp. 180-81.
22. J. Pattnaik, Rakta Tirtha Eram, Swadhinata Sangramara Eka Marmantuda Adhyaya (O), Cuttack, 1986, pp. 5-71.

themselves in other houses. Local Congress offices were opened even in private houses. The small boys were taught to sing the patriotic poems of Banchhanidhi Mohanty. Women of the villages were also taught how to blow counch in a special way to inform the people about the arrival of the police in their areas.

The so-called independent government formed at Eram ordered the boatmen not to ferry their boats for the police, who were approaching there to arrest some local Gandhians. The women of nearby villages started blowing counches. People assembled in number and requested the police repeatedly to return. But the police did not listen to them and proceeded to Eram where a meeting had been organised by the activists. The place was packed to its capacity. To disperse the mob the police suddenly started firing, killing 28 persons on the spot including a woman and infuring 56. The Zamindar Radhakanta Padhy, who until 1942AD was a regular supporter and primary member of the Congress, turned anti-Congress. The slogan' Quit India' irritated him. Because it provoked the people against the British and to the dominance of the Zamindars.[23]

At Lunia in Balasore district the Gandhians selected six villages to form independent government. People boycotted the British government, court and held meetings to denounce the excesses of the police. Local richmen were directed to provide work for their labourers. The villagers gheraoed the police and took away their fire-arms subsequently. When they returned them on the request of the local *Satyagrahis*, the police out of anger and vengeance suddenly fired at them killing 6 on the spot. Three persons died later. A collective fine of Rs. 2,225 was also imposed on the villagers.[24]

---

23. J.N. Pattnaik, *op.cit.*; Souvenir, Orissa Pradesh Congress Committee, BBSR, 1988, p. 40.
24. Souvenir, Struggle For Freedom And Orissa, BBSR, 1990, p. 129; Prajatantra, Saptahiki, 1st July, 1989, p. 35.

In Jaleswar the activists destroyed railway line, burnt effigies of local white officials and declared historic Raibania Fort independent. The police could not enter the area for fifteen days. The sensitive areas were supervised by the *Satyagrahis*. Some pro-people policemen also helped the agitators. The workers used the house of common villagers as their hide-outs.[25]

In Bari, where Ramadevi and Gopabandhu Chaudhury had opened an *Ashram* of great repute, the movement became very intense. After the arrest of the leaders the teachers and students of the basic schools closed the institutions and joined the movement. But the most surprising fact was that these constructive workers who were well-known staunch Gandhians and had immense popularity among the local people, could not stop the people from a violent and bloody movement. They repeatedly requested the people not to be violent. The excited people were not prepared to listen to them. Cyclostyled pamphlets were circulated in the areas secretly. The people went to Kalamatia to hold a meeting in protest of police arrest and on they way were confronted by the police. The public wanted the police to release the Gandhians. But some of them were whipped and driven out. The mob was enraged. One Hadibandhu Panda in order to release a *Satyagrahi* forcibly snatched away the rifle of the police. He was stabbed by buyonet to death. The furious people became mad and pounced upon the police consequently three of them died on the spot by the bullet fire and seventeen were wounded. Still the people with their traditional martial style charged the police with *lathis* and preferred death. Though *lathi* was nothing in front of fire-arms, [26] the martial spirit of the Oriyas at that time definitely would have spellbounded the British force.

25. D.K. Panda, Mukti Sangramare Jaleswar (O), Jaleswar, 1985, pp. 31-35.
26. A.T. Mohanty and D.R. Samal, Mukti Sangramare Bari Andolana (O), Cuttack, 1989, pp. 30-35.

In Tirtol, the *Satyagrahis* started intensive propaganda. The police entered villages to search the *Satyagrahi* and inflicted punishments on both workers and people. The people in retaliation, set the post office on fire. Telegraph line was also cut off.[27]

Everywhere the students and elder *Banarasenas* used the sing the following,

"The kick of the while sergeant,
has to be answered,
we are the offsprings of the—great 'Dhruva and Prahallad'.
Shame to us!
If we had to die one day, then
why not with glory today."[28]

The youths of Govindpur in the district of Cuttack organised by the local Gandhians formed a club where they were trained in martial art. The people at various places set the government offices on fire. The *Satyagrahis* considered to ablaze the police station of Govindpur. Nripen Sengupta was entrusted with this task as he was tall and lanky. But the police got the news before he could do anything and arrested many *Satyagrahis* and sympathisers. Some furious youths were also trying to kill the police.[29]

In the district of Koraput, the leaders were arrested soon. But the local Gandhians who remained outside the urban centres, instigated the people. The tribals under Laxman Naik of Tentuligumma of Malkanagiri *Taluk* of Bepariguda Police Station joined the movement. Many tribals became Congress Primary members. Laxman Naik was the president of this village primary Congress

27. *Utkal* Prasanga, Republic Day Special, 1989, pp. 29-34.
 The child heroes of Puranas who braved pain against injustice.
28. Quoted in Binod Kanungo, Bandha Tuma Pedi Putula (O), Cuttack, 1983.
29. Interview—Bibhutibhusan Acharya; H.K. Mahtab, *op.cit.*, p. 93.

committee and also a member of the DCC. Under his leadership many constructive centres were opened. He was son of a middle class tribal village-head and had a little school education. He was so devoted to Gandhi that people used to call him 'Gandhi of Malkanagari'. Laxman Naik decided to capture Mathili Police Station and collected hundreds of people with flags and *lathis* to march to the police station. On the way they destroyed liquor shops and other station at Kengrebeda. Chandrabeda and Kuntipalli. There Laxman Naik cautioned people not to resort to violence even if the police took recourse to repressive action.[30] But Laxman Naik was mercilessly beaten by the police. He lay unconscious. In the skirmish a forest guard was killed. The police opened fire killing five on the spot and wounding seventeen. Later on Laxman Naik was charged with the murder of the forest guard and was arrested. In area of Nawarangpur, an armed police party obstructed the people and shot down fifteen dead. Thus twenty-five people were killed from Koraput district and fifty people died in jails.[31]

As the jails were over-crowded, most of the political prisoners were kept in Berhmapur and Cuttack jails. While the prisoners hoisted national flag and shouted slogans in spite of police brutalities, [32] in Puri jail, some *Satyagrahis* jumped out of the jail wall.[33]

But the most melancholic incident in Berhampur Central jail was the hanging of Laxman Naik. The innocent *Adivasi* leader was hanged to death on 29th March,1943. The excitement , frustration and anger of the prisoners were beyond limit. They on they day did not take their meals and started singing patriotic songs in chorus throughout

30. H.K. Mahtab, *op.cit.*, p. 129; Proc. IHC, 1980, Vol. III, pp. 712-15; N.R. Pattnaik, *op.cit.*, pp. 95-101.
31. H.K. Mahtab, *op.cit.*; N.R. Pattnaik, *op.cit.*
32. R.C.Ram, Sangrami (O), Cuttack, 1986, p. 59.
33. Sradhanjali Nabakrushna Chaudhury, Rourkela, 1984, pp. 77-78.

the night before the Fateful Day. 'Right upto his very last breath, he was found to have chanted *'Mahatma Gandhi Ki Jai'* which reverberated the jail campus'.[34] Thus a great Gandhian revolutionary passed away from the political scene and it was a great loss for the tribals of Orissa, particularly.

The movement subsided due to unprecedented police oppression. But it proved that the common Indians were no longer feeble and not unable to understand their rights. The mission which Gandhi had started in 1920 AD. and those Gandhian workers who, in spite of their many drawbacks, had laboured hard and sacrificed a lot, became successful in awakening the people and strengthening their confidence to a large extent.

The activities of Subhash Chandra Bose could not influence the common Oriya Gandhians in a considerable way. Only Nilakantha Das and a few of his associates formed the branch of Forward Bloc but could not become a threat to the Congress regional organisation. In spite of their affection, admiration and respect to Subhash Chandra Bose, the Gandhians did not support him. Although they realised that Subhash Bose's effort might strengthen the national movement, they could not admire his point of argument that to get independence from one aggressor, Indians should take the help of another. In spite of their reservations for Subhash Chandra Bose's political strategy to free the country, they expressed grief on his tragic departure from the political science.[35] Even primary Congress Committees held condolence meetings for the Indians who died in the war in favour of INA. Haratals were observed against the trial of INA prisoners. Funds were raised and Oriya INA men were felicitated by the

34. B. Parida, Mukti Sangram O Orissa, 1803-1948 (O), Jagatsinghpur, Cuttack, 1979, p. 51; R.C. Ram, *op.cit.*, p. 69.
35. Questionnaire—Baidhar Swain, Prasadi Mehre and Advaitaballav Ray.

common Gandhians.[36]

II

THE GANDHIANS AND THE COMMUNISTS, CONSTRUCTIVE PROGRAMMES AND *GARHJAT* MOVEMENTS

The Communists were criticising the Congress because it did not launch any agitation against the British before 1938 AD. But they themselves became no more hostile against the British when Russia entered in the war in favour of the Allies. Their mysterious silence and lost from political scene was ridiculed by the contemporary newspapers. Their effort to use the leadership of some Congress socialists was also criticised.[37] Even contemporary literature reflected the inability of the Communists to provide proper direction and solution to their movement.[38] They lacked proper co-ordination and direction and were restless due to strong Gandhian influence among the people. However, some dedicated Communists in Orissa partook in the Quit India Movement alongwith the Congress and were imprisoned.

In jails communists and other Gandhian workers lived together. But some staunch supporters of the Congress including the socialist turned Communists due to naked groupism and power politics among the Gandhians in jails even. The status and false prestige enjoyed and imposed by some top Congress leaders on the common workers created a peculiar condition. The infitration of non-committed hypocrite Gandhians to the Congress and their growing dominance also made them frustrated.

36. Dagar, 9th year, No. 5, 1946; p. 33; OSA, Home (pol.), Confidential, File No. 25, Part-2, 13th September, 28th November, 12th December and 16th December, 1945.
37. Dagar, 3rd year, No.1, 1940.
38. G.Chhotray, Pheria (O), Cuttack, 1947, p. 58; K.C. Pattnaik, Raktamati (O), Cuttack, 1987, p. 106; S.N. Dwivedi August Biplaba (O), *op.cit.*, p. 196.

Unnecessary ego of 'A' grade and 'B' grade prisoners humiliated these workers and they left the party.[39] As a result, the Orissa Communist party in Berhampur Jail was born.

However, the communists failed to be a threat to the Congress in Orissa. The *'Dagar'* reported, "The Communists failed to enlist the people in their organisation after much effort, as nobody became their prey".[40] In spite of vigorous efforts by the Communists, the common Gandhians could not be detracted from their Gandhian path. The movement and sacrifice of Gandhi and common Gandhians was still fresh among the people. And the so-called power-loving Gandhians did not also leave the party as their political future seemed bright. On the other hand, in some areas, the Congress workers tried to bring[41] back those Communists, who were once supporters of Gandhi, to the regional organisation, in which they had some success.

Constructive Programmes

The constructive workers who had postponed their activities due to Quit India Movement returned to their *Ashrams* which were destroyed by the police. Among others the Bari *Ashram* had played a prominent role.[42] Some of the old Ashramites like Braj Kishore Singh (Chatu Babu) after release from the jail went to their respective native places. But they faced many difficulties in villages. These local Ashramites returned to Bari and started a new house for the *Ashram*. They quickly engaged themselves in relief work in their areas. The houses of the various basic schools were reconstructed.[43] Funds were collected

39. *Samaj*, Death Anniversary Special, *op.cit.*
40. Dagar, 10th year, No. 13, 1946.
41. OSA, Home (Pol), Home (Pol), Confidential, *op.cit.*, 13th January, 1945.
42. Questionnaire, Sarat Chandra Maharana.
43. M.N. Das (ed), Sidelights of History and Culture of Orissa, Cuttack, 1977, p. 271; Prajatantra, Mahtab Jayanti Special, 1988, p. 37; Souvenir, Chatu Babu (O), Chatrapur, Ganjam, 1986.

even from Sambalpur district to improve the condition of Bari *Ashram* and the Basic schools. Some young Gandhians stayed in the *Ashram* to learn villages handicrafts. For the children of political activists and prisoners, schools and hostels were opened to make them self-sufficient in life. Consequently, many children of common Gandhians joined the schools.[44]

The children were taught spinning and weaving. Some were sent to Wardha to get higher education. It was their primary education at Bari which made them about to earn their livelihood. They joined different spinning centres and institutions of basic education in many places of Orissa. Some workers were sent to Koraput to open *Ashrams*.[45] With the help of local carpenters spinning wheels and weaving machines were made and for this one factory was opened at Kendupatna in Cuttack district. Ramadevi accompanied by Sarat Chandra Maharana arrived at Sambalpur. They reviewed the progress of the spinning centres at Samalaipad and at other places of the district and gave instructions to the workers about the village reconstruction. She addressed meetings and collected funds for 'Kasturaba National Trust' and opened a branch at Sambalpur. A women training centre was opened at Barhgoan.[46]

Some Gandhians also reviewed the old *Ashrams* and training centres in different places. Gaurang Charan Das, after release from jail, went to his village, offered the *Harijans* scope for entry into the village temple and also started co-operative farming.[47] Uma Charan Pattnaik, being disgusted with the Congress power politics, went to the lands of the tribals and opened an *Ashram* in Udayagari and induced the *Khonds* to cultivate cotton in

44. A.T. Mohanty, Dasarathi Samal, *op.cit.*, pp. 36-39.
45. Ramadevi, *op.cit.*, p. 130; Questionnaire—Parvati Giri.
46. OSA, Home (pol.), Confidential, *op.cit.*, 18th March, 1945, 13th May, 1945, 28th May, 1945.
47. Souvenir, Gauranga Charan Das, Cuttack, 1987.

their area.[48] Binod Kanungo opened an *Ashram* in his village Mallipur of Cuttack district.[49] Mohan Nayak and Damodar Nayak went to villages of Ganjam, opened an *Ashram* there and started *Harijan* movement.[50] Malati Chaudhury settled in an *Ashram* at Angul and devoted her life in the service of the tribals.[51]

These Ashramites were, however, feeling lonely. Though they were working for the development of the common people, their activities were gradually seen as only pious and symbolic in nature. Social usefulness of their works were not genuinely seen by many Congressites in power. Even in the limited nature of power, they enjoyed, the leaders became busy in groupism. They highlighted Gandhism ideas only to maintain their Gandhian status. *Ashrams* helped constructive Gandhians to have asylums to spend the rest of their life. They created Gandhian atmosphere in the *Ashrams* until their death as they were used to such types of ideas and atmosphere in the *Ashrams* until their death as they were used to such types of ideas and atmosphere. They felt restless for the growing power-politics in the Congress. Its impact felt in the villages which further frustrated them. They were deserted and forced to lead a lonely life in *Ashrams*.

Anti-Feudal and Anti-British Movements in *Garhjats*

The impact of pre-war movements of many *Garhjats* was felt in other *Garhjats* of Orissa. Quit India Movement intensified the zeal of the workers in these areas. In Gangpur, Bonai, Sonepur, Athagarh, Baud, people continued their agitation.[52] The movement in Talcher, Dhenkanal was in most intensive stage. The Gandhians among the states' people had opened centres for

48. OSA, Home (pol) Confidential, File No. 25/45, 29th July, 1945.
49. A.T. Mohanty and D.R. Samal, *op.cit.*, p. 41.
50. Nabin, 24th September, 1946.
51. R.D. Chaudhury, p. 123.
52. S.S. Pradhan, Agrarian and Political Movement The States of Orissa, 1931-49, Delhi, 1986, pp. 129-44.

constructive programmes and used different Gandhian tactics to awaken the people. They reached a stage of violent movement. This violent confrontation of the activists became more intensified and bold. In some *Garhjats*, alongwith Gandhian tactics of *satyagrahs, hartal* and marches, the people started guerilla warfare leaving altogether Gandhian way of un-armed confrontation.

In Dhenkanal, the leaders started armed rabellion. Mahesh Chandra Subabhu Singh, Krutibash Pradhan, Baisnab Charan Pattnaik where the most active leaders. Unlike others, Baisanab Charan Pattnaik was a believer of violence and directly asked the people to drive out the *Raja*.[53] A typical idea entered into the mind of the people that Mahatma Gandhi was dying in prison and it would shame on the part of state employees to serve the autocrat.[54] So they joined the agitators, and shouting *'Gandhi Mahatma Ki Jai'*, the Congress volunteers with Gandhi cap on their heads entered neighbouring *Garhjats* to incite these people. They started the constructive programmes of anti-untouchability and village sanitation. A *Harijan* Volunteers' Army was formed. The volunteers used to sing thus,

"We are human beings,
but don't have prestige,
Our daughters and daughter-in-laws are-
sisters-in-law (*sail*) of those oppressing us-
and we are bloody *'sala'* Satans."[55]

However after the movement, a faction developed because of the difference of opinions among the socialists, local activists and the communists. It affected the movement. Prisoners got released taking different pleas and it became difficult for the leaders to keep contact with

53. *Ibid.*, p. 148; B. Mohanty, *op.cit.*, p. 137.
54. S.B. Pati, Democratic Movement in India, Delhi, 1987, pp. 134-35.
55. B.K. Dhai, Bhulibu Nahin (O), BBSR, 1980, pp. 116-23.

the workers. When Harekrushna Mahtab formed ministry in 1946 AD, after winning the election, the *Praja Mandal* became more faction-ridden. Both the Congress workers and the Communists formed States' people's student forums. Finding this opportunity, the *Raja* of Dhenkanal used his weapon to weaken the agitation.[56]

Under the leadership of Pabitra Mohan Pradhan, the Gandhian *Prajamandal* workers started agitation against the king of Talcher. Pabitramohan Pradhan jumbed out of the jail and fled to Calcutta to avoid arrest. The agitated people surrounded King's palace. The Gandhian workers formed *Panchayats* and established *Chasi Mulia Raj*. The movement, however, unlike the earlier years, could not retain its non-violent character. The activists at last used weapons.[57]

In Mayurbhanj, Sarat Chandra Das, a staunch committed Gandhian, formed a *Prajamandal* and demanded concession from the king. He was popularly called as 'Sarat Gandhi'. Teachers and students joined him. Gandhian methods of popaganda and constructive programmes made him very popular in the state. To combat him the king formed another *prajamandal* with the help of his tax collectors and revenue officials. They even used Congress flag and Congress name to misguide the people. Sarat Chandra Das opened Schools, training camps, formed *Panchayats*, and propagated for the cotton cultivation. His movement was purely non-violent. Meanwhile, the agitation of the *paik-s* or the peasant militia largely helped the movement because many *paik* leaders also were close associates of Sarat Chandra Das.[58]

56. Compilation, Dhenkanala Andolanara Sankhitpa Itihas, p. 26; H.M. Pattnaik, Dhenkanal Andolana (O), Dhenkanal, 1983, p. 55.
57. P.M. Pradhan, Muktipathe Sainika (O), Cuttack, 1949. pp. 98-140 and 196-204; Souvenir, Biplabi Jananayak Pabitramohan, Rourkela, 1990.
58. S. Pradhan, *op.cit.*, pp. 154-162; NMML, AISPC, File No. 112, Part-1 (Letter from Umakanta Pattnaik on Mayurbhanj Prajamandal Movement).

These movements in the *Garhjats* were Gandhian in nature in many respects. The fate of these movements depended largely upon the fate of Gandhian movement which aimed at national independence. Many of the *Garhjat* activists were Gandhians like those of British Orissa. It was due to Gandhi's influence they joined the movement. The activists used Gandhian techniques of *hartals,* picketings and marches and started constructive programmes to uplift weaker section of the society. Their non-violent and not so non-violent *Satyagrahas* in this last phases of the movement tamed the kings and the British at a time. Gandhi's techniques helped these once very ignorant and backward people to impose their resolutions on the kings.

III

CONGRESS POWER POLITICS : 1944—47 AD

By 1944 AD almost all prisoners were freed. The tempo of the Quit India Movement was still fresh among them. They observed Independence Days, and August Day to commemorate August Revolution (Quit India) regularly till 1946 AD.[59] Power politics within the organisation raised its head again when the temperature of the Quit India Movement was subsided. The hypocrites or so-called Gandhians became active. The bright political future of the Congress was clearly seen at the nearest horizon. Such type of people entered the Congress in numbers. The common people were no more required. During District Board and Congress organisational elections some people helped[60] the leaders to enter the party to grab power. Though rest of the Gandhians were against these, they could not do anything. Because their main aim was to keep the temperature of the movement alive to achieve independence.

It was a felling among these unwanted members even

59. Nabin, 30th July 1946, 20th August, and 26th August, 1946.
60. Interview—Bibhutibhusan Acharya.

in 1941 AD that if anybody used *Khadar*, his three generations,—after and before him—would be branded honest and truthful.[61] This practice became so phenomenal that in 1946 AD, the *'Dagar'*—a Satirical Oriya Weekly reported,

> "Mahatma Gandhi does not like theft, lottery, filthyness, dishonesty and hypocricy. But it is seen that in his name the people of India are aiming for something else.... In the name of politics some people are becoming dishonest, cunning and ill-charactered...."[62]

It was also indicated by the weekly that there emerged two types of disciples of Gandhi—One who looked towards metaphysical direction of the revolution and worked for it and other, who by their quickness and oratory capacity, misguided the people. "Perhaps after Gandhi's death", the weekly professised, "another revolution will break-out among the disciples of Gandhi. They will be divided into two distinct groups. ....one will be westward where the other will be eastward" .[63] It was indicating the orthodox Gandhians who were believers in basic village improvements and constructive programmes and were practising many Gandhian doctrines in personal life to their level best. They were thus branded as east-ward; and the other progressive but not down-to-earth and power loving Gandhians who only believed him as a political strategist and many of whom were not committed to the people were called west-ward.

The politics became a matter of 'purchase and sale'[64] even during Gandhi's era when he was the generalissimo of the Congress. His sway over the Congress members was receding with the end of mass-based movement and

61. Dagar, 4th year, No. 4, 1941.
62. *Ibid.*, 10th year, No.6/7, 1946-47.
63. Dagara, *op.cit.*
64. *Samaj*, Death Anniversary Special Issue, (Gopabandhu Das), 1945.

growing dominance of power politics. The elections for different Local and District Boards in Orissa were held in 1945 AD.[65] Again Congress local organisations became active. The Congress had to face the communists, the party of expelled Congress members of Nilakantha Group and others. In December, 1945 AD, election was held for Ganjam District Board. Even stalwarts like Dibakar Pattnaik of Nilakantha's group himself was defeated decisively by a comparatively non-entity from the Congress camp.[66] But this election was not free from controversy so far as the selection of the candidates was concerned. In the Kudala taluk, there was some dissatisfaction among the members of the Congress over the arrangements made by Harekrushna Mahtab with the *Raja* of Khalikotte.[67] It was not necessary as the Congress popularity was very strong and further, this type of political bargaining was an unhealthy practice.

In Sambalpur the Congress was making intensive efforts to capture the Board. A business man was taking a prominent part in organising the Congress. It was reported that he had spend Rs. 2,000/- from his pocket. It was also alleged that he did so to create his supporters to get a Congress ticket in the fourthcoming Assembly election.[68] There had been an internal dissension among the workers.[69] Nabakrushna Chaudhury came to enquire into the case of a candidate in Sambalpur, who according to Sri Laxminarayan Mishra, was not fit to be a nominee of the Assembly on account of his involvement in black marketing. His action of feeding all the Congress workers during a meeting was also criticised. The Congress workers were dissatisfied with the result of the last District Board election in which Congress did not have a walk-

65. S.N. Pattnaik, *op.cit.*, p. 193.
66. OSA, *op.cit.*, 29th December, 1945.
67. *Ibid.*, 12th December, 1945.
68. *Ibid.*, File No. 25, Part-II, 12th October, 1945.
69. *Ibid.*, 29th December, 1945.

over. Sri Gouri Sankar Mishra and Sankar Prasad Mishra, two prominent personalities in Sambalpur, who had been professing independent views,[70] joined the Congress. It was alleged that their move appared to be same as might be expected from many similar people 'who changed their loyality after seeing which way the wind blows'.[71]

Election to Puri District Board was also held. The Board first introduced basic education in the schools under its supervision. Primary teachers were trained for a month in Basic Education. Training centres were opened in many places.[72] But the growing groupism and dominance of power politicians in these years could not be avoided.[73] The condition in Cuttack and Balasore DCCs also became same.[74] The PCC witnessed tussle between different groups. The battle for power also affected many PCC members.[75] Many new members were restless and impatient to grab power.[76]

Talking about the pious attitude and commitment of some Board members for the people, one Gandhian observed that at that time there was no feeling of big or small among the members of the Board. Though he was a common member of the Board, he could dare to indicate the chaiman's short-coming without any hesitation.[77] This was, of course, a rare event, because very few lower-level Gandhians could be members of the Boards. They were severely affected and disturbed by the groupism within the district organisations. New non-committed Gandhians started their preparations to grab power by using their monthly and social influence. The periodicals and

70. *Ibid.*
71. *Ibid.*
72. Prajatantra, Mahtab Jayanti Special, *op.cit.*, p. 40.
73. Niankhunta, 8th year, No.7/8, 1946.
74. Interview—Advaitaballav Ray, Bibhutibhusan Acharya, Harekrushna Biswal.
75. Dagar, 10th year, No. 17, 1946-47.
76. *Ibid.*

newspapers ridiculed these elections as dramas. 'The *Niankhunta'*, the most popular satirical Oriya weekly, reported thus,

> "In the political stage of Orissa, a new dance drama had been started. Violence, jealousy, short-sightedness and groupism has affected the leaders. To grab power the vocal unworthy men are displaying their muscles. Keeping their feet on the empty belly of the poor, the zamindars and rich has started dalliance of the false drama of *Swadeshi*".[78]

Ridiculing leaders the weekly further expressed the view that the leaders were forgetting their promises quickly.[79] The zamindars and wealthy persons, who were opposing Congress earlier, entered the Congress organisation.

In DCC elections also the groupism became prominent because of their close relationship with the office bearers of the Board of local-self government. Some members of the Ganjam DCC, who were trying to replace some committed Gandhians, called a special meeting to move a no-confidence motion against the office bearers. As the Congress had no such provisions and procedures, it could not happen. But some of the honest office-bearers became very emotional and expressed the following views,

> "Those who had not touched the boundary of the Congress and helped the British during the war and also during the national movement, and those who had filled up their boxes by black marketing while many Indians were dying of hunger, those who are always busy to inflict pain and oppression on the people by exploiting them-against whom the Congress is fighting—those by using the mark of patriotism on their forehead have encircled the Congress like ants

77. Prajatantra, *op.cit.*
78. Niankhunta, 8th year, *op.cit.*
79. *Ibid.*

seeing the power in Congress hand. Not only that, by using these ill-equipped wealth in different ways and tactics they are trying to control the institution of the Congress to make their ways clear. Their illusion and cleverness have made some of us blind. With the help of some established leaders they are creating the nasty game of 'group and clique politics'. They are trying to influence many members of the Congress by the help of wealth and other temptations. In this critical juncture of Nation's fate everybody should be alert against these creature. But to our misfortune we feel that in the district of Ganjam there is factionalism among the Congressmen, and beneath this disturbances there are the disguised hands of some established leaders."[80]

This was not only the case of Ganjam Congress organisation. Power had made many of the workers blind to lose their self-respect. Though the committed Gandhians were still alive and even old workers of the Congress of 1920s were witnessing these developments, their policy of appeasement for the sustenance of Congress movement until independence made them inactive, and this inactivity and silence proved very costly for the Congress organisation. Even some committed Gandhians of yester year became interested [81] in power politics. The socialists were no more active like the previous decade. A few constructive workers also isolated themselves from the Congress activities and took shelter in the Village *Ashrams*.

The Election of 1946 AD

On the basis of the recommendation of the Cabinet Mission, the Congress participated in the election of 1946 AD. This time the victory of the party was crystal clear. But the aim of the Congress was something else, which in

80. Nabin, 11th February, 1947.
81. Interview—Ghanashyam Pati, Bibhutibhusan Acharya.

form of the Congress circular was issued to the PCCs thus,

> "Election in a country under foreign military rule have no great importance and yet in the present context the country may not neglect them. The elections are contested primarily to keep away traitors and swislings from posing as the true representatives of the country".[82]

As the concept of Indian independence was in much more clearer shape by the time when the Congress nominated its candidates to contest the election, no importance was given to Congress fundamental ideas and procedures. Power-politicians played the game well to sabotage the power. Many non-committed Gandhians were selected by the party. Whether the candidates believed in prohibition of intoxicants and whether he was a member of the primary committee was not examined. Whether he used *Khadar* or in the past had done something for the Congress and went to jail, or believed in the stand Congress took during the Second World War was not taken into consideration. No importance was given to these basic directives of the Congress to select its candidates. Kings were accepted as Congress candidates who were never sympathisers of the Congress. Importance was given how to win the contest, but other basic vital issues became very minor.[84] In this context, Sradhakar Supakar remarked,

> "In the fire of political battle who proved pure gold their place and position suddenly changed in the society. At the dawn of independence, this was an unfortunate development. The weight of *`Gunjar'* became more than gold."[85]

82. N.N. Mitra (ed), Indian Annual Register, January-June, Vol. 1, Calcutta, 1945, p. 236.
83. *Samaj*, Death Anniversary Special Issue, 1991.
84. *Ibid*.
85. *Ibid*.

This electioneering process became increasingly a matter of cunning and disturbing activities. The satirical periodicals found interesting informations to make their pages salty. One of these periodicals *'Dagar'* wrote,

> "This election drama was totally an illusion. The people would invite disease by taking the injection of election. Though the Congress had emphasised on fair and honest politics, but nobody followed it. Even the *Satyagrahis* of the Congress instigated the people to take bribe from the opponents and to vote for the Congress—the practice which in future would prove dangerous".[86]

It was also reported that a dog could win election in the name of Congress.[87] Those who had been opposing the Congress and its leaders in the past, approached the Congress leaders with the explanation that they were true Congressites.[88] The office of the PCC became crowded where the candidates were selected. The number of aspirents was very big. All has come with the bagful of sacrifices they had done for the country.[89] But who weighted more were considered for the candidature.

The Congress won 47 out of total 60 seats of the Orissa Assembly.[90] Harekrushna Mahtab was considered to be the premier but he was reluctant as it would personally harm his interest. It opened him to criticism which, he thought, would lower his prestige in the long run. 'He was aware of the fact that most of the Congress candidates had no knowledge as to how to run an administration'.[91] Anyhow, under his leadership the Congress ministry was formed. Socialists like Nabakrushna Chaudhury joined his ministry. The ministry tried to take some drastic steps

86. Dagar, 9th year, No. 19/20, 1946.
87. *Ibid.*
88. *Ibid.*, No. 26, 1946.
89. *Ibid.*, No. 17/18, 1946.
90. N.N. Mitra (ed), *op.cit.*, p. 229.
91. OSA, Home (Pol), Confidential, File No. 81, 22nd January, 1946.

to provide the people the articles of daily-use through fairer means.[92] It targetted the dealers and black marketers to curb their activities. Fot this, village committees were formed through which daily-use commodities in concessional rates were distributed properly. But this process failed in its mission as it became more complicated and ill-managed. It failed to check black-marketing and the number of black marketers grew.[93]

The necessity of the control of District Board over these committees was questioned. The number of dishonest and cunning people grew in number.[94] So also grew the number of some supporters of illegal nature of the power-loving leaders in villages who created strong bases for the leaders to continue their hold over the people and party. Thus, the intensity of power politics grew with the passages of time.

In 1947 AD, when the top Congress leaders were finalising the plans of independence of India and Gandhi was busy at Nuakhali—the riot-affected area of Bengal—the Gandhians in Orissa were eagerly waiting for the prevailing situation. The independence came along with the partition of the country, which deeply hury the Gandhians. The Gandhians had to celebrate the Independence Day on 15th August, 1947 AD of course, half-heartedly.

When India got independence, the Oriya population, except in one or two cases, remained peaceful being free from communal tension, genocide and unprecedented cruelty. The sufferings of the refugees in other boarder provinces of India did not occur in Orissa. In this respect Orissa was lucky. But surprisingly when Indian independence was celebrated, many princes of *Garhjats* also openly celebrated the occasion and congratulated the

92. Dagar, 10th year, No. 1, 1946.
93. *Ibid.*, No. 9, 1946.
94. Dagar, 10th year, No. 13, 1946.

subjects for this purpose. The kings also started to praise Gandhi. They also claimed their direct and indirect support in making the Gandhian movement successful. The temples of the *quillas* were lighted and poor were served with food.[95] The successors of oppressive princes were by then changing their tune according to the change of the situation.

The dramatists like Monaranjan Das wrote a drama called *'August Biplab'* which was played by leading groups in Cuttack town. Eminent story writer Rajkishore Ray published an article *"Nutan Prabhat"* or "New Morning" in which he had hoped to forget old taults and think for a new beautiful and seren India. He had also wished the forty crores of children of India to be energetic for this purpose.[96] Oriya literature suddenly got a boost and making decades of national movement in Orissa as background, new aspiration hopes and ideas where being appeared in literary pages.

Reacting to the question on partition, Gandhians expressed the view that it was the divide and rule policy of the British that created such problem. But many of them also blamed those so-called power hankering Gandhians who were restless to get power. These Gandhians never blamed their leader for partition because for them Gandhi was dead against the proposal of partition and he failed to annule athis proposal because he was terribly hury due to unprecedented communal tension and bloodshed and growth of power-war within the Congress, surprisingly, the common Gandhians' opinions were not taken or they were not considered necessary in this critical juncture in spite of their long years of valuable contributions. Curiously enough the transaction for independence remained confined within the top Congress elites. And at last the Gandhian movement for Independence ended with

95. Navin, 19th August, 1947.
96. Dagar, 15th August, 1946.

the freedom and partition of India. The Gandhian force in Orissa like other provinces had their break after long period of hectic political activities and high patriotic temperature.

IV

In 1942 AD, during the Quit India Movement, the Gandhians proved their capabilities as the leaders of common masses. Gandhians of all types—constructive workers, socialists, states peoples activists, politicians both committed and non-committed—made the movement quite successful for which Orissa got an exalted place in the annals of the struggle for Indian independence. Again the Gandhians won confidence of common people to lead them in a movement. They really made the people, in many respects, alert, organised, self-conscious and brave. People had reached at a stage of unprecedented boldness in demanding their rights, which proved the success of Gandhian movement. The Gandhians in their effort too succeeded to a great extent in mobilising the people. Continuous and step-by-step activities of the Gandhians and the common people through political and social movements changed the Indian scenario rapidly.

But their decades of effort had its by-product in the shape of alarmingly growing groupism and power politics within the Congress. The Congress was no longer becoming a party of devoted full time or part time social workers who really loved or respected Gandhi. Rather, the non-committed hypocrited becoming Gandhians, entered Congress and pushed the real and committed Gandhians to the background in the final years of the struggle to monopolise power. They were not committed to Gandhi's ideas but became respected leaders of the masses using *Khadar* dress. Such Congress politicians were mushroomed in place of social-workers. At the same time Gandhi was losing his sway over the Congress organisation and was busy single-handedly in riot-affected areas of Communalism. The real-Gandhians remained only silent spectators of this usurption.

Sensing that this type of exploitation might be adoped by the Congress workers in post-independence era, the great nationalist Oriya poet, *Jatiyhakabi* Bira Kishore Das, while in the jail, in 1943—when he was interned because of participating in the Quit India Movement, cautioned the people of India thus,

> "I can see clearly
> the flood of Independence is coming quickly,
> But don't drink it out of greed,
> It is just like the water of first flood of the-
> month of *Asadha*-which contains all the bubbling
> and attractive white filths.
> ....
> If the white leese turns black,
> the sufferings of the poor would not be changed,
> with the bones of the skulls of crores of people,
> the *Darbar* hall of Delhi would be built.
> The rich, kings, money-lenders and zamindars-
> would come out wearing the sacred beads of sacrifice.
> But don't be misguided by false sacred beads of sacrifice,
> dress and pleasing talks".[97]

97. As quoted in R.C. Ram, *op.cit.*, p. 64.

6

Conclusion

From 1920 AD to 1947 AD, the Gandhians of Orissa worked for the emancipation of the society-both politically and socially under the leadership of Gandhi. While making the people gradually conscious of their rights and duties towards the country they also represented the class interest of the poor society to which most of them belonged. When the general public in Orissa came out spontaneously without any hesitation and asked for their due rights, it proved that the Gandhians were successful in their mission in mobilising the poor, ignorant and inert Oriyas to the maximum.

Before 1920 AD, the condition of Oriyas was worst due to political turmoils, social stagnation and material instabilities. British administration in Orissa could not improve the condition of the people because of indifferent attitude of the officials. Political vivisection, dominance of the neighbouring non-Oriya speaking provinces, lack of education and commercial activities made the society completely inert and submissive. Lakhs of people died of hunger when the Great Famine of Orissa visited the region in 1866 AD.

But after the famine, some Oriyas became conscious of their condition. They became organised and wanted the unification of Orissa under one political unit. Dominance of the neighbouring provinces and their heinous attempt to destroy Oriya culture and language were properly answered. Language agitation destroyed the age-old isolation of Oriyas of different districts and birth of vernacular newspapers and modern literature forged the feeling of oneness among the then educated oriyas. The *'Utkal Sammilani'* formed under the leadership of Madhusudan Das in December, 1903 AD spearheaded the Oriya movement for achieving a complete goal.

But the poor common and ignorant people were far away from this development. Poverty, illiteracy and backwardness still had their dominances on the society. Meanwhile, a man of great capability, Pandit Gopabandhu Das, came to the socio-political scene of Orissa who urged the common people to take their part in shaping the future of their region. A full-time social worker and a great nationalist poet of high calibre, Gopabandhu Das with close associates, heralded a new era of hope in the poor people.

Gandhi's rise to fame and popularity in 1920 AD infatuated Gapabandhu Das to merge the *'Utkal Sammilani'* with the National Congress and to adopt non-violent non-co-operation method to achieve both national and regional salvation simultaneously. In spite of the reluctance of the old guards of the 19th century Oriya nationalism, Gapabandhu continued his faith in Congress movement and completed the process of political linkage of Orissa with the national mainstream by joining the Indian National Movement under Gandhi's leadership.

Gandhi's policy of non-violence greatly suited to the common Oriyas to be his followers. Non-violence suited to the physically and mentally inert people join the movement. As peoples' inertia and fear to British might was very high, very few could turn violent agitators, so non-violent way proved physically, financially and mentally feasible for any Oriya to be a gentle anarchist. Agrarian society which was very unstable financially, could only aspire to join a movement of Gandhian type in which any willing soul could be even a part-timer. Absence of communal disturbances allowed Gandhism to dominate the political life of Oriyas of these years without any challenge from disturbing forces. Absence of caste movements could not produce any hindrance to the dominance of Gandhian movement as the lower castes lacked awareness of class-consciousness due to acute general poverty, illiteracy and isolation. The presence of intermediary castes also lessened the pressure of segregation on them, thus, preventing bipolarisation as evolved in South India. Championing their causes in a big way Gandhi captured their imagination from the beginning and no other movement could induce them in later years till the independence of the country.

Religiousness of Gandhi's doctrines, his emphasis on some tenets of Hinduism made him a Godly man among the common Oriyas who were under the strong spell of medieval bhakti cult and were religious and fatalist by nature. Gandhi's special concern for the poor people, particularly for the poverty-striken populace of Orissa, made him immensely popular. The highly educated ones thought of him a great political strategist. But the semi-educated, literate and illiterate rural people realised him as the true representative of their hope and interest. They joined his movement in numbers and became the standing force in villages. Hindu joint-family system provided many of full-time activists the security and shelter for the sustainance and growth of the movement. Role of Gopabandhu Das and his associates also influenced many youngmen to be common Gandhians. The rank nationalists opened Gandhian *Ashrams* and institutions and trained the young Gandhians in the line of self-respect and self-sufficiency. Provincial Congress leaders like Gopabandhu Das, Nilakantha Das, Harekrushna Mahtab, Gopabandhu Chaudhury, Rama Devi and etc. could attract many young people to join the national movement. When Gandhi himself took the cause of Oriyas in a big way he naturally got the support of the people of Orissa.

The people who joined the national movement and worked for Gandhiji became Gandhians. They wore

Khadar, talked about Gandhi's doctrines, arranged meetings for the visiting leaders and participated in different programmes of Gandhi. In the Non-Co-Operation Movement they participated in picketings and marches. Young school boys joined the movement. Both adults and youngs formed the group of common Gandhians who were both part-timers and full-time activists. Many Gandhian *Ashrams* and Congress institutions grew in different corners of Orissa, which provided the needed asylum to the budding Gandhians. It was due to these common Gandhians in Villages boycott of British courts and foreign clothes became successful.

In 1921 AD, the Gandhians were very few in number in spite of the primary membership of the PCC rose to 52,000. Around 3,000 were active full-timers in districts of the region though more were part-time activists. After the suspension of the movement the number of full-timers reduced to even one thousand only, who were mostly constructive workers. Though the village level Gandhians were indulged in different political activities in urban areas, the impact of national movement was felt in the villages gradually.

A new era of Gandhian movement ushered from 1930 AD when it turned to a completely mass-based one. Civil Disobedience Movement in Orissa became quite successful and the experience of Gandhians in the previous decade widened the scope and reach of Gandhi in the countryside. Many more men and teenagers joined the movement as Gandhians representing different castes. Women participants increased in number. The class interest of the poor Gandhians was clearly reflected in this mass-based movement of Salt agitation. The poverty-striken agrarian society of Orissa completely joined the movement both mentally and physically.

The movement was followed by mass-based peasant movements. Some Gandhians of previous years turned socialist to champion the causes of the peasants. Though did not agree with some of Gandhian ideas, in totality, they kept abiding with different Gandhian doctrines. Due to their relationship with the Congress and Gandhi, they became known as socialist Gandhians. They used Gandhian techniques of *Satyagraha*, marches, *hartals*, and utilised the popularity of Gandhi to mobilise the peasants.

In the previous decade the Gandhians were mostly from higher caste *Brahmins* and *Karanas*. But in the subsequent period of the movement, the Gandhians were from different castes though the number from higher castes, including *Khandayats* was more, the peasant agitations saw the common people who joined the movement in numbers. In the previous decade, very few *Harijans* joined as common Gandhians; but this time, their number increased, though not very big, as compared to their population in the region.

In Gandhian *Ashrams*, some staunch Gandhians stayed and became full-time social workers. They adopted different Gandhian doctrines in their own personal lives and were known as 'constructive Gandhians'. They worked against untouchability and for the upliftment of women. They propagated *Khadar*, popularised spinning, fought against intoxicants and held different exhibitions to attract popular interest. Though other Gandhians were not exclusively involved in these activities, they were great supporters of them, and practised these in their personal lives.

The Gandhians were imprisoned and loved in various jails. The leaders got many facilities because of their status as 'A' grade or 'B' grade prisoners. But the common Gandhians were 'C' grade prisoners. In the jails they suffered a lot. The jails became overcrowded due to the sudden growth of Gandhian prisoners. Women and teenagers also went to jails. Within jail premises, the Gandhians observed different national days and hoisted flags in spite of the restriction of the authorities. The learned Gandhians tought other Gandhians about different doctrines of Gandhi. Instructions were given on different subjects to educate the budding and novice Gandhians. When returned, the leaders did not face any social ostracism, because of their status and influence; but the common Gandhians—particularly the women, suffered in the villages. They were socially boycotted and were forced to perform purifying customs which were costly and humiliating.

In these years of 1930 AD to 1936 AD the constructive Gandhians became extremely busy in different programmes of Gandhi. They popularised spinning, held exhibitions and fought against intoxicants. Different camps were opened to train the Gandhian volunteers in the line of self-sufficiency. Many women volunteers also joined these camps. When Gandhi started his *padyatra* in Orissa in 1934 AD against untouchability, Gandhians of Orissa worked hard to make his visit successful. Although they achieved little success, they could be able to bring awareness among the Oriyas through their different social programmes.

One 1st April, 1936 the separate Orissa province was formed. The Gandhians of the province and especially, of the outlying tracts, through their respective forums, highlighted the cause of amalgamation, in spite of the indifferent attitude of some leaders of the PCC. After the formation of the province, the Orissa Congress organisation entered the electoral battle in 1937 AD. The Gandhians worked hard to elect their party candidates. Their popularity among the villagers enabled them to get the support of the lower—middle-class-peasants who formed bulk of the limited voters.

But the election saw the growth of groupism and power politics among the Congress members. Sensing the bright political career ahead many unwanted hypocrites overnight turned Gandhians and entered the Congress organisation. The number of primary committees grew tremendously, so also the number of primary members.

They were nearly two lakhs. When the Congress won the election with a clear majority and formed the ministry, the number of non-committed members of the Congress in Orissa increased further. Petty power-brokers tried to dominate the local Congress organisations by enlisting their own men as Congress primary members. Self-less social workers were gradually outnumbered by the selfish politicians who had no commitment for the people.

The elections of DCCs and local Congress Committees became faction-ridden because of the role of the DCCs in selecting the party candidates for local Boards, District Boards and various municipalities. Many workers were openly indulged in immoral ways and accumulated illegal money. The committed Gandhians—mostly constructive workers, were gradually alienating themselves from the political activities. The socialists turned bitter critics of the ministry and the power politicians. They could mobilise the public support from behind and forced the ministry to take some drastic steps to raise the standard of the common people. But finally they remained silent because of their limited number and dominance of the power-politicians in the provincial Congress. Even the committed Congresites who were not truly Gandhians, like Nilakantha Das, left the Congress because of the growing groupism and naked politics in it.

In September, 1939 AD, with the outbreak of Second World War, the political scenario of India changed rapidly. The Congress ministries of different provinces in India resigned in protest when the British declared India as a member of the Allies, without consulting the Congress. The committed Gandhians at this critical time were eagerly awaiting Gandhi to start a fresh movement. When the Congress rejected August Offer in 1940 AD, Gandhi advised his followers to start individual *Satyagraha* which was only symbolic in nature in protesting illegal British war policy. But it could not raise the political temperature to their expectation.

However, Gandhi took the boldest and final step of his political career on 9th August, 1942 AD when he launched the historic 'Quit India Movement'. The tremendous excitement and the spontaneous involvement of large number of people proved the untiring efforts of the Gandhians of Orissa in successfully mobilising the mass. The inert, submissive and poor Oriyas at last joined the political movement and bravely claimed their due rights from the colonialists. The 'Quit India Movement' turned violent only after leaders of all ranks were arrested. The rest of the Gandhians without caring Gandhi's policy of non-violence led the people to start arsons and riots. Official buildings, police *thanas* and post offices were set on fire. The authorities while suppressing the movement, killed and arrested many Gandhians and the common people who supported them.

In the *Garhjats*, which were ruled by the kings, the movement also had its impact. The Post-Salt Movement years saw the growth of awareness among the *Garhjat* people. The local educated people were influenced by Gandhi's rise and popularity. Many of them organised the people and followed Gandhian doctrines. Different constructive programmes were implemented and many *Ashrams* were opened. The *Garhjat* Congress *Karmis* propagated Gandhi's ideas among the people and used Gandhi's popularity and techniques of *Satyagraha*, marches and *hartals* to start agitation. Though the *Garhjat* people turned violent, among the activists many were Gandhians and hence the movements here were, in many respects, Gandhian in nature.

With the disappearance of patriotic zeal of 'Quit India Movement', the dominance of power-politicians were again felt in the Congress organisation. The socialista were no more vocal. The constructive Gandhians gradually became isolated. Their works were occasionally highlighted by other Gandhians. The non-committed members made the DCCs big structures of different small groups having allegiance to different leaders. Many people who were enemies of the Congress and had worked against the Gandhians in the earlier years, became *congressias*. The *Khadar* dress became a symbolic fashion. Gandhism was losing its ground which was so strong even upto 1942 AD. The process of power politics which was started in 1937 AD became very strong with sound foundation by 1946 AD. Though the election of 1946 AD saw the victory of the Congress, the common Gandhians were made sidetract. Power politics and nepotism grew in spite of the effort by some committed Gandhian leaders. District and Local Boards, and municipalities came under the strong influence of the ministers and power-brokers who had their strong position in the Congress organisation. Simultaneously village level power brokers-called 'touts' who crowded Congress offices and ministerial chambers started polluting the political atmosphere.

Thus, though, there was success of the Gandhian movement for the independence of the country, Gandhism lost its sway over the Congress organisation in Orissa, and the true followers of Gandhi, were gradually pushed to the background unnoticed and uncared for. Power politics became the only career in the Congress as it gradually shed its revolutionary shape to be a political party in Independent India.

Glossary

Adivasi	Tribal people
Amla	Clerks, Native Judicial or Revenue Officials
Anna	Six paise
Ardhapagala	Half Mad
Arth	Material Possession
Asadha	First Month of Indian Rainy Season
Asahajogira Atma Katha	Autobiography of Non-co-operator
Ashram	Refuse, Hermitage, Also The four Stages of Hindu Life
Astalohakarmi	Metal - Smith Caste
Atta	Flour
Avtar	Incarnation
Avtarvad	Theory of Incarnation
Babu	Educated Government Servant
Badhei	Carpenter Caste
Balua	Peasant Militias
Banarsena	Brigade of Monkey
Banayat	Peasant Militia
Bande Matram	I Bow to Thee, Motherland
Bania	Goldamith Caste
Bata	Banyan tree
Bauri	Untouchable Caste of Orissa
Behera	Head of the Caste
Benami	Absentee
Bethi	Forced Labour

Bhagwan	The God
Bhagabata	The Oriya pronounciation of 'Bhagvat Gita'
Bhandari	Barber
Bhakti	Devotion
Bharatvarsha	India, Its Traditional name after the great ancient king Bharat
Bichhuati	One Type of Irritating Shrub
Bidi	Country-made Cigar Made up Tabacco and Kendu Leafs
Bidrohi	Revolutionary
Biplab	Revolution
Biplabi	Revolutionary
Bopa	Oriya coloquial Derivation From 'Bapa' *i.e.* Father
Brahman, Brahmin	The First in Rank Among the Four Castes of Hindu Society
Brahman Samaj	Priest Society
Bustee	Lane
Chakada	Area
Charakha	Spinning Wheel
Charakha Sangha	Council of Spinning Centres
Chasa	Traditional Cultivating Peasant Militia Caste
Chasi Mulia Raj	Rule of Peasants and Labourers
Chaukidar	The Village Watchman
Chellah	Disciple
Chattiar	Moneyed merchants of Madras
Chupse Baithe Raho (Hindi)	Sit Silently
Chuda	Pressed Rice

Congressia, Congressilok or Congresswala	Congress workers
Cowery	Traditional Oriya Currency
Dafadar	The Village Official Appointed by the British Who Reports on Bulglary, Theft, Death and Birth
Dagar	Messenger
Dama	Untouchable Caste, (Basket Makers)
Dandia	Folk Dance of Gujrat
Darbar	Royal Court
Daraji	Tailor
Dasakatia Karmi	The Worker who Gets Ten Rupees
Deshakatha	Story of the Country
Dewan	Revenue Minister
Devata	God
Devati	Goddesses
Dharana	Sitting for a Cause Demanding Immediate Action
Dhengura	Drum Beating
Dhoba	Washerman Caste
Dhoti	Male Cloth
Diwas	The Day
Firingi	British
Gajapati	The Tittle of the King of Orissa
Gandhiwala	Followers of Gandhi
Gandhivadi	Believers in Gandhism
Gandhi ki jai	Victory to Gandhi
Garba	The Folk Dance of Gujrat
Garhjat	The Princely States of Orissa
Garhua	The Soldiers Stationed in Forts
Gauda, Gopal	The Mikman Caste

Gita	The Bhagabat Gita of Mahabharat
Giti	Song
Ghaita	Oriya Coloquial form of the word 'Husband'
Gramasabha	Village Council
Gudakhu	One Type of Toothpaste of Intoxicating Nature
Gudia	Sweet-Maker Caste
Gujrati	People of Gujrat
Guru	Teacher
Harijan	The word used by Gandhi for the Untouchables, *i.e.* Children of God
Harijan Sevak Sangha	Scheduled Caste Welfare Organisation
Hartal	Strike
Hindusthani Seva Dal	Indian Voluntrary Organisation
Hiteishini	Well-Wisher
Hukum	Prescription or Order
Jagannath	The God or Orissa (Lord of Universe)
Jagannath Dharma	The Cult of Jagannath
Janani	Mother
Jat	Farmer Caste of Haryana, Punjab or U.P.
Jati	Sub-Caste
Jatiya Kabi	National Poet
Jatiya Vidyalaya	National School
Jyotisha	Astrologer Caste
Kabir Panthi	Followers of Kabir
Kalingi	The Peasants of Ganjam
Kaliyug	The Hindu Era of Injustice
Kamara	Black Smith Caste

Kandara	Scheduled Caste who are Traditional Village Watchman
Karana	Writer Caste of India
Karma Mandir	The Temple of Action
Karmi	The Devoted Workers
Katakia	The People of Coastal Orissa were Generally Known in Western Orissa
Keuta	Fisherman Caste
Kendra	Centre
Khadara, Khadi	Hand-Spun Coarse Cloth
Khadaria	The Man Uses Khadara, The Gandhians
Khadi Kendra	Khadi Centre
Khajuri	Date Palm
Khandayat, Khandayat-Kshyatriya	Traditional Warrior Caste of Orrisa
Khilafat	Relating to Caliphate of Muslims
Kirtan, Sankirtan	Devotional Singing
Kirtan Mandali	Devotional Singing Music Troupes
Krishak	Farmer
Krishak Bahini	Farmers' Army
Krishak Sammilani	Farmers' Conference
Kondh, Khond	A Tribe of Orissa
Kothia	Who Works For a Year on Contract Basis as Agricultural Labourer
Kulthi	One Type of Pulse
Kumbhi Patia	The followers of Alekha Dharma *i.e.* the Cult of Formless
Kumbhara	The Potter
Lala	Merchant Community of Punjab
Lathi	Stick

Lathial	Stickman, Goon
Lokamata	Opinion of the People
Mahadev	The God Shiva
Mahajana	Village Money Lender
Mahanayak	Present Militia of Orissa
Mahanta	The Head of the Religious Endowment
Mahaprasad	The Holy Boiled Rice Prepared in Jagannath Temple at Puri
Mahar	Un-touchable caste of Maharastra
Maharaj	The Great Soul
Mahatma	The Great Soul
Mahima Dharma	The Sect Propagated by Mahima Gossain
Mandia	One Type of Millet
Mandira	Temple
Maratha	The People of Maharastra
Marawari	People of Marwar of Rajasthan
Maqdami	Villages under a Tex Collecter Called Maqdam
Masari	Mosquito Net
Matha	A Religious Institution
Mela	Fair
Moghulbandi	Coastal Area which were Under Direct Administration of Moghuls
Mukti	Salvation, Freedom
Mundial	Village Headman
Muthihandi	Arthen Pot to Collect Rice
Nai Talim	New Education of Gandhi
Narayana	The God Vishnu
Navjiban	New Life
Nikamma	Workless

Nutan Prabhat	New Morning
Odhana	Veil
Odra or Orh	The Traditional Peasants of Orissa from which the name 'Orissa' has been Derived
Padayatra	Pilgrimage on Foot
Paik	Foot Soldier
Pakhal	Cold Watered-Rice
Pana	Scheduled Caste of Orissa (The Bambo Workers and Drum Beaters)
Panchasakha	The Five Associates
Panchubarni	Multi Coloured
Panchayat	Traditional Village Council
Pata	Hand Woven Silk Sharee
Pataka	Caste
Patidars	Forming Caste of Gujarat
Pathasala	Traditional Village Primary Educational Institution
Pitha	Oriya Cake
Prajamandal	Organisation of the States Poeple
Prajatantra	The Rule of the People
Punga	Funnel
Punjabi	The People of Punjab
Purana	Epic
Purdah	Veil
Purnaswaraj	Complete Independence
Purusartha	Four Important Objectives of Hindu Life *i.e.* Dharma (Reghteousness), Arth (Material Gain), Kama (Desire) and Moskhya (Salvation)
Putuli Bania	Merchants of Medicinal Herbs
Quilla	Fort

Radhi	Scheduled Caste of Orissa who prepares Chuda
Raj	Rule
Raja	King
Rajput	The Famous Warrior Castes of Medieval Rajasthan
Rakta Bahini	Blood Sacrificers
Rama Rajya	Rule of Rama, a Great Mythological Ruler who was a Great Benefactor
Ranaveri	The Triumpet of War
Rana Nimantran	Invitation to Fight
Rani	Queen
Rasad	Food Materials
Rathayatra	Car Festival of Jagannath
Rishi	Saint
Ryots	Farmers
Sabha	Council
Sadhav	Traditional Oriya Merchant
Sahitya	Literature
Sahu	The Surname of Many Higher Castes of Orissa Meaning 'honest'
Sala	Brother-in-law, (Generally used to degrade others)
Sali	Sister-in-law
Samaj	Society
Samaja Sebi	Social Worker
Sambad Bahika	Messenger of News
Sambalpuri	Product of Sambalpur particularly Sharee
Samanta	Feudals
Samyavadi	The Believers of the Concept of Equality (Socialists)

Sammilani	Conference
Santan Dharma	Council of Defend Hindu Religion.
Rakhini Sabha	Sangha, Council
Santisena	Army of Peacekeepers
Sanyasi	Sage
Sarakari Loka	Government Servant
Sarathi	Charioter
Saru	Arum
Sasan	Brahmin Villages
Sati	Custom of Widow Burning
Satyagraha	Adherence to Truth, Also Protest Demonstration in a Peaceful Manner
Satyagrahi	Who Adheres to Truth or who Participate in Peaceful Demonstration
Satya Samachar	True News
Satyayug	The Age of Satya (Virtue)
Seer	Traditional Unit or Weitht
Seva	Service
Sudh	One kind of soldiers of Orissa, One Militia Caste
Swadeshi	Indigenous
Swaraj	Self-Government
Swaraj Mandir	The Temple of Self-Rule
Tadi	Country Liquor
Tahasildar	The Tax Collector
Taluk	Area
Tanti	Weaver
Teli	Oilman Caste
Thana	The Police Station
Thalari	The Metal-Smith, Brace-Smith

Theki	Pot
Thoria	Grain Merchant Caste
Tole	Residential Sanskrit School
Uthakankal	Rise, O Skeletons !
Utkal	The Land of Excellent Arts, Orissa
Utkal Gandhi Sevasangha	Orissa Branch of Gandhi's Voluntary Organisation
Utkal Laxmi	Utkal, The Goddess of Prosperity
Utkal Sammilani	Utkal Union Conference
Vaishnavism	The Cult of Vishnu
Varnashram	Four Fold Life of a Hindu
Vellala	Farming Caste of Tamilnadu
Yatra	Traditional Oriya Folkdance
Zilla	District

Bibliography

A. INTERVIEWS

1. *With Gandhians :*

Acharya, Bibhuti Bhusan, Brahmansailo, Cuttack.
Biswal, Harekrushna, Nagpur, Cuttak.
Bose, Rajakrushna, Bangali Sahi, Cuttack.
Chudamani, Gokul Mohan Rai, Sundara Sahi, Puri, Cuttack.
Maharana, Annapurna, Gramasevak Press, Cuttack.
Maharana, Sarat Chandra, Gramasevak Press, Cuttack.
Mohanty, Nilamani, Banagli Sahi, Cuttack.
Mohapatra, Shyamakanta, Sailo Jharpada, Cuttack.
Pati, Ghanshyam, Govindpur, Cuttack.
Patra, Bauribandhu, Waubarai, Cuttack.
Patra, Gunabidhi, Majurai, Cuttack.
Pradhan, Iswara Chandra, Waubarai, Cuttack.
Ray, Advaitaballav, Manik Ghosh Bazar, Cuttack.
Sarangi, Udayanath, Narayan Mishra Lane, Cuttack.

2. *With Old Villages :*

Dixit, Jayakrushna, Adaspur, Cuttack.
Mohanty, Loknath, Ghodansh, Jagatsinghpur.
Mohaparta, Achyutananda, Adaspur, Cuttack.
Mohaparta, Mayadhar, Adaspur, Cuttack.
Pradhan, Prahllad, Adaspur, Cuttack.
Sahoo, Uchhab, Adaspur, Cuttack.

B. STRUCTURED QUESTIONNAIRE

Behera, Biswambar, Rambha, Ganjam,
Behera, Rusi, Rankia, Cuttack.
Berma, Hari Charan, Kusupur, Cuttack.
Biswal, Harekrushna, Nagpur, Cuttack.

Chudamani, Gokul Mohan Rai, Sundara Sahi, Khurda, Puri.
Das, Braja Sundar, Hakim Para, Dhenkanal.
Das, Golak Chandra, Haladia Patna, Cuttack.
Das, Rabindra Mohan, Gopalgaon, Cuttack.
Devi, Godabari, Gopalgaon, Cuttack.
Dey, Priyanath, Purnagram, Cuttack.
Dhal, Nakulananda, Uttanagara, Cuttack.
Giri, Prabati, Samalai Padar, Sabalpur.
Jena, Akrura, Anandpur, Cuttack.
Majumdar, Mukunda Prasad, Indupur, Cuttack.
Mehre, Prasadi, Gudabhelipadar, Phulbani.
Mishra Suresh Chandra, Sakhigopal, Puri.
Mohanty, Baikuntha Nath, Deuli Sahi, Cuttack.
Mohanty, Bholanth, Kania, Cuttack.
Mohanty, Gobind Chandra, Nua dunia, Cuttack.
Mohaparta, Goura Chandra, Bhadrak, Balasore.
Mohapatra, Nityananda, Bhubaneswar, Puri.
Maharana, Annapurna, Grama Sevak Press, Cuttack.
Maharana, Bhimasena, Itamati, Cuttack.
Maharana, Sarat Chandra, Grama Sevak Press, Cuttack.
Nath, Mathurananda, Govindpur, Garadpur, Cuttack.
Nayak, Baidya Nath, Terjang, Cuttack.
Nayak, Bala Krushna, Rankia, Cuttack.
Nayak, Srinath, Terjang, Cuttack.
Panda, Balaram, Baguli Sahi, Ganjam.
Pani, Nitya Nanda, Dharadharpur.
Parida, Chemru, Panimara, Sambalpur.
Patra, Alekha, Basulipada, Sambalpur.
Prusti, Gourahari, Baphapur, Cuttack.
Rath, Barabara, Dharpur, Cuttack.
Rai, Bira Kishore, Kisan Nagar, Cuttack.
Samal, Basudev, Balipala, Cuttack.
Samal, Nrusingha Charan, Haladi, Basant, Cuttack.
Samant, Birabar Narayan, Paradip Garh, Cuttack.
Samant, Raghunath Singh, Khandapara, Puri.
Sarangi, Udayanath, Narayan Mishra Lane, Cuttack.
Senapati, Lokanath, Bhiligram, Puri.
Swain, Baidhar, Bali Gorada, Dhenkanal.

Tripathy, Jagannath, Nabarangpur, Koraput.

C. DOCUMENTS AND RECORDS

(i) National Archives, Delhi :

Published :

Census of India, 1901.
Census of India, 1921.

Non-Published :

Judicial, File No. 830 (The Registrar, Nizamat Adalat, 1836)

(ii) Orissa State Archives, Bhubaneswar :

Published :

Census of India, 1951, Vol. XI, a. Ahmed (ed.), Cuttack, 1953.
Final Report on the Survey and Settlement of the Province of Orissa, 1890-1900.
Gandhiji in Orissa, Publication Division, Director of Public Relation, Orissa, 1970.

Non-Published :

Home (Political) Confidential, File No. 1, 1927, (Office of the Deputy Commissioner, Sambalpur).
Home (Political) Confidential, File No. 4, 1932, (Office of the Deputy Commissioner, Sambalpur).
Home (Political) Confidential, File No. 5, 1937, (Orrisa Police Abstract of Intelligence).
Home (Political) Confidential, File No. 6, 1937, (Police Arrangements for the Election to Legislative Assembly).
Home (Political) Confidential, File No. 25/45, 1945, (Fortnightly Report from the District Magistrate, Ganjam).
Home (Political) Confidential, File No. 25/Part-II, 1945, (Fortnightly Report from the Deputy Commissioner, Sambalpur).
Home (Political) Confidential, File No. 81, 1946, (Special Section, Reports of Special Branch on the Formation of Ministry of Orissa).

(iii) Delhi University Library System, Delhi University :

Published :

Annual Register, 1929-47, N.N. Mitra (ed.), Annual Register Office, Caltutta, 1929-48.
Collected works of Mahatma Gandhi, Vol. XVII-XLI, The Publication Division, Ministry of Information and Broadcasting, Government of India, Delhi, 1965-73.
Indian Quarterly Register, H.N. Mitra (ed.) Annual Register Office, Calcutta, 1924-29.

(iv) Ratan Tata Library Delhi :

Published :

Bihar and Orissa District Gazetteers, L.S.S.O' Malley (ed.), Government Printing, Patna, 1932.
District Gazetteers, Bihar and Orissa, 1900-1911.
Bihar and Orissa Secretariat, Patna, 1915-16.
District Gazetteers, Orissa, R.C.S.Bell (ed.), Cuttack, 1945.
Orissa District Gazetteers, Nilamani Senapati, Durga Prasad Kuanr (ed.), Government of Orissa, Cuttack, 1977.

(v) Nehru Momorial Museum and Library, Teenmurti Bhavan, Delhi :

Non-Published :

AISPC, (States' Peoples' Movement in Orissa)
File No. 35.
File No. 112/Part-I
File No. 127/157
File No. 127/251, File No. 127/255
File No. 127/277
File No. 206.
Andhra-Utkal Boundary Disputes, File No. 16/64/1925.

D. LITERATURE (Autobiography, Biography, Drama, Short Stories, Novels and Poetry)

(i) Delhi University Library System, Delhi :

Das, M.R. : *August 9* (O), (Drama), Nalanda, Cuttack, 1947.

Das, N.K. : *Atma Jibani* (O), (Autobiography), Nilakantha Granthavalli, Students' Store, Cuttack, 1963, Friends Publishers, Cuttack, 1971.

Mehtab, H.K.: *Prativa* (O), (Novel), Students' Store, Cuttack, 1962.

Sadhanara Pathe (O), (Autobiography), Students' Store, Cuttack, 1972.

Mohanty, G.N. : *Mati Matala* (O), (Novel), Bidyapuri, Cuttack, 1977.

(ii) Sahitya Academy Library, New Delhi :

Chhotray, G. : *Pheria* (O), (Drama), Cuttack Trading Company, Cuttack, 1947.

Mohanty, S. : *Andha Diganata* (O), (Novel), Cuttack Students' Store, Cuttack, 1964.

Krushna Chuda O Anyanya Galpa (O), (Store Stories), Cuttack, 1965.

Maralara Mrutya O Anyanaya Galpa (O), (Short Stories), Cuttack, 1962.

Patha, O Pruthibi (O), (Autobiography), Eastern Media Prakashan, Bhubaneswar, 1986.

Mishra, G.B. : *Ardha Satabdira Ithas O Tanhire Mo Sthana* (O), (Autobiography), Granthamandir, Cuttack, 1958.

Pradhan, P.M. : *Mukti Pathe Sainika* (O), (Autobiography), Nabajivan Press, Cuttack, 1979.

(iii) Orissa Sahitya Samaj Library, Cuttack :

Das, G.B. : *Bandira Atma Katha* (O), *Kara Kabita* (O), (Poetry), Gopabandhu Grandhavali, Satyabadi Press, Cuttack, 1948.

Das, K.B. : *Jivani O Jivan* (O), Friends Publishers, Cuttack, 1981.

Mohapatra, L.K. : *Kanta Sahityamala* (O), Part-I, Orissa Book Emporium, Cuttack, 1964.

Pattnaik, K.C. : *Kumbhara Chaka* (O), (Autobiography), Students' Store, Cuttack, 1975.

Rakta Mati (O), (Drama), Students' Store, Cuttack, 1987.

Senapati, F.M. : *Fakir Mohan Granthabali*, Friends Publishers, Cuttack, 1963.

(iv) Orissa State Archives, Bhubaneswar :

Chaudhury, R.D. : *Jibana Pathe* (O), (Autobiography), Grantha Mandira, Cuttack, 1984.

Champati Ray, K. : *Paika Kheda* (O), Jagannath Gaveshana Sankruti, Puri, 1953.

Das, G.B. : *Bhima Bhuyan* (O), (Novel), Vidyapuri, Cuttack, 1988.

Dwivedi, S.N. : *Mo Jibana Sangram, Ardha Satabdira Samajabadi Andolanara Kahani* (O), (Autobiography), Grantha Mandira, Cuttack, 1984.

Mohanty, G.N. : *Dhuli Matira Santha* (O), (Biography of Gopabandhu Chaudhury), Bidyapuri, Cuttack, 1985.

Panigrahi, K.C. : *Matira Manisha* (O), *Luhara Manisha* (O), (Novel), Kalindi Rachanachaya, Part-I, New Student's Store, Cuttack, 1971.

Routray, N.M. : *Smruti O Anubhuti* (O), (Autobiography), Granthamandira, Cuttack, 1986.

Senapati, F.M. : *Atmajivani* (O), (Autobiography), Cuttack, Student's Store, Cuttack, 1963.

E. NEWSPAPERS

(i) Orissa Sahitya Samaj Library, Cuttack :

Asha, 1914-40.
Deshakatha, 1936-39.
Lokamata, 1937-39.
Prajatantra, 1931.
Ratnakar, 1920.
Samaj, 1921-38.
Sambalpur Hiteisini, 1895.
Sayta Samachar, 1936-37.
Seva, 1922-23.
Utkal Dipika, 1870-1920.
Utkal Putra, 1973-74.
Utkal Sevak, 1870, 1921, 1931.

(ii) Orissa State Archives, Bhubaneswar :

Nabin, 1937-47.
Utkal Dipika, 1920-33.

F. SOUVENIRS

(i) ***Prajatantra Prachara Samiti Library, Cuttack :***

Agrani Sangrami Niranjan Pattnaik (O), K.C. Acharya (ed.), Berhampur, 1980.

Baishnab Charan Nayak (O), Baripada, 1987.

Biplabi Biswanath (O), Kanasha, Puri, 1983.

Biplabi Jananayak Pabitramohan (O), Srujani Sahitya Sansad, Rourkela, 1990.

Chatu Babu (Braja Mohan Singh) (O), Chhatrapur, Ganjam, 1986.

Compilation, Nilagiri State peoples' Movement (O), Balasore, 1982.

Dhenkanal Itihas Committee (O), Dhenkanal.

Gouranga Charan Das (O), Cuttack, 1982, 1987, 1988.

Jatiya Kavi Abhinandan (O), Chandrasekhar Mohapatra (ed.), Satakshi Press, Cuttack, 1973.

Kavi Banchhanidhi (O), Cuttack, 1987.

Mahanti Pradhan (O), Dhendanal, 1987.

Mahtab Jayanti Smaraki (O), Cuttack, 1988.

Orissa Province Freedom Fighters' Sammittee, Cuttack, 1986.

Orissa State Freedom Fighters' Association, BBSR, 1986.

Pradesh Congress Committee, Orissa, BBSR, 1988.

Prajatantra Rajat Jayanti (O), Cuttack, 1972.

Rajendra Verma (O), Nirupama Das (ed.).

Ramachandra Mohapatra (O) Jharapada, Cuttack, 1984.

Sachi Jena (O), 1987.

Sangrami Suryamani Nayak (O), Cuttack, 1989.

Silver Jubilee, National Independence, Chandrasekhar Mohapatra (ed.), Cuttack, 1971.

Sradhanjali, Nabakrushna Chaudhury (O), S.N. Dwivedi (ed), Rourkela, 1984.

Sridhar Sahoo (O), Kendrapara, Cuttack, 1984.

Struggle for Freedom in Orissa, BBSR, 1989.

G. PERIODICALS

(i) ***Delhi University Library System, Delhi :***

Journals of the Orissa and Bihar Research Society,

	Vol. XIII, 1927, Patna, 1927.	
Proc. IHC	Vol. II,	Session-39, Delhi, 1978.
	Vol. III,	Session-40, Delhi, 1979.
	Vol. III,	Session-41, Delhi, 1980.
	Vol. III,	Session-44, Delhi, 1984.
	Vol. III,	Session-45, Delhi, 1985.
	Vol. III,	Session-46, Delhi, 1986.
IHRC,	Vol. XI,	Madrass, 1970.
OHC,	Vol. III,	No. 2, 1977.
	Vol. IV,	No. 2, July, 1982.
	Vol. XX,	No. 1, 1995.
JOH,	Vol. XIII-XIV,	1995.
	Vol. XV.	1996.
OHRJ,	Vol. III,	No. 1st, June, 1954.
	Vol. VI,	No. 1, April, 1957.
	Vol. VII,	No. 2, July, 1959.
	Vol. IX,	No. 1-2, April-July, 1960.
	Vol. IX,	No. 2, January, 1961.
	Vol. X,	No. 4, 1962.
	Vol. XXVIII,No. 1-4, 1978.	

Studies from Africa and Asia, W.W. Morris Jones (ed.), University of London, Atnole Press, 1976.

(ii) *Prajatantra Prachara Samiti Library, Cuttack :*

Orrisa Review,	Vol. XLII,	No. 1, August, 1986.
	Vol. XLII,	No, 8, April, 1988.
Utkal Prasanga (O),	Vol. 37,	No. 9, April, 1980.
	Vol. 47,	No. 1, August, 1986.

Republic Day special Issue, January, 1989.

(iii) *Jadumani Sahitya Sansada, Udaipur, Nuagaon, Puri :*

Dagar, Bhadrak, 1940-47.

Niankhunta, Cuttack, 1942-48.

Prajatantra, Mahtab Jayanti Special, 1988. Saptahili (O), June 18, 1989, July 1, 1989.

Samaj, Death Anniversary Special Issue (Gopabandhu Das), July, 1945 and July, 1991.

Sarvodaya, Cuttack, July-August, 1991.

(iv) Padhiary Pathagara, Cuttack :

Sucharita, 12th and 13th Year, July-December, BBSR., 1987.

H. NON-PUBLISHED THESIS OR DISSERTATION

Non-Published- (M.Phil. Dissertation, Department of History, Delhi University, 1980).

Pati, B. : *Peasants Tribals and the National Movement in Orissa*, 1921-36.

I. BOOKS

Acharya, B.C. : *Godabaris Mohapatra Parikrama* (O), Students' Store, Cuttack, 1969.

Odiya Sahitya Sankshipta Parichaya (O), Granthamandira, Cuttack, 1975.

Achrya, P.N. : *Odisara Itihas* (O), (ed.) S.K.M. Ali, Orissa Book Store, Cuttack, 1977.

Baliarsingh, S. : *Ranpur Bidrohaa* (O), Rastrabhasa Samabaya Prakasan, Cuttack, 1985.

Banerjee, R.D. : *History of Orissa*, Vol. I, Bharatiya Publshing House, Calcutta, 1930.

History of Orissa, Vol. II, Banares Hindu University Press, 1929.

Behera, G.D. : *Kanika Biplaba (Panchamuka Praja Andolana)* (O), Chandabali, Balasore, 1987.

Beteille, A. : *Essays in Social Structure and Social Stratification*, Asia Publishing House, Bombay, 1969.

Brown, J.M. : *Gandhi's Risc to Power, Indian Politics*, 1915-22, Cambridge University Press, London, 1972.

Gandhi and Civil Disobedience, The Mahatma in Indian Politics, 1928-34, Cambridge University Press, London, 1977.

Das, B.S. : *Studies in the Economic History of Orissa, from Ancient Times to 1833*, Firma KLM Pvt. Ltd., Calcutta, 1978.

Das, C.M. : *Aitihasika Krupasindhu* (O), Gopabandhu Sahitya Mandira, Cuttack, 1962.

Kabi Gopabandhu (O), Students, Store, Cuttack, 1966.

Das, M.N.(ed) : *A Century of the Indian National Congress*, Vol. III, 1935-47, Vikash Publishers, New Delhi, 1985.

Sidelights of History and Culture of Orissa, Vidyapuri, Cuttack, 1977.

Das, S.K. : *Swadhinata Sangramara Bhumi Eram* (O), Cuttack, 1988.

Das, S.N. : *Desaprana Madhusudan*, Orissa Book Store, Cuttack, 1971.

Unnabinsa Satabdira Odisha (O), Das Publishers, Cuttack, 1962.

Yuga Purusa Gopabandhu Das, Orissa Book Store, Cuttack, 1972.

Das, S.S. : *Utkalara Laban Tirtha Ba Biplabini Inchudi* (O), Balasore, 1980.

Dhal, B.K. : *Bhulibu Nahin* (O), Book Land Internationl, Bhubaneswar, 1980.

Dwivedi, S.N. : *August Biplaba* (O), Cuttack Trading Co., Cuttack, 1989.

Eschmann, A., Kulke, H., Tripathy, G.C. : *The Cult of Jagannath and the Regional Tradition of Orissa*, Manohar, New Delhi, 1978.

Grover, V. (ed) : *Political Thinkers of Modern India, M.K. Gandhi*, Deep & Deep Publication, New Delhi, 1990.

Guru, Raj. : *Agni Path* (O), Pragati Prakasana, Cuttack, 1985.

Hoque, M.A. : *Muslim Administration in Orissa, 1568-1751 AD.*, Punthi Pustak, Calcutta, 1980.

Hunter, W.W. : *History of Orissa*, Vol-I and Vol-II, Smith Edder & Co., London,1872.

Statistical Account of Bengal, Vol-XVII-XiX, Concept Publication,Delhi-1877.

Hutton : *Castes in India*, Oxford, Bombay, 1986.

Irschick, E.F. : *Politics and Social Conflict in South India; The Non- Brahmin's Movement and Tamil Separatism*, 1916-1924. Oxford University Press, Bombay,1969.

Jain, Prativa : *Gandhian Ideas, Social Movement and Creativity*, Rawat Publication, Jaipur, 1985.

Jit N.K. : *The Agrarian Life and Economy of Orissa : A Survey*, 1833-97, Calcutta, 1984.

Jena, K.C. : *History of Modern Orissa*, Punthi Pustak, Calcutta, 1985.

Social- Economic Condition of Orissa (19th Century), Sandeep Prakasan, Delhi 1978.

Kanungo, B. : *Bandha Tuma Pedi Putula* (O), Dipak Press, Cuttack, 1983.

Dariya Dakhal (O), Rastra Bhasa Press, Cuttack, 1983.

Labana Saytagraha Orissa (O), BBSR., 1986.

Runa Parisodha (O), Gyana Mandal Prakasani, Cuttack, 1979.

Lohia, R.M. : *Marx, Gandhi, and Socialism*, Samta Bidyalaya, Nyasa, Hydrabad, 1978.

Mahtab, H.K.(ed.) : *History of the Freedom Movement in Orissa*, State Committee for Compilation, History of Freedom Movement, Orissa, 1957.

Utkal University History of Orissa, Vol. III, Cuttack, 1964.

Malik, M.D. : *Biplabi Chakradhar* (O), Haladia, Cuttack, 1973.

Mishra, A. : *Talacher Andolana* (O), Talcher, 1986.

Mishra, C.R. : *Freedom Movement in Sambalpur*, B.R. Publishing Corporation, Delhi, 1986.

Mishra, K.C. : *The Cult of Jagannath*, Firma KLM, Calcutta, 1971.

Mishra, N.M. : *Adhunika Odiya Katha Sahitya* (Upanyasa) (O), Orissa Sahitya Academi, 1982.

Mishra, P.K. : *Political History of Orissa, 1900-1936*, Oriental Publishers and Distributors, Delhi, 1979.

Mishra, P.K. : *Political Unrest in Orissa, In the 19th Century, (Anti-Feudal, Anti-British and Agrarian Rising)*, Punthi Pustak, Calcutta, 1983.

Mohanty, A.B., Samal, D.R. (ed.) : *Mukti Sangramare Bari Andolana*, Grama Sevak Samabaya, Cuttack, 1989.

Mohanty, B.R. : *August Biplaba* (O), Kalinga Grantha Mandir, Cuttack, 1962.

Orissa Andolanara Itihasa (O), Rastrabhasa Prakasana, Cuttack, 1988.

Swadhinata Sangrama Orissa (O), Modern Bharati, Cuttack, 1978.

Mohanty, J.N. : *There Where Trees Flower; Essays on*

Modern Orissa Literature, Book Land International, Bhubaneswar, 1980.

Mohapatra, J.N. : *Orissa in 1936-37 to 38-39*, Government Press, 1941.

Mokherjee, P. (ed.) : *Utkal University History of Orissa*, Vol. VI, Pattnaik Press, Cuttack, 1964.

Nanda, B.R., Joshi, V.C. (ed.) : *Studies in Modern Indian History*, No. 1, Orient Longman, Delhi, 1972.

Norman Dorothy : *Nehru; The First Sixty Years*, Vol. I, London, 1965.

Padhi, B.M. : *Puratana Kalingara Samajika Itibruti* (O), Grantha Mandira, Cuttack, 1992.

Panda, D.K. : *Mukti Sangramare Jaleswar* (O), Durga Printers, Balasore, 1985.

Panigrahi, K.C. : *History of Orissa*, Kitab Mahal, Cuttack, 1981.

Parida, B. : *Mukti Sangrama O Odiisa, 1803-1938* (O), Aloka Prakashani, Jagatsinghpur, Cuttack, 1979.

Pati, S.B. : *Democratic Movements in India*, Discovery Publishing House, Delhi, 1987.

Patra, K.M. : *Orissa State Legislature and Freedom Struggle, 1912-47*, Indian Council of Historical Research, Delhi, 1979.

Patra, S.C. : *Formation of the Province of Orissa, The Success of the First Linguistic Movement in India*, Punthi Pustak, Calcutta, 1979.

Pattnaik, B.M. : *Amari Gan Kahani* (O), Sarada Printers, Bhubaneswar, 1989.

Pattnaik, H.M. : *Dhankanala Andolana* (O), Dhenkanala, 1983.

Pattnaik, J. : *Rakta Titha Eram O Swadhinata Sangramara Eka, Marmantuda Adhyaya* (O), Nalanda, Cuttack, 1986.

Pattnaik, N. : *Cultural Traditions in Puri, Structure and Origanisation of a Pilgrim Centre*, India Institute of Advance Studies, Simla, 1977.

Pattnaik, N.R. : *Swadhinata Andolanare Odisara Adivasi O Sahid Laxman Naik* (O), Adivashi Bhasa O Sanskruti Academy, Bhubaneswar, 1990.

Pattnaik, S.N. : *Odisare Swadhinatara Andolan* (O), Grantha Mandira, Cuttack, 1972.

Pradhan, S.S. : *Agrarian and Political Movements; States of Orissa*, 1931-49, Inter-Indian Publishers, Delhi, 1986.

Ram, R.C. : *Sangrami* (O), Nabayuga Granthalaya, Cuttack, 1986.

Sahu, N.K., Dey, S.C. : *Who's who of Freedom Workers in Orissa*, State Committee for Compilation of Freedom Workers, BBSR, 1967.

Sahu, Mishra & Sahu : *History of Orissa*, Kitab Mahal, Cuttack, 1980.

Sahoo, B. : *Weaker Section, Poverty and Development*, New Era, Bhubaneswar, 1985.

Samal, J.K. : *Princely States of Orissa*, Vohra Publishers, Allahabad, 1988.

Samantaray, N.B. : *Odiya Shityara Itihas, 1803-1920* (O), P.K. Dhal, Bhubaneswar, 1964.

Sarkar, S. : *Modern India, 1885-1947*, Mac Millan Publishers, Delhi, 1983.

Shah, A.P. : *Life in Medieval Orissa, 600-1200*, Chaukhamba Orientalia, Varanasi, 1976.

Sharp, G. : *Gandhi as a Political Strategist. Porter Sergest, Boston*, 1979.

Gandhi Wields The Weapon of Moral Power, Navajivan Publishing House, Ahmedabad,1960.

Singh, P.T. : *Swadhinata Sangramare Banara Sena* (O), Sri Press, Cuttack, 1986.

Stirling, A. : *An Account (Geographical,Statistical & Historical of Orissa Proper or Cuttack*, 1886 (Reprinted by Bengal Secretariat Press, Calcutta, 1904).

Supakar, S.K. : *Madhyama Purusha* (O), Cuttack Writers Co-Operative Ltd. Cuttack, 1982.

Toynobee, A.G. : *A Sketch of the History of Orissa, From 1803-28*, (Reprinted in OHRJ, Vol. IX, April- July, 1960).

Verma, M.M. : *Gandhi's Techniques of Mass Mobilization*, R.K. Gupta & Co. Delhi, 1990.

Index